CHESAPEAKE STRIPERS

by Keith Walters

ROCKFISHING TACKLE & TECHNIQUES
THE WAY IT WAS ▪ THE CRASH
MORATORIUM ▪ RESTORATION
YOY CONTROVERSY ▪ RE-OPENING ▪ GAMEFISH
RECIPES ▪ AND MORE...

CHESAPEAKE STRIPERS

First Printing—September 1990.
Second Printing—April 1992. 799.17
Wal

Published in the United States of America by AERIE HOUSE,
P.O. Box 279, Bozman, Maryland 21612.

Library of Congress Catalog Number 90-90280

ISBN 0-9627039-0-7

Cover Photo: The author holds a 22-inch striper caught on an
Atom popping plug. The fish was released. Photo by Carole Walters.

For my wife of 35 years,
Jean Carole Walters

My ray of sunshine
On the cloudiest day,

My brightest beacon
In the darkest night.

Acknowledgements

First and foremost, credit for this book must go to my wife, Carole. She organized many years of clippings and great sticky gobs of my illegible field notes. She not only edited the text, but yanked me back on track whenever I went astray. She took care of all the business of producing a book while I did the writing. Without a partner like Carole, there would be no *Chesapeake Stripers* book.

Second, there are so many people who helped me along the way by sharing fishing information and providing the basis for interesting anecdotes that it would be impossible to name you all. Suffice to say that if your name is in this book, I thank you for your help. If your name does not appear here, I thank you anyway. You will be in my next fishing opus, absolutely guaranteed.

Third, thanks to *Attraction*, *Chesapeake Bay Magazine*, *The Fisherman*, *Fishing Tackle Trade News*, *Maryland Magazine*, *Salt Water Sportsman*, *Striper*, MSSA's *Tidelines*, and the U.S. Fish & Wildlife Service for permission to use portions of material I originally wrote for them.

Fourth, many thanks to the Fourth Estate—the press—most particularly the other outdoor writers who have helped me every step of the way. I hope that some day, in some way I can pay it all back.

And last to the fish that made it all possible, the greatest gamefish of all, the striped bass. May he ever reign as:

"King of the Chesapeake"

Contents

Chapter 3 THE WHALER YEARS (1964–1974)

Chapter 4 THE MAKO YEARS (1974–1981)

Chapter 5 EASTERN SHORE

Chapter 6 LEARNING FROM THE LOCALS

Chapter 7 THE CRASH

Chapter 8 A MORATORIUM

Chapter 9   RESTORATION

Chapter 10   STRIPED BASS AND THE HATCHERY

Chapter 11   STRIPER TAGGING

Chapter 12   YOUNG-OF-THE-YEAR INDEX

Chapter 13   FRESH WATER STRIPERS

Chapter 19 GAMEFISH?

Chapter 20 STRIPER TACKLE AND TECHNIQUES

Chapter 21 WINTER WORKSHOP

Chapter 22 RECIPES BY CAROLE WALTERS

EPILOGUE

REFERENCES

Introduction

Chesapeake Stripers is about my 37-year love affair with striped bass. If that sounds a little kinky to you, so be it.

I absolutely *had* to write this book. Some are aware of my all-consuming interest in stripers. This book describes only *my* personal experiences, and some of the knowledge I've gained over the years. There is simply too much material to tell it all. Even after a third of a century, I am still learning.

By a rare stroke of luck, I lived in the very center of great rockfishing in the halcyon days, from 1958 to 1981. Our home on the Little Magothy River in Cape St. Claire was 11 minutes from the Bay Bridge/s by fast boat and even closer to other great striper areas.

To give the reader a clue about my fishing frequency, I bought popping plugs by the gross, made my own bucktail jigs by the hundreds and bought my live eels 200 at a time.

About the time the striper fishery began to crash in the late 1970s, I retired from NASA after a 30-year career in photography. We moved to a quiet creek off Maryland's Choptank River, which again put me in the center of striped bass activity—another lucky break.

A new career in outdoor writing gave me the opportunity to interview striper biologists, and accompany them in the field on Young-of-the-Year (YOY) surveys; hook-and-line mortality studies; and gathering big brood stripers to spawn them at the hatchery. I watched as tag returns unfolded a story about striper migrations. Striper fishing, management, and politics are told from my point of view as one of Maryland's 750,000 recreational anglers.

Beginning with catching my first small rockfish on grass shrimp in the Magothy River, then following my striper fishing education through plugging, bucktailing, eeling, chumming, trolling, and travelling, I hope the reader will find many helpful hints for his own striper fishing. Conservation-minded anglers will find plenty of material about the striper crash, moratorium, restoration, YOY controversy, reopening, and the possibility of gamefish status for our favorite fish. Craftsmen will find off-the-wall hints about caring for tackle and making striper lures in "Winter Workshop."

When you *do* catch a "keeper," try the recipes for coordinated striper meals that my wife, Carole, has developed in our 35 years of marriage. If you need an inducement to try her recipes, consider this: I tip the scales at 220 pounds. The gal can cook. Trust me.

Chapters in the book mostly follow a time line rather than a story line, since so many things happened at once. Chapters and sub-chapters are titled, allowing the reader to jump about and read whatever is of interest at that moment. If you like, you can use VCR terminology: "Hit that fast-forward, willya honey?" You can "replay" any chapter later.

If some of the stories are told with a wry twist or some humor may pop into the narration, it is because I wanted to accent the good times, as well as share my flubs and a few fabulous fishing facts I've learned from other striper anglers.

You can't help but improve your knowledge of striperology if you *memorize every word* of –

Chesapeake Stripers

Foreword

Anyone can write about anything. But to write authoritatively about anything, one has to know his subject. Keith Walters knows striped bass, and he knows the Chesapeake; thus it is appropriate that he wrote this book.

This is no ordinary book about a fish; or fishing. It is about a particular fish, and primarily about a particular tidewater complex—the Chesapeake Bay and its tributaries. It is about subjects Keith Walters knows well.

He also knows well the art of catching stripers—better known in Chesapeake Bay Country as rockfish. He can be considered an expert fisher of rock, and not just because in 1964 he won the season-long Maryland Saltwater Sportfishing Tournament with the catch of a 32½-pounder on a ⅞-ounce Atom swimming plug.

As anyone can write a book, anyone can get lucky and catch a winning or trophy fish. What separates the men from the boys is consistency. And Keith Walters was, until the rockfish moratorium was implemented, a consistent catcher of rock. And, he will be again when the ban is lifted later this year because he has learned his fishing well.

The angler, whether casual or serious, can learn much about catching rock in this book because the author lets the reader in on his techniques, places, his thinking, even his secrets.

But, all of us can learn much more than just fishing for rockfish from *Chesapeake Stripers*. We can be informed about the fish itself, its biology, its habitat, and many other aspects of this delightful species including man's management and mismanagement of the rockfish.

This is in a way a love story of a man and his fish; a man who has dedicated a good part of his life in volunteer fisheries work, and other studious aspects of lending a hand to a wonderful fish in a heap of trouble.

We will never see fishing for the striped bass as it was in the hey days enjoyed by Keith Walters, and the writer of this foreword. But through the pages of this book, we can re-live those days while getting a better understanding of why things have become what they have.

Always a photographer, Keith Walters took to serious outdoor writing only in recent years. Too bad he didn't do so earlier. The right word is worth a thousand pictures.

— Bill Burton, Outdoor Editor
The Evening Sun, Baltimore, MD
July, 1990

Carole and Keith at Grays Creek, 1955.

IN THE BEGINNING (1955–1958)

Getting Hooked on Rockfishing

It was all Jimmy Tracey's fault. At least that's what my wife, Carole, said after Jimmy introduced me to rockfishing. Actually, it started a bit more slowly than that.

Carole Stewart and her cousins, Shirley and Jimmy Tracey, and I spent some beautiful summer days at the Tracey shore on Grays Creek off the Magothy River. Swimming and putting about in Jimmy's father's rowboat was about as pleasant a way to pass the time as one could imagine. Actually, I dated Shirley first, but when she showed me a photograph of her cousin, Carole, something inside me said, "That's her. That's the one!"

Just back from the Korean War, I was regaining some stability after some very destabilizing things in my life. The lady in the picture exuded stability and class. Shirley introduced me to Carole, and that was it. Actually, I think they traded me for a sweater or something, but we really have to get back to the fishing.

I'm not sure if Carole ever forgave Jimmy for this: Soon after Carole and I were married on June 17, 1955, we were invited to the Tracey's shore. Jimmy said he just happened to have some grass shrimp and minnows and offered to take me fishing. Jimmy always preferred "female minners" though I could never tell the difference. I had no tackle, but he said "no problem."

Jimmy and I putt-putted out into the Magothy River and found the edge of the grass along the inside of Gibson Island. Jimmy set anchors fore and aft so the boat was parallel to the grass, and about a short cast away. He showed me how to bait a hook with grass shrimp and cast with a spinning outfit. We used a spreader under a float, with a minnow on one hook and a grass shrimp on the other.

Either the fish were dumb, or Somebody Up There was determined to hook me. We caught a nice mess of yellow and white perch. Then, a small rockfish nailed my grass shrimp. The cork went under with no hesitation, no nibbling bites like perch are wont to do. Just a slamming hit, and the float was headed for Mountain Point.

The rockfish fought harder than a perch, though it wasn't much bigger. I held it up in admiration. Silver with seven lateral stripes, the little guy was one of the prettiest things I'd ever seen (except Carole).

Another thing I noticed was that the tiny striped bass did not smell fishy. It had a different, distinctive aroma that was somehow pleasing. To this day, I can't describe it.

Jimmy said the minimum size for rockfish was 12 inches (then), so I slipped it back overboard. It would not be the last striper I released. But from that point on, I was hooked on striped bass. I was about as close to Heaven as any rockfisherman is allowed to get.

Keith and Jim Tracey building a fire to fry perch.

An Understanding Wife is the Key to a Full Tacklebox

Though Carole and I were both working, we were trying to save to buy a starter house. So, when she agreed that I should take advantage of a big sale on Mitchell 300 spinning reels at Montgomery Ward's on Monroe Street in Baltimore, I was there in a flash. A new rod, reel, line, and some hooks for perch fishing, and I was in hog heaven.

Later, Jimmy Tracey took me to Tochterman's fishing tackle store in Baltimore. Jimmy laughed as I marvelled over extensive displays of tackle I didn't know existed—and didn't have the money to buy. I must have bought something, but I felt like a kid in a candy store with no money. I still feel like that young kid when I go into a tackle store, though now I walk out with an armload of goodies.

Two events in our lives shoved Carole and I in a direction that later worked out in our favor: First, we both loved the water. Second, we didn't get to the Tracey's shore as frequently as before we were married. We spent a few hot summer weekends in our tiny apartment in Glen Burnie. That did it. We *had* to get out on the water.

So, our next purchase was a 5-HP Wizard outboard motor (and, of course, fishing tackle for Carole). We carried the motor in the trunk of the car. Remembering that cantankerous %#@&%$ motor, it still amazes me when my modern 15-HP Johnson starts on the first pull. With an outboard motor we had mobility. We could rent rowboats most anywhere there was fishing.

Carole runs the boat near Herald Harbor.

One summer day near Herald Harbor off the Severn River, everything went wrong. We were fishing along the edge of the grass on Long Point at Little Round Bay with peeler crab bait for perch when a school of rockfish moved in. Suddenly, we were both hooked to rampaging rockfish, and neither one of us knew what to do about it. The two fish expertly crossed our lines. I said a few words my young bride didn't know I knew, and I didn't know that she knew what they meant. It was pandemonium. It was also one of our first fights. I don't remember if we landed any stripers, but I still remember that wonderful shot of adrenalin when we tangled with those fish.

Cape St. Claire

"Let's go look at this waterfront property," I suggested one Sunday after scanning *The Baltimore Sun* ads. Carole was a bit surprised. Neither one of us knew why I had picked that particular day to look at real estate ads, or found that particular ad. I called the agent to show us the house. That's all she did when we got there. She sat in the kitchen and we explored everything on our own. The agent just answered questions. We sold ourselves the house. We asked Carole's father, Gil, to look it over, and then we signed a contract. Whew!

Of course, we had to do some financial finagling, but we swung the deal. We didn't know it then, but we were on a waterfront real estate escalator that has continued until now. No thought of that then. We were on the water!

Well, actually, we were on a shallow slough that drained into the Little Magothy River in Cape St. Claire. As a bonus we were only a few minutes from our workplace at the U.S. Naval Engineering Experiment Station (USNEES) across the Severn River from the Naval Academy. Locals called it "The Station" then. Carole was a secretary in one of the technical divisions and I was a photographer.

Later we bought two lots next to our starter house and built a larger house when Carole's sister, Debbie, came to live with us after their mother died.

With my boat in front of the house on the Little Magothy just off Chesapeake Bay, fishing possibilities were unlimited. And tempting. There were many conflicts when obligations and fishing confronted each other, face-to-face. Luckily for me, fishing usually won.

Fishing at the Station

The neatest thing about the Station, aside from its laid-back ambience, was the fact that I could fish from the riprap seawall after work for—you guessed it—rockfish. In those days, you could park your car next to Building 120, then fish from the rocks for a quarter mile to the next cove. I learned a lot about rockfishing by trying different lures and techniques from that riprap. Also, I learned that some people can jinx you from a mile away.

Keith with an 8-pounder caught at "The Station."

Lois Clarken worked in our Technical Information Division (TID). She and Carole became friends, and Lois' husband, Warren, became my close pal. I could be fishing from the riprap, catching one striper after another, but when Warren arrived the fish stopped biting. Warren walked along the rocks until he was out of sight around the point, casting a #15 or #17 Tony Acetta spoon into the Severn River as he went.

I began to catch fish as soon as he disappeared! I hadn't changed my pattern of fishing. There was something weird about that. I cast my Tony spoon out and let it sink to the bottom. Then, I began a slow retrieve, timing my reeling speed to get the most wobble out of the lure. I could feel lure wobble through the rod. There was some sort of structure straight out from my favorite spot, a long cast from shore. Since stripers are structure-oriented animals, I had the best luck there. The best fishing was on the downtide side of the obstruction. I pulled several nice stripers out of that hole.

Then everything stopped! Warren had come into view around the point. Warren hadn't caught a thing. I showed him my pile of rockfish, and told him I caught them all when he was out of sight, but they had stopped biting when he came back into view. He thought I was kidding. No way! I had the fish to prove it.

For some reason, Warren never became a die-hard striper fisherman like me. In fact, he gave up fishing.

Warren Clarken and Keith with stripers.

Zapping the Competition

We had a recurring problem in fishing from the Station riprap. One angler trolled right through our best fishing spot every evening from a small runabout. He stood in the back and steered his outboard motor with his legs as he trolled a bucktail jig next to the shoreline. He caught a lot of stripers.

When he trolled past us, we always stopped casting and glared at him. If he caught a rockfish, he'd keep coming back until the fish stopped biting. This gave us a lot of heartburn, since we were not mobile. We had no other place to fish. This guy had the whole Bay. I had a brainstorm.

"Carole, cast right there, as close to the stern of that boat as you can," I said as the boat went past 30 feet out from us. Carole did as I directed. She was not as sophisticated in the devious ways of anglers then. Her line crossed and tangled with our antagonist's line. He untangled the resulting mess and handed her back her lure. What could he say to a young woman? I grinned at him, friendly-like. He mumbled something and sped away. He never came back when we were fishing from the riprap.

The halcyon days of fishing from the riprap were coming to a close. I had pointed out to Ensign Roe, Station Security Officer, that one could walk along the riprap from the parking lot at Building 120 to the cove upriver, and thence off the naval base through an employee park without encountering a fence or guard. The thought must have occurred to him that spies could travel the reverse route just as easily. Roe had a fence installed, cutting us off from our great fishing. I was torn between rockfishing and patriotism, and I have since wondered if maybe the wrong thing won.

The Contest

I was getting a reputation as a fishing nut, more particularly a rockfishing nut. The boys in TID at the Station; Pat Fairall, Julius Pincus, Gene Carter, and George Listman in the Photo Lab; Hal Kumer and Dick Meers in the Art Section; plus our Division Chief, George Gary, began to rag me a bit about my fishing prowess.

With the brash assurance of irrepressible youth, I allowed as how I could catch a rockfish "in your bathtub, if necessary." Hal Kumer had taken up an interest in fishing, and he bet he could outfish me (what, beat the Champ?) any lunchtime I chose, and right from the seawall behind the building where Dr. Robert Goddard had done some early experiments on rocket engines. I took Hal up on that. Couldn't lose. I studied the tide charts. Finally, I named the day.

Remember that old saying about kissing something in Macy's window and giving someone an hour to draw a crowd? Well, I didn't know so many people would be out at lunchtime, but there was a mighty big gang turned out to see me or Hal go down in defeat. Hal wore the white hat, and I, being a cocky brash kid, had to wear the black hat.

I unlimbered my favorite rig, an 8-foot Actionrod and a 306 Mitchell spinning reel I was mighty proud of. I snapped on my favorite lure of the time, a #15 Tony spoon with a brilliant yellow feather. I might have flexed my muscles and showed off with long casts a bit more than necessary. Hal had a similar spinning rig, but I think he used a bucktail jig. We began to cast and reel, cast and reel. Hal was casting to a certain spot not far out. There were a lot of jokes from the sidelines. Hal allowed as how he was going to beat my knickers off.

"Ho-Ho," I said.

Hal caught a rockfish. As fight announcers say, the crowd went nuts. Hal played it up real good. He let his drag slip more than necessary, and hollered a lot. Score one for Hal's white hat.

I redoubled my casting efforts, but I may have also sped up my lure in the excitement. Maybe too fast for a rockfish to catch. Hal stayed cool. I caught nothing. Hal caught another rockfish, enough for his family dinner, he said, yawning. Two for the white hat. Black hat, zero.

As smart politicians do, I admitted defeat before the Station bell rang announcing the end of lunchtime. Hal's admirers made much of his success, and Hal ragged me for weeks about my lack of piscatorial prowess.

Pugnose Striper

Ed Talbot brought in a strange-looking striper one day. It looked like a boxer who had his nose smashed in too many times. Ed said he caught it off Tolly Point on a bucktail. I photographed it for Ed, and sent a copy, with a description, to Captain Frank Moss of *Sportfishing* Magazine, my first sportfishing article.

Later, I found that Dr. Romeo J. Mansueti wrote a paper in 1960 (Chesapeake Sci. 1(2):111-3, for those who are interested) about: "Large pugheaded striped bass, *Roccus saxatilis* [since renamed *Morone saxatilis*], from Chesapeake Bay." The paper "describes these fish, not particularly uncommon, as being due to natural causes during early development."

Pugnose striper.

In the Small World Department, I never knew the late Dr. Mansueti, but his former wife, Alice Jane "A.J.", who helped Dr. Mansueti with his striper research, is now married to Dr. Robert Lippson, Assistant Northeast

Regional Director of the National Marine Fisheries Service (NMFS), and now (1990) they live just six houses down Broad Creek from us. A.J. made many of the illustrations that are still used in striper literature today, and she also designed the cap that is given as a reward for returning striper tags to the U.S. Fish and Wildlife Service (USFWS).

An Eerie Evening at Sandy Point

A gentle mist hung in the evening air. It was early spring and wintering Chesapeake stripers were beginning to stir. A few had been caught from the beach at Sandy Point State Park on bloodworms. It had been a long winter. As my personal spring sap rose, striper fishing was uppermost in my mind.

Carole and I picked up a dozen bloodworms at Angler's, and drove to Sandy Point at dusk. A few anglers had surf rods in sand spikes when we got there.

I figured the best fishing would be right at the point. Why does it always seem that points of land are best, even if the fish are tearing up the water a mile down the beach? I pushed my homemade pipe sand spikes into the beach in a good location on the sandbar and put our rods in them.

We baited 1/0 hooks with a gob of bloodworms and cast our sliding sinker "fish finder" rigs right at the edge of dusk. Our rods were placed in their holders to await certain bites. I had rigged a small bell near the tip of each rod to signal bites after dark. We carried a flashlight, but to save batteries we didn't use it unless necessary. Several anglers on the beach had gas lanterns. Their portable lights made a cheery circle of light around them, but it was dark where we fished.

We were dressed for the damp cold, but it was uncomfortable. You couldn't see very far in the mist. It was a little spooky, like being lost in a fog. Our only connection with the real world was the sight and sound of small wavelets washing up on the beach, and occasional traffic noise on the nearby Bay Bridge that was lost in the mist. Not far from us, Sandy Point Light sounded its mournful warning to passing ships too far out on the Bay for us to see through the mists.

About 20 feet from us, another angler set up. He used two rods set in sand spikes, and baited up by the light of his gas lantern. He was a big fellow, maybe six-foot five or so, built like a pro football lineman. His movements were slow and deliberate as he set up. He made no sound. It was like watching a movie with no sound track. When he had both rods set to his satisfaction, he stood quietly with his hands in his jacket pockets and stared out at the Bay, waiting.

Fishing was slow. We saw no fish being unhooked in other anglers' amber-colored circles of light. Our rod tip bells made no sound. We checked our baits occasionally and refreshed them with a new gob of bloodworm, but no fish nibbled our offerings. It was quiet. Very quiet. Carole and I talked about small stuff, maybe to ward off the chill, maybe to bolster our courage in the spooky darkness.

I strolled over to the silent angler and said "howdy."

"Any luck?," I asked.

"Nope, not yet."

Carole materialized at my side in the lantern glow.

The guy had a way of looking at us that made me uncomfortable. I still can't describe it. Sort of like a cat watching two birds, looking from one of us to the other through slitted eyes, as if deciding where and when to pounce. Maybe it was the mist and the darkness, but I was getting very uncomfortable about having taken my young wife on a dark beach where possibly hostile people lurked.

In conversation I may have mentioned I was a Korean War vet.

"See any combat?" the big guy asked.

"Yup, didn't like it either. Scared spitless most of the time."

"I liked it," he said quietly. "I liked to kill Germans. Snuck up on them with a homemade garrote. Cut their windpipes before they could make a sound."

He went into some detail about how he made his strangling device; a length of piano wire with a wooden handle at each end. How he waited silently in the dark until he had figured out the movements of a German guard until he could sneak up behind him. How he could whip his garrote over the head of the unsuspecting soldier and kill him before he could make a sound.

This was getting weirder by the minute. I saw two possibilities. One, he was trying to assure himself a solitary evening of striper fishing by scaring us off. Or worse, he was only partly rehabilitated, an ex-combat soldier who had handled his battle fatigue a whole lot differently than I did.

I knew guys like him in Korea. Quiet, brooding loners who rarely spoke to the others. They slept in the daytime and headed out across the MLR (Main Line of Resistance) at night, alone. They'd come in at daybreak, like skulking Count Draculas in dirty fatigues returning to their coffins to sleep. They always had a human ear or two to show for their night's work. Most of us stayed away from these ghoulish types. We had some serious doubts whether those ears were all Oriental. Some looked a little Caucasian.

Carole and I bid this WWII veteran good night, backing away as quickly as possible toward our fishing outfits. The vet looked back out across the Bay with the same 500-mile stare I had seen in Korea.

Trying not to look obvious, we alternately cast and retrieved our baits as we moved progressively farther down the beach until we could just barely see the mist-shrouded glow of his lantern. Then, we headed for our car on the parking lot, jumped in, locked the doors and lit out for home.

One thing I was curious about, though. Every time he had reeled in to check his bloodworm baits, I strained my eyes in the misty darkness, trying to see if he used piano wire leaders.

A Spinning-Man I Will Be

When we look back at some of the things that influenced our early tackle selections, a large part of the credit (or blame) must go to those outdoor writers who pen glowing words about this or that great reel or rod.

When Carole gave me "Spinning for Salt Water Game Fish" by Joseph D. Bates, Jr. in 1958, I couldn't put it down. Bates talked about spinning tackle, sure, but he also wrote interesting anecdotes about how he used it, and what he caught with it. He made a case for light tackle spinfishing that has lasted me all my fishing life.

While others coped with conventional rotating spool gear, and the resultant backlashes, I went happily on my way, catching loads of stripers with my spinners. It was not until recent years that revolving spool reels got sophisticated enough for me to avoid most backlashes.

I named my boat *Backlash*. Does that tell you something?

2

THE TIN BOAT YEARS (1958–1963)

At Last, Mobility

I remember the 12-foot aluminum V-hull like it was yesterday. It was leaning against the outside wall of the Monroe Street Montgomery Wards, transom resting on the pavement and bow sticking up in the air, which made it seem bigger. I think we paid $189 for the hull, plus cushions, oars, anchor, and other small stuff.

We were living in our starter house on the Little Magothy in Cape St. Claire. The slough in front of our house was too shallow, but Levi and Mary Young next door had just enough water to float my new tin boat. Levi gave us permission to put my boat at the end of his plank dock and I was in business.

Inky guarded the tin boat.

13

The old 5-HP Wizard wheezed its last, and I bought a used 12-horse Johnson. With one exception, I bought Johnson/Evinrude motors for the next 30 years—with no regrets.

The Little Magothy channel had a shoaling problem. Sand drifted from the Bay side of the inlet into the inlet itself, making for an average depth at medium tide of 18 inches or so. Several dredgings temporarily deepened the inlet, but shallow water rarely stopped me from going fishing in the tin boat.

A One-Lure Rockfisherman

Only one rockfish lure graced my tackle box in the early days, the Tony Acetta Pet spoon. Favored sizes ran from the tiny #12 to #19. If there was any fish I couldn't catch on a Tony, I didn't want to hear about it. I had Tonys with yellow feathers or no feathers, and a few of the double thickness jobs—which cast like a bullet but didn't catch stripers. With the Tony I caught stripers, bluefish, white and yellow perch, crappie, largemouth and smallmouth bass, pickerel, white shad, longnose gar, and too many others to remember.

Tony Acetta Pet Spoon.

I didn't find another single-lure fanatic until Carole and I vacationed at the Hotel Purnell in Ocean City, Maryland one summer. I got to talking with the owner, who was a kindred spirit, a striper nut. He motioned me to his station wagon in back of the hotel, where he kept his fishing gear. He had two wooden tackle boxes. He opened the first one. It was packed solid with Mirrolure swimming plugs! I asked him if he ever used any other lure.

"Sure, look at this," he said, opening the second box. It was full to overflowing with Mirrolures, too—but in different colors. He fished the Ocean City inlet for stripers with that one type of lure, and was very secretive about the exact times, tides, and spots. But he caught rockfish on his plugs just as I caught stripers on spoons.

Mouth-of-Magothy Rockfish

There was a lot of good rockfishing within a short distance of the Little Magothy inlet. A grass bed ran from inside the black can in the mouth of the Magothy River to Fairwinds Marina at the mouth of Deep Creek. Jimmy Tracey and I trolled the edge of this grass bed with small white bucktails from my boat or his. Jimmy had bow and stern lights powered by D-cell batteries. A little dim, but legal then.

Jim and I stayed after dark one night, trolling the edge of the grass. We were catching stripers on every pass. After dark, we had marks to go by. We lined up the Magothy River entrance black can with Baltimore Light, which put our track just on the edge of the grass.

The fish continued to hit until we quit at 10 p.m., though it was one of the blackest nights I ever experienced. No starlight, nothing. Black as pitch. I never knew how the rockfish could find our lures on that darkest of nights, but they did. It was something to remember for the future.

Jim Tracey and Keith with Magothy stripers.

We trolled the same spot in daylight, too. Jimmy got a little sleepy when fish were not biting and took little naps on the bow seat as I steered the boat from the stern. I waited until he was really cutting some Z's and slowly changed course until his fishing line was close enough to reach. I grabbed his line and give a mighty yank, as if an IGFA world-class striper struck Jimmy's lure. He awoke like a shot and started cranking. Each time he detected the ruse, he made up some new words.

Gil and Ethel Pumphrey bought a sleepy little rowboat marina near the mouth of Deep Creek, named it Fairwinds Marina, and built it into what it is today, with their sons running the business. Later, Gil bought a charter-boat, the *Fairwinds Lady*, and took anglers rockfishing. The reason I mention all this is one quote I remember from those days. Gil said, "If I don't have half a box of rockfish by 10 a.m., I get a knot in my stomach." I never forgot that, and that is the reason I will never take people fishing for money. If I don't catch fish, I only have myself to please. I enjoy the fishing, even if there is no catching.

Upriver/Inriver Magothy Rockfish

There were many stories about rockfish in the Magothy River. One was a winter fishing tale. Tony DiBartolo (Tony pronounced it Dee-bart-low), who was head of the plumbing shop at NASA Goddard Space Flight Center, where I then worked as a photographer, told me about catching stripers through the ice off Indian Village in the winter. I never tried it, but he said they had good success there.

One September day, I got a call from Jimmy Tracey. He was very cagey about some big rockfish they found upriver. I met them in the "secret spot" that evening. If it was so hush-hush, why was every boat from Grays Creek that could still float parked over Jimmy's secret grass bed when I got there?

It was next to a long pier between Ulmstead Point and the mouth of Deep Creek. There were extensive grass beds on each side. You could only fish there at high tide, because the fish were rooting around in the thick grass, and it was impractical to plug there at low tide.

The drill was to run shallow-running Rebel swimming plugs slowly above the grass. When 10- to 20-pound stripers hit the plugs with a mighty splash, the angler had to keep the fish's head up so he wouldn't dig down into the grass and scrub the plug off. We had a ball with those fish for two or three weeks, and it was all over. The spot never paid off again even though I checked it many times afterward.

Jimmy Tracey found good rockfishing on several sandbars not far from Grays Creek. He used grass shrimp bottom-fished and he moved around a lot. In those days, rockfish ran 12 to 15 inches in the Magothy.

There was another story about a successful troller in the Magothy that I could never check out. Seems this guy knew about every deep hole in the river. He trolled with one rod, fishing deep. When he went over a deep hole, he free-spooled line so his lure drifted down into the hole that held stripers, then he re-engaged the reel and brought the lure sharply up out of the hole— just so. Anyway, he was rumored to be a very good rockfisherman, the stuff of legends. I never found out who he was.

Mountain Point Bar to the Boilers

One of my favorite after-work evening trips in the tin boat was to troll the shallows from the river side of Mountain Point Bar along the high cliffs there. One evening, I caught a 13-pound rockfish just inside the bar on a #14 Tony. I was so excited I nearly forgot how to net the fish.

From Mountain Point Bar I trolled off the Gibson Island shoreline toward Sillery Bay to the "boilers" that show on some charts as three wrecks together off the high cliffs.

In those days, the boilers stuck up above the water on a medium tide. When I reached the boilers, I stopped and cast my spoon on all sides of the wrecked machinery. Rockfish would lay alongside the boilers and dart out to grab my lure, then try to regain the safety of the barnacle-encrusted iron. Sometimes they made off with my lure, sometimes not. It was an expensive game for a poor government photographer. I soon gave it up to fight fish in more open waters.

Later, I plugged these wrecks, but they either sunk deeper or rusted away, and became harder to find. Tracey sometimes plugged there too, with good success.

Atom Plugs Make a Big Splash

Returning fishless from the boilers one evening, I decided to troll around the bar on the Bay side. There were about four small boats anchored in shallow water near the swimming pavilion on Mountain Point Bar. Everyone was into fish, but I couldn't tell what they were doing. I cut my motor and drifted along far enough away to see what was going on without disturbing their fishing. Looking back, this was the best thing I could have done. I learned more by being polite than if I had barged in on the anglers and ruined their sport.

The boats were in a circle and the anglers were casting something that was driving the stripers crazy on the surface. Fish would hit their plugs in a shower of spray, blasting the little lure into the air, then the stripers would grab it as soon as it hit the water.

The anglers were using light spinning gear. It took some time to get a fish in. I was fascinated. My adrenalin was really pumping, but I still didn't horn in.

In about an hour, the sun was setting. The fish stopped biting. The boats began to leave. One of them came past me slowly and the angler thanked me for not messing up the fishing. I asked the guy what lure he was using. He looked around to see if anyone was listening, and in a conspiratorial tone, he almost whispered: "Atom plugs, the ⅝-ounce ones." Hot damn! It took me less than 10 minutes to get home, tie up my boat, and zip up to Angler's.

"What's a A-damn Plug?" I anxiously asked Joe Habel, "I want one."

"You mean Atom plug?" he asked.

"I dunno," I replied, "some guys were tearing hell out of rockfish near Mountain Point Bar on a small surface plug. I want one bad."

Joe Habel sold me the first of the jillion surface lures I bought over the years, but there was nothing as wondrous as that first little blue-and-white 5/8-ounce Atom popper.

The next night, I went back, armed with my one Atom popper. So did the other boats. The fish didn't show. No matter, I went back every evening for a week until I hit the fish. By the time the fish came back, the other anglers had given up. I had the fish to myself.

It was pandemonium and adrenalin all over again. There is no thrill in fishing equal to catching stripers on the surface. It is still my favorite kind of fishing, and the striper is still my favorite gamefish.

I called Jimmy Tracey about my new hot spot. Jim knew how to keep a secret—he only told Buddy Scott, Buddy's brother, and eleven others from Grays Creek, so my secret place was safe. Jimmy and I (and the Grays Creek gang) fished there regularly for years.

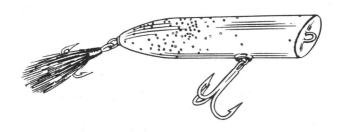

Atom popping plug.

There was a little cove near the pavilion. We often caught stripers there on popping plugs, right next to the shoreline. Jimmy would anchor there all day and wait for the fish to show. I had less patience, and roamed all over the area, from the Gibson Island causeway to Sandy Point, checking out all of the likely-looking shallow water in between with Atom plugs.

Jimmy often caught more rockfish by simply waiting them out. I had an empty gas tank and an empty fishbox, but I think we both enjoyed our fishing equally. We often named the spots we fished. This cove was the "first house." Other places included the "jetties", the "preacher's house" and the aforementioned "boilers." It was like speaking another language when other anglers, possible competitors, were within earshot.

Spooky Stripers Light Up the Water

Carole and I often plugged the Gibson Island shoreline at dusk, then fished peeler crab baits on the bottom after dark. Sometimes we would take just a sandwich for our supper. One night we were anchored in calm, shallow water off the "first house." It was dark as pitch. Carole and I looked up at the stars and tried to pick out the Big Dipper, Orion, and others. It was one of those quiet times, away from traffic, TV, and ringing phones. Beautiful!

Suddenly, we heard what sounded like rain hitting the water 100 yards out in the Bay. It was weird. The stars were still visible because there were no clouds. We strained our eyes looking for something, but nothing showed itself. The sound came closer. This was getting spooky, like some horror movie where a big blob of ectoplasm materializes and gobbles up the Brooklyn Bridge or everything in your tackle box.

As we stared into the darkness, a great white light appeared in the shallow water, coming right for us. The light split and part of it went around our boat on each side. I had a bite, but didn't hook whatever it was. Probably too scared to set the hook.

Then I figured out what it was. A school of rockfish had come toward us moving at high speed, following a school of baitfish. Their feeding accounted for the splashing noises we heard. The light we saw was the fish outlined by tiny organisms that fluoresce when they are disturbed. I never experienced such a weird thing before or since.

Many times since I have seen my prop wash illuminated as I ran home alone from fishing the bridges at night. One night I was so entranced with watching my lighted wake I almost ran into my neighbor, Levi, as he headed into the Little Magothy inlet in his outboard cabin cruiser. It scared me as much as it did him.

Swampings and Cats that Fish

Inky was an outdoorsman's sort of a cat. He was altered as a kitten, which gave him weight advantage enough to intimidate all the cats in the neighborhood, and most of the dogs. His lack of libido also left him more time for the important things in life, hunting and fishing. He watched the incoming tide from the end of Levi's plank pier, waiting for his favorite dessert, minnows, to appear. He could grab and guzzle a minnow in a heartbeat.

I thought Inky deserved a trip or two in the tin boat. He hated the noisy outboard, but was content to sit on the bow seat and regally accept the occasional minnow bait that he considered was his due. Carole even photographed Inky and I out yellow perch fishing in the Little Magothy in the tin boat. I had to draw the line at taking him rockfishing. He was too swift of paw. I was afraid he would grab a treble-hooked Atom plug before I could cast it beyond his reach.

Inky watches Keith perch fish from the bow of the tin boat.
(20x enlargement from old Ektachrome slide)

Inky could tell the distinctive sound of my tin boat and outboard motor when I came in through the Little Magothy channel and would run to the dock to meet me.

One evening I didn't come home the way I'd planned.

It was like any other evening after work. I jumped in the tin boat and planed out through the channel looking for rockfish. I tossed surface plugs along the shoreline near Sandy Point, then decided to troll back toward the Little Magothy. When I was just in front of Bay Head I heard a big slurping noise behind me. I looked over my shoulder to find a six-foot wave about to break over me. It was too late to do anything. The first wave tossed me out of the boat and drowned the motor, luckily. An unoccupied boat with the motor in gear can come back at you and cut you to pieces.

The second wave tossed me back in the boat headfirst. Succeeding waves were smaller. I was in a bit of a daze. I lost my glasses. Without them I couldn't see past my nose.

A lady on the shore saw what was about to happen. She called to me, but I didn't hear her over my outboard motor. She sent her son out to see if I was all right. He helped me get the floating stuff together, and we walked the boat to his dock. My neighbors in the Cape, Jim Lock and Orville Appleton, picked up the tin boat later in Jim's truck. I was badly shaken. The lady called me later. Her son had found my favorite Centaure reel and Actionrod.

Breakers along the Bay Head shore are caused by ships heading down the Bay from Baltimore. Their bow waves advance across the water until they hit the shallow sandbar, then stand straight up and break as they move toward shore. I started to think about a bigger boat.

Movie Stars: Love That Love Point Wreck

Carole and I were asked to appear in a movie that Hamm's Beer made in 1962 about rockfishing. It was titled: "Rockfish, King of the Chesapeake."

The movie crew (two men) was from Minnesota, Hamm's home port. Their advisors were Bob Pond of Atom fishing lures, and Joe Boone, a Maryland DNR biologist.

Why were Carole and I asked to be in the movie? How did they pick us? They were looking for someone who surface plugged for rockfish, and I guess I had bought about as many Atom plugs from Angler's as anyone. We were young then, too.

We made an appointment to meet the crew at daybreak one October morning in our tin boat on the Bay side of Mountain Bar, a place where I had been steadily catching big stripers on Atom plugs. They would film from another boat. I was so sure of myself, I told the crew it wouldn't take long.

Carole and I met the movie crew and Bob Pond as planned. They shot some great scenes of us casting Atom plugs, silhouetted against the rising sun. The main problem was they were anchored in the exact spot where I had been catching rockfish!

We gave it the old college try, but couldn't catch a fish for the cameras that morning. A busted trip. That's the way it is with fishing, I told them, ha ha. The Minnesotans were not amused.

We agreed to meet at a motel on Kent Island before dawn the next morning. Bob Pond had a hot spot to try, one that Annapolis *Evening Capital* outdoor columnist, Don Carpenter, had showed him. I'll be forever glad he did.

Fishing stories should always begin at dawn. Our Love Point odyssey began at dawn on October 9, 1962—my 32nd birthday. The rising sun peeked through scattered low-hanging clouds. The wind had picked up since we had met in the early hours, but there we were in a leaky 22-foot wooden scow, tossing plugs at the old Love Point wreck. It was so rough it was hard to see surface plugs work in between whitecaps, so I used a $7/8$-ounce blue and white Atom swimming plug.

Our mission was to capture several really big rockfish that Joe Boone would keep alive until the sun came up enough for a good exposure on the slow motion picture films in use then. Light levels at dawn precluded getting good exposures. We would photograph our rockfish being "caught" later, with the sun high and bright.

The wreck was about a third of the way from the Love Point lighthouse to the shore, in about six feet of water. A wooden tug or coasting freighter, it had washed ashore on the bar. Its ribs stuck up into the air like the bleached bones of a whale left to rot. At medium tide, a huge propeller protruded from whitecapping Bay waters like the disappearing tail of a whale. Aboard our scow were Al from the movie company; Joe Boone, Bob Pond, and myself. We used medium spinning tackle to cast our $1^{1}/4$-ounce popping plugs and $7/8$-ounce swimmers.

"Put your lure as close to the wreck as you can," Pond advised us, "don't worry about losing lures. I've got plenty." The fire drill began. The fish were big, some over 20 pounds. A determined striper can play a lot of tricks around barnacle-encrusted wrecks. Another problem we endured was the jerky reel drags of that day. Popped lines were commonplace as big fish gave that final tug.

We had at least four stripers over 20 pounds aboard when the action stopped as suddenly as it began. Pond was convinced that the fish only hit at dawn, and I expect he was right. I filed that data away for later use.

Joe Boone "walking" big stripers.

Author (center) on dock holds bow line near camera tripod. Movie crew concerned about camera. Bob Pond in bow of boat, Joe Boone on right.

We plugged around the rocks protecting the Love Point Lighthouse before running for shore. Pond assured us he had caught big rock casting plugs around the rocks at the lighthouse in the past, but no such luck that day.

When we reached the big commercial docks inside the hook at Love Point the sun was high. Joe Boone got out to "walk" his big fish and keep them alive in the shallow water until the movie-makers set up their cameras.

In the meantime my wife, Carole, met us so she could clamber into a 12-foot aluminum boat with me and "catch" the fish we caught earlier. The movie camera looked down from the high dock into our boat. Carole and I plugged the water near the dock for close-up and "action" shots. We hammed it up (for Hamm's?) by "setting" the hook, and generally looking happy. When the movie-makers had enough of those shots, Joe Boone tied on a big striper, and we "fought" it to boatside and netted it. We had caught enough big stripers on our own to know how it was done, so it might have looked pretty good on the screen.

I made up my mind to come back another October. First, I needed a more substantial boat to cross the Chesapeake from our home in Cape St. Claire. The 12-foot aluminum was a bit iffy.

Cape Cod

One of the first books I bought after catching rockfish fever was *Striped Bass Fishing* by Henry Lyman and Frank Woolner, published in 1954. Lyman and Woolner were the high priests of striper fishing in the high surf. They also published *Salt Water Sportsman* magazine, and I subscribed to that. Reading about striper fishing was the next best thing to doing it, and the information I gleaned from their book was priceless. It also made me want to travel to the mystic land of big stripers, and see for myself.

Cape Cod, Massachusetts was *the* mecca for those who wanted trophy stripers in the summer of 1961. Of course, Carole and I had differing ideas about what comprised a vacation. She wanted to sightsee, and I wanted to at least dunk a lure in some of the fabled striper holes I'd been reading about. We compromised. I looked at some of the places, made a few casts, talked to some anglers, and we saw a lot of sights.

We stayed in a motel near the Bourne Bridge to Cape Cod. I tossed every manner of lure I knew about then into the rapid currents of the Cape Cod Canal. I was a bit leery about getting my bucktail jigs too deep, because I'd lose them on the rock-strewn bottom. Naturally, I was a green angler, and new to that area. I caught nothing.

Nearly 30 years later, I found out why. Bob Pond said he always let his jigs bounce along the bottom in the canal. "The jigs hitting those rocks must make a tick-tick sound," Bob said, "That's what turns the fish on."

Oh, well, we did find Sandy's, a great place to get lobster. It was right across from the motel, and we had the best lobster dinner we ever had before or since.

I tried slack and moving tides in the canal, with no luck. No matter, the fishing is sometimes more important than the catching. And, what would I have done with a 50-pound striper in a motel room, anyway?

We moved our base of operations out on the Cape, to a motel I'd rather not mention. The people there were about as friendly as boa constrictors. From there, we took in all the sights. Well, all the beaches where stripers were likely to lurk. Again, we were fishing the wrong tides with the wrong equipment, at the wrong times. But, we could say we fished there. The very name, Nauset Beach, conjured up visions of striper blitzes and beach buggies. Later, I bought a boat that bore the Nauset name. We made quite a few casts from Nauset Beach, with no takers. There is always the chance, and that's what keeps the adrenalin flowing.

Carole surfcasting at Nauset Beach, Cape Cod.

We dunked our lures at famed Race Point off Provincetown, then Truro, near Orleans, even Sandwich. Standing ankle-deep in what seemed like zero degree water on Sandwich Beach dunking bloodworms, we were surprised by a bus-load of kids who ran screaming and splashing with delight into water a polar bear might have second thoughts about. Wow!

A Ton of Big Stripers

On our way off the Cape, we stopped at the well-known Red Top tackle shop in Buzzard's Bay. The guys behind the counter were friendly enough, but didn't offer any information to help a novice Marylander catch a "bass." (New Englanders pronounce it "BAAASS"). We didn't have the money to hire a guide or a charterboat.

On the parking lot outside, I struck up a conversation with a red-eyed striper fanatic. His car was festooned with the long rods they call "high surf" sticks adorned with Penn Squidder reels. His clothes looked like they had been slept in—or fished in—for a decade, and he had a heroic growth of stubble. For some reason, he took a liking to me, and we compared Cape Cod and Chesapeake Bay striper fishing. He didn't like me enough to divulge any Cape Cod striper secrets, but he nodded his head toward two coolers in the back of his station wagon.

"C'mere, look at this," he said. He lifted the lids on the two huge coolers. They were packed solid with iced-down "bass" that ran from 20 to 50 pounds or more! He had fished all night for several days, and just last night, he'd lucked into a blitz. He was the only one on that stretch of beach. He said he was a commercial hook-and-liner, and those fish were destined for market.

"What did you catch them on?" I asked with innocence of someone too dumb to know they shouldn't. He scanned the parking lot to make sure no one could hear, and dug into an old wooden tackle box with brass hinges. He held up something I'd never seen before. I guess you could call it an eelskin jig/rig. It had a four- or five-ounce lead head with a circular ring attached. The ring had a groove around its circumference. A piece of brass sash chain was threaded through the ring. A 9/0 or so hook was attached to the end of the chain.

Metalure Eelskin Rig.

He explained how a preserved eelskin is slipped over the hook and chain and the open end is brought over the ring and tied. The hook is pushed through the eelskin near the tail. In use, water pressure through the open ring keeps the eelskin ballooned out. A less messy rig that has now disappeared from the market is the Alou rigged plastic eel.

My new friend gave me one of the real eelskin rigs, minus the smelly skin itself, but darned if I can find it.

Cuttyhunk, and Other Spots I Haven't Fished

On our way home, we drove through New Bedford, an old whaling town that seemed, in 1961, to be economically depressed. With all that valuable waterfront, I expect it is not that way today. Naturally, I had to sniff around the waterfront a bit. We pulled into a parking lot near a dock, and got out to stretch our legs and take a few slides of this picturesque area. It was mid-morning.

By luck, a striper charterboat pulled up to the dock where we were standing. It was called the *Strad*, captained by Charley Haag, a concert violinist who quit the New York Philharmonic to go striper fishing.

Charlie Haag in his Cuttyhunk bass boat.

Haag had three anglers on board. The *Strad* was an open, lapstrake wooden inboard boat, about 28-feet, a classic hull sometimes referred to as a "Cuttyhunk bass boat," but it also had the lines of a Jersey sea skiff. They had been out all night fishing the rips off Nashawena and Cuttyhunk Islands. This was the area where Charles Church caught his long-standing record 73-pound striper in 1913, a record that stood for decades. The *Strad* anglers had several big stripers, and one of them held up a 50-pounder for me to photograph.

Frank Woolner of *Salt Water Sportsman* magazine later told me he had fished with Haag many times.

"He built his own boat, you know," Woolner said. "And, he was a NUT the way he fished. He wouldn't let you pull in a bass on the same side of another boat in sight, even a mile away. He was one of the best bass fishermen, though."

I expect I should have tried to book into a trip with Captain Haag, but he did night fishing. I had visions of my bride spending a night in a strange motel worrying about me tossing around in six-foot waves trying to land a striper I didn't have the money to have mounted, anyway.

Between the fish the Cape Cod surf angler showed us, and those I saw the *Strad* anglers land, I knew there were stripers bigger than I would ever catch out there. But, that wouldn't stop me from trying. It was far from a wasted vacation.

One of Charlie Haag's anglers with a big striper.

3

THE WHALER YEARS (1964–1974)

An Understanding Wife is the Key to a New Boat

Getting swamped in a small tin boat is a safety lesson learned the hard way. I started looking for a new and safer boat to ease my bride's mind about my solitary after-dark fishing. Coincidentally, she had just gone back to work, and she somehow connected her re-employment with my boat buying.

Boston Whaler was then running ads in the fishing magazines showing a Whaler sawed in three pieces, with a guy standing in each floating slice of boat. One guy wore a big smile and a chain saw. That seemed safe enough for me. I did the winter shows, looking at boats.

My new Whaler, Carole's new house.

At a Baltimore boat show I was standing alongside a novel boat that appealed to me, when my knee buckled the unsupported plywood side inward about six inches. The salesman was a marvel of quick thinking. "We make 'em like that so they'll flex," he said with a straight face when I pointed out the ribs were two feet apart. I went back to looking at fiberglass hulls.

Montgomery Ward had a sale on 40-HP Gale (OMC) outboard motors. Next, I was able to get a good price (full retail) on a 16-foot Nauset model Boston Whaler and trailer from Harvey Gates.

The Bay Bridge Gang

At NASA Goddard Space Flight Center, I photographed all sorts of satellite tests. That brought me into contact with a lot of NASA engineers and technicians. Many of them fished. Many fished for striped bass. How convenient! We'd meet after work, in our respective boats, under the Bay Bridge.

Jim Stephens and John Webb usually fished together in Jim's boat, sometimes in Webb's. Warren Boerum, Paul Henley, Paul King, Paul Butler, Bob Young, and other NASA types fished the bridge. It seemed there was always someone we knew fishing around the pilings or rock piles.

Some of the "Bay Bridge Gang" with their 1965 rockfish trophies. Left to right: Warren Boerum, John Henley, Paul Henley, and Jim Stephens.

Bay Spray is Good for the Soul

One rough evening, Goddard technician Don Bauer fished with me in my Whaler. Like most anglers in a hurry, I had one speed, wide open. Rough or calm, always wide open. It was rough. Like any good host, I put my guest on the downwind side so he wouldn't get as wet as me. When we got to the bridge and I finally slowed down, he was slightly shaken, and as wet as I.

"What do you think of my nice safe Whaler?" I asked Don.

He looked around the boat slowly, water droplets forming on the end of his nose. Finally, he voiced an opinion:

"It's like a bathtub with a piano in the middle," he said. He never went fishing with me after that. I don't know why.

Love Point Revisited

Talk about luck! On October 10, 1964, I tossed a ⅞-ounce blue and white Atom swimming plug at the propeller of the old Love Point Wreck, and in less time than it takes to tell it, I was into a monster striper.

Love Point Wreck, October 10, 1964.

Then, my problems began. My Mitchell 306 reel had a jerky drag, and threatened to pop my line with every rush the striper made. The 306's bail spring broke and I had to alternately hold the bail closed and try to crank the reel handle with my left hand as I played the fish. The fish seesawed my line back and forth across the propeller and hull, which was coated with razor-sharp barnacles. I loosened the drag as much as I could. The fish finally swam away from the wreck, and I breathed a sigh of relief. Now I had a chance.

We continued the seesaw battle as the incoming tide carried us up the Chester River. It seemed like hours, but was probably only 20 or 30 minutes before the big fish was at boatside. When it showed color, it was obviously a monster striper.

"Look at the size of that rockfish!" said my angling companion, Jerry Rayburn, when he spied the huge fish thrashing around at boatside. Jerry didn't want to gaff it for me. He was afraid if he missed it, I would toss *him* overboard. I finally talked Jerry into gaffing the fish.

Not far away, two elderly gents in a runabout watched the battle. When we brought the fish aboard, we were even more amazed at its size. We had never seen a rockfish that big. Neither had the gents.

"What did you catch that fish on?" asked one gent. I showed him my ⅞-ounce Atom swimmer, now broken in two from the fight. Atom plugs (and any other heavy-duty lure worth using in the salt) have a wire running through the plug that connects the hooks, so the lure held the fish. The belly treble hook had been broken off by the monster fish, but luckily the lure's tail hook had grabbed him by the cheek.

The ⅞-ounce Atom swimmer that caught the author's 32½-pound tournament-winning striper.

"Hot dog!" one gent said when he saw my lure, "I've got one of those!" He dove into his tackle box while his buddy tossed their anchor overboard, right there. I didn't have the heart to tell them I caught the fish back at the wreck, now two miles away.

Jerry and I motored back to the wreck, and showed the fish to Stephens and the others. They couldn't get over the size, either. They had caught several big stripers in our absence, but nothing that big. Jerry made a cast and caught an 18-pounder, which I was happy to gaff for him.

I had more luck that day than might be assumed from simply catching a big rockfish. Like many anglers of that day, when you had something good, you let your buddies in on it. Before this trip, I had told Stephens about the big fish on Love Point, and how Bob Pond had showed us how to catch them in October, 1962.

On this October morning in 1964, Jim and I had decided to run our boats across from the Little Magothy River to Love Point together. He had a 19-foot boat with a 40-horsepower motor. He remembers two passengers, Tom Raley and Bob Young. I had a 16-foot Whaler with a 40-horse Johnson, and one passenger, Jerry Rayburn. Both boats left the Little Magothy inlet together, but my smaller hull was just a tad faster, and I got to the wreck first. My lure was the first one in the water. Luck of the draw.

The guys raved about the size of the fish. Jim told me I should enter it in the then-new Maryland Sportfishing Tournament that the DNR began in August, 1964 with Bill Perry as Director.

I dragged the monster striper into Chuck and Don's Tackle Store in Parole near Annapolis. The fish's giant tail left a wide, wet trail on the floor. A slightly amazed Chuck Prahl weighed the animal for me. Chuck's official, calibrated tournament scale showed the striper weighed 32-pounds, 8-ounces!

The author holds his tournament-winning striper.

"I think you've won the tournament," Chuck said, somewhat prematurely I thought. He had been following the tourney, and I hadn't even known there was a tournament until Jim Stephens told me.

Helen Giblo wrote the outdoors column for the Annapolis *Evening Capital* newspaper. She asked if I could bring the fish to her house in Bay Ridge so she could get a photograph. She was running late for another appointment, and would I do her that favor? Sure. She took a picture of me with the fish on her dock and wrote a story for her paper.

Back home, Carole took a few pictures of me holding the big striper. Then, I cleaned the fish, and we ate it. Dumb. Should have had it mounted. Clearly, 20/20 hindsight. Several good things followed, though.

Chuck's prediction was correct. Mine *was* the largest rockfish registered in that first tournament.

Bill Burton of *The Baltimore Sun* called. I gave him the details of my catch, and he wrote a nice story. Actually, I was very impressed with his ability to write a good story from a short interview. He was also doing some public relations work for Bob Pond's Atom plugs, so he asked if Bob could use my photograph with the tournament-winning striper in Atom plug ads. He offered to send me some Atom plugs for my trouble. Since we lost several lures a week, that was like manna from Heaven. I sent Bill some pictures, and they used two of them in a 1965 Fishing in Maryland magazine Atom plug ad.

The awards banquet for the tournament was held in February, 1965 at the elegant old Carvel Hall in Annapolis, which has since been demolished. Bill Perry organized the affair and Bill Burton was master of ceremonies. Hal Lyman of *Salt Water Sportsman* Magazine was the keynote speaker. Friendship with Perry and Burton have continued to this date. And, ironically, I now write articles for Hal Lyman's *Salt Water Sportsman* Magazine.

Other winners in that tourney were: Richard S. Gatti received a cup for his 8-lb 2-oz bluefish. Doris H. Gray had a 4-lb hardhead. Charles Everly had a 72-lb black drum, and John Gootee had a 76-lb channel bass. Alfred R. Wallach had a 1-lb 11-oz white perch, and Ernest J. Gibbs caught a 60-lb cobia.

Governor J. Millard Tawes presented me with a silver wine goblet engraved, "Rock, 32 Lbs. 8 Oz., Keith Walters, 1964."

But that wasn't the best of it. Banquets and publicity are fun, but only for the moment. Through rockfishing, I met many lifetime friends who continued to turn up even after we moved to the Eastern Shore in 1981.

We'll meet these folks again.

Podickory Point Plugging

Carole and I spent some beautiful summer and fall evenings plugging the shoreline between Cape St. Claire and Sandy Point State Park. I always looked forward to the 4th of July. The weekend closest to that holiday began plugging time. Then, stripers moved into shallow water, not more than four feet deep.

We drifted along with the breeze or tide, casting popping plugs like the Atom. If we had a hit or swirl behind the plug, I'd toss out a small anchor on a 20-foot line to hold us near that spot. I still fish that way today, only now for bluefish in May.

Certain places along that shore always held fish. There were sandstone outcroppings that provided enough structure for a rockfish or two. Fishing was good on both sides of the seawall that enclosed Podickory Point Marina.

Carole with Podickory stripers.

Finally, a Use for Those Humongous 14-Inch Plugs

One evening just at dark, with an outgoing tide, I noticed a cabin cruiser, the *Mallard* having more luck than average. The captain trolled parallel to the Bay Bridge on the down-tide side of the pilings.

He and his lady constantly fought big stripers as they made a big circle to return to their pattern. I hung back and watched.

As they went past, they hollered they were trolling their #21 Tony spoons with no weight. That size Tony is BIG. I needed a big lure.

I frantically rooted through the tackle box and came up with an 800 series Creek Chub swimming plug that measured 14 inches. It was the only really BIG lure I had aboard.

I snapped it on my big spinning outfit, and trolled well behind the *Mallard*. A moose of a fish grabbed the plug (I have caught many fish smaller than that plug). The striper began to end-over-end cartwheel behind the boat, trying to dislodge that lure. No way. It had three treble hooks. I went home that night with a 30-pounder.

I followed John Webb's suggestion for a low budget mount: I put the big striper on a piece of plywood, outlined it with a pencil, then cut around the outline with a saber saw. That fish silhouette still hangs on my wall, painted yellow and lettered:

> ## "TIME SPENT IN ACTIVITIES OTHER THAN FISHING IS TIME WASTED"

— Izaak Walters

A 14-inch Creek Chub swimming plug with ¹/₂-ounce Rat-L-Trap for comparison.

The next evening I was back with several big Creek Chub plugs. I had two fish on at the same time, but as I fought the first fish that hit, the other headed for the bottom and scrubbed off my plug. I did land a big striper. The second one would have been over my legal limit.

Soft Crabs are Edible Fishbait

Jim Lock, a neighbor in the Cape, frequently fished with me. If we didn't catch a few rockfish plugging the shoreline, we'd motor down to the Bay Bridge and plug the rockpiles. Often, we would carry a few live soft crabs with us and stay after dark to float the baits next to the rockpiles.

If there was a secret about where to fish the rocks and when, I failed to find it. Sometimes the fish would be lying in the slack water inside an eddy current, sometimes on the uptide side where they had to fight current, occasionally on the downtide side where there was no current. Mostly, they could be found in a place we called the "front corner." On the uptide side of the rockpile, each "corner" of the rocks had a place where fish could lay just out of the current, where they could dart out and grab morsels whisked past their noses by the tide.

The neat part of soft crab floating was that if the fish didn't bite, you still had a few live soft crabs to eat when you got home. *We never ate dead soft crabs*. Never!

The author and Jim Lock with stripers that fell for soft crabs.

Ace Lace from the Space Place and the UFO

As a photographer, I had a lot of dealings with the NASA Goddard Public Affairs Office, run by Ed "Moose" Mason. Ed was (and is) big enough to warrant that nickname.

One of Ed's top PIO guns at Goddard was James Lacey. Lacey was bigger than life. Actually, bigger than the universe. Like many a PR guy, he came on strong. And kept going. A nice guy, he sometimes jolted folks a bit off balance by shoving out a glad hand and introducing himself, "Hi, there, I'm Ace Lace from the Space Place."

Lace, an outdoorsman and an avid shotgunner, wanted to experience rockfishing. I told him to be at my house soon after work, and we'd have a shot at the Bay Bridge with live eels.

I didn't invite Lace to dinner, as I told him later, because I didn't want to spring him on Carole all at once. He grabbed a couple of Macs and showed up at the door. I introduced him to Carole and hustled him out the door.

The Bay was ROUGH. For once, I had to slow down and rock back and forth in the waves a bit. I didn't think it would bother Lace because he'd flown fighter planes from carriers in WW II. But, the Macs were not sitting too well on his hiatus hernia. He turned a nice shade of green and stayed that color most of the evening.

The water was really churning at the bridge. The Whaler bounced and lurched in three-foot seas. Lace put his head down on the console and begged to die.

"Should I stop fishing?" I asked, dangling a live eel alongside a bridge piling. No reply.

"You came all this way. Don't you wanna fish?" Lace gurgled a polite, "No, you go ahead and fish." It was the only time I ever saw him that subdued.

I caught a couple of eight- or 10-pound rockfish around a bridge piling. Lace finally barfed over the side. Then, he perked up. We were on our way home, then, at dusk. The Bay had calmed down about the same time as Lace's stomach.

As we headed up the Bay past Sandy Point Light, we saw a big light in the sky. Since we both worked for NASA, we made a few jokes about UFOs. We had a lot of fun, but the light didn't go away. It was about halfway between Gibson Island and Baltimore Light. We decided to investigate. As we got closer, we saw the light was suspended under a helicopter, which seemed to be looking for something. I poured on the coal, thinking maybe we could help.

Just off Gibson Island, we saw a small outboard runabout motoring southward, in gear, with all its lights on, trolling rods set in holders. There was no one on board.

The adrenalin started pumping. We got the message. Some poor fisherman had fallen overboard. I ran north in the boat's wake. Lace scanned the water with a flashlight. The chopper pilot followed us with that HUMONGOUS skylight, flying a Zee pattern ahead of our bow. It was like a big sun up there, it was so bright. We stayed a couple of hours, looking. We saw nothing. No life preserver, nothing floating. It was a sobering experience. When the chopper left, we did. Police took the runabout.

Lace had recovered entirely from his recent stomach problems. He asked for a beer at the house. We were still shook about that poor rascal from the runabout. We were both thinking, "There, but for the Grace of God, go I."

Lace took the fish.

Soft Crabs Under the Bridge, Under the Moon
... August, 1964

We bought our soft crabs from Cantler's on Mill Creek. They knew we were fishermen. They preferred to sell peeler crabs rather than soft crabs as fish bait. Both were the same price then. Even though they had to stay up all night shedding out their peelers to get soft crabs. Don't look for that courtesy now.

I think Mrs. Cantler knew we were using the soft crabs as rockfish bait, but she never let on. We'd admire the soft crabs, and feel how soft they were, and comment on the fact that they were all alive, and how delicious they'd be in the frying pan—an accurate statement if we didn't use them all catching fish.

Mrs. Cantler asked us once, scowling, "You boys aren't using these nice soft crabs for *fishing* are you?" She sort of spit out the word "fishing," like it was something really disgusting.

"No, ma'am, we wouldn't do nothing like that!" It was a little game she and I played every time I bought soft crabs, which was almost every night.

We left with our crabs in a cloud of dust. Time's a wasting!

Bill Smith (he liked to spell it "Smiff" like he was related to Snuffy) was my partner in grime at Goddard (we did a lot of nasty, dirty high-speed camera set-ups in vacuum chambers and stuff). Bill and I were in my Whaler, and Bob Young and Jerry Rayburn joined Jim Stephens in

Jim's boat. We met under the old bridge on the Eastern Shore side. I think we were between pilings 56 and 57. Jim anchored between the pilings to our east.

It was a beautiful moonlit night in August, 1964. The tide was running out at a good clip. You could see the water boil in rips and eddy currents on the downtide side of the pilings. We began to float our soft crab baits.

In this fishing, we used medium spinning tackle, about 15-pound test line. Most of us had disabled the drag clickers on our reels, because when you are fishing on a still night you don't want to draw a lot of company. A two-foot leader of 30-pound test line was tied to a 2/0 stainless steel hook. The stainless O'Shaughnessy hooks, we believed, were stronger, though brown Aberdeen hooks would have held anything we caught. A pinch-on sinker of the proper size on the line end of the leader completed the rig. We cut our crabs into six or more baits, and saved the claws and back flippers for emergencies.

I heard the hum of a taut line in the next boat. Someone was into a fish over there. A lot of grunting and swearing. The fish were big that night, mostly 10-pounders or better. Then, Bill had a hit. Then me. Then, someone in the next boat. It went like that for several hours, with some slack periods when the tide's speed changed.

Left to right: Jerry Rayburn, Bill Smith, Bob Young, Jim Stephens, and the author.

I didn't figure the slack periods out until later, though I knew it had something to do with having our baits in the striper's feeding range. The fish were not on the bottom, but suspended somewhere above it.

It was one beautiful night, and the best action we had on stripers for some time. Everyone was elated, and we were joking back and forth between the boats about running out of bait. Finally, Bill and I were crawling around on the deck, looking for left over crab parts for bait. I remember putting my last tiny back flipper on that big hook—and I caught a striper on it!

Jim ran his boat back to my place that night, and we had a picture taking session. A group of happy rockfisherman.

"Bring the Wheelbarrow, Carole"

Citizen's Band (C.B.) radio was coming into wide use about the time I began to range a bit farther in search of rockfish. All of the Bay Bridge gang had a set in their boats. We stayed away from the truckers by avoiding channel 19, though sometimes when we were fishing under the Bay Bridge, the truckers above us would blast over into our channels with their big linear amplifiers. Linears were illegal, but effective.

C.B. was like a party line then. It seemed everyone had a set at home, in the car, and in the boat. People listened in, others talked to entertain them. It was a nice way to communicate until language on the radios got so foul many gave up on C.B.

Some of our fishing buddies had colorful C.B. "handles." Jim Stephens was "Bucktail," alluding to a favorite lure. Paul Henley was "Nightcrawler," because he stayed out half the night showing eels and soft crabs to stripers under the bridge.

Al Smith was "Whaleboat." My handle came from John Webb ("Rowboat"), who insisted I should be "Mathew Brady" because I was a photographer, an old one at that. I changed my handle to something more in line with my capabilities—"Backlash."

Henley later had a heart attack (we shared the same doctor), and after a short recovery period, Paul asked Dr. if he was allowed to go fishing. I had taken Dr. white perch fishing, so I guess the good doc thought what I showed him was pretty tame stuff. Dr. gave Paul the go-ahead to "go fishing." Little did doc know that Paul was spending most of the night fighting big animals, then cleaning fish before reporting to work the next morning.

My home C.B. antenna wasn't getting out, so I bought one big enough to dwarf my three-stack chimney. Jim Stephens and John Webb helped me erect the monster. It was snowing when we clambered up on the roof. I don't like heights. We slipped around a little, but got the job done. Think about it. How many of YOUR friends would spend a cold weekend day on a slippery roof, with snow swirling around? These guys are special.

Many a time the C.B. radios came in handy. Emergencies or general communications, they were handy if you could get through the noise.

I used to call Carole from the boat with a fishing report as I ran home from the bridge.

"Carole, bring the wheelbarrow to the dock," I said into the mike.

"Yeah, sure," she snickered. She thought I was showing off because everyone monitored C.B. Not so. That night, I got lucky.

NASA engineer, Gil Bullock, once told me he would come all the way from Laurel to Cape St. Claire any night I had fish for him. He had a big family. I asked Carole to call Gil and tell him to come and get the six rockfish I had for him. She called. I could imagine what was running through Gil's mind. "Go all the way to %$#@$ Cape St. Claire for six little fish. Fooey!" he probably thought.

When Gil arrived, I trundled the wheelbarrow out to his car with six 10- to 12-pound stripers in it. Sixty pounds of fish, easy. You can imagine Gil's expression. After that, he always came for fish when I called.

Polite is Class, Rude is Crude

Carole and I saw Jimmy Tracey plugging a small area in front of the "preacher's house" along the Bay Head shoreline in three feet of water. We pulled up on the outside of his boat and cut our motor.

"They're right in there," he said, pointing to an area near shore, "Pull in beside me, and cast where I tell you."

"I don't want to mess you up."

"You won't, move over just off my stern and cast right where I show you." Jimmy made a cast and a rockfish grabbed his popping plug in a shower of spray. Hot Dog! The adrenalin was flowing. I moved.

Now, this was a tiny spot we were casting to, no bigger than a bathtub. Later, I found a small outcropping of sandstone there. Rockfish have to hang around something, no matter how small.

Another secret Jimmy told us was not to crank our plugs across the water fast. You had to give the plug as much action as possible with as little forward movement as possible. Dance it in one place. That's the only way they would hit it.

Carole got a hit. She stood up to fight the fish, probably a mistake. The fish gave her quite a fight, bent rod, singing drag, the whole works. I netted her fish.

Oh, oh! There was a skiff coming at us full speed. He saw Carole catch the fish. Jimmy and I had been through this before. We simply stopped fishing. The guy was a real slob, no fishing couth. He pulled in next to Jimmy and began to rip his plug across the surface where he thought Carole's fish hit. He had no hits. He kept it up, moving in closer to us.

Finally, Jimmy had to say something to him about his running up on top of us and messing us up. Now, remember, if the guy had been polite, we might have told him what we were doing. His brusk manner and his remark that "I'll fish anywhere in the Bay I want" made us mad. We clammed up. Finally, Jimmy had it.

"Why don't you go down to the Bay Bridge with the %$&*# snaggers?" he asked. A Bay Bridge rockfish snagger was the lowest form of life to Jimmy, the "cream of the crap," he said once.

Our antagonist finally got mad and roared off across what he must have thought was our fishing hole. It wasn't. After he left, we waited until he was nearly to the Bay Bridge before we began fishing again. We caught more fish, too. Big ones.

Go Slow, Snaggers at Work

You could see them any time of day or night around Bay Bridge pilings, the rockfish snaggers. They used all manner of treble-hooked devices to snag stripers in the side, gut, or tail. They didn't have the patience or good sportsmanship to try and catch stripers that wouldn't bite on plugs, jigs or bait.

I remember seeing one guy I knew standing on the bow of his boat, as close as he could get to a bridge piling, jerking his rod tip up and down with great vigor. I called his name and said something to him about it. He laughed.

Snagging rockfish is illegal now. In fact, you may not use "a treble hook that is not an intrinsic part of a floating lure within 1,200 feet of any pier that supports either span of the William Preston Lane, Jr. Memorial Bridge," according to the DNR's Maryland Tidewater Sport Fishing Guide. I don't know if snagging rockfish was illegal in the past, but it sure is now. It didn't suit me.

Over the years we caught a lot of big stripers around Bay Bridge pilings. It was not unusual to catch one with its sides all ripped up where it had been raked by a snagger's treble hooks.

I remember a hot summer day when a buddy (I'll call him "Sam" in case being mentioned in the same paragraph with "snagging" would embarrass him) and I were casting bucktails around the western rockpile. Sam hooked a big rockfish, but it acted crazy, as if it was foul-hooked. It was much more powerful than any we had seen.

Fishing boats anchored around the rockpile were thick, hardly any room between them. Sam's fish led us a merry chase between anchor lines and fishing lines. I ran the boat while he battled his fish.

Then, I noticed a DNR Police cabin cruiser following us.

"Sam," I said, "If that fish is foul-hooked, and I think it might be, I want you to break it off."

Sam didn't want to give up his trophy fish, and we discussed it loudly and at great length. I explained that the DNR Police were on the lookout for snaggers and had made several arrests. And if his fish, even though it wasn't purposely snagged with an illegal device, didn't have the lure in its mouth all legal like, he'd better bust it off at boatside or we'd likely get a ticket from that nice gentleman in that boat over there marked "POLICE."

Sam got the fish up near the boat. It was BIG, maybe 30 pounds. The biggest Sam had ever caught. A lifetime trophy. The DNR boat was closing fast. Sam's bucktail was outside the fish's mouth, hung in its cheek. Marginal. If the DNR officer was in a bad mood, he would write Sam's name on a form with several copies. I had visions of forfeiting my boat. Now, we hadn't set out to snag rockfish. We weren't using the snagger's usual weapons.

It was decision time for Sam. The officer was getting close enough to see the lure in Sam's fish. I turned the boat away so the fish was on the side away from the officer, who began to circle us.

It was up to Sam. I think he made the right decision.

Sam grabbed his fishing line and held it. The fish gave a lunge and broke the line. Sam snapped to attention and started to swear at the disappearing fish. It was not an act for the officer. Sam was really upset about turning loose the biggest striper he ever caught.

Chumming on Poplar Island Flats

Tony DiBartolo heard there was a big school of rockfish responding to chummed clams north of Poplar Island on the flats in September, 1969. We waited for a nice evening to try for them. The trip would be 18 miles one way—nautical miles. I didn't relish riding 36 miles in rough water in an open Whaler. Most of it after dark.

We lucked out. The evening was slick calm. We had a bushel of clams aboard and that lucky feeling.

We were alone at the "hotspot." If the fish were really here, where was everyone? It was a pretty night.

We picked a place near a dropoff, anchored, and started to chum with the clams. First, we half-filled a bucket with clams, then smashed their papery shells with a cut-off piece of oar handle. We mixed a little water with this glop, and tossed handfuls of the mixture overboard at short intervals until we got a few hits. Then, we slowed the frequency of our chumming. Fresh clams were opened for bait. Some anglers used both the clam snout and the stomach for bait, but I only used the snout.

Medium spinning gear and a 24-inch leader of 30-pound test tied to a 2/0 hook was the standard rig. Sinkers were as small as possible, enough to keep the bait on bottom, but not too heavy to detect bites. I tried egg sinkers with my running line passed through the sinker's center with good success. The free-running sinker was stopped by a terminal snap swivel. It was a fishfinder rig that allowed the egg sinker to run up the line so the fish wouldn't feel the weight.

It wasn't long before we got bites, and fish. They were big stripers, running up to 12 or 14 pounds. We had a ball.

Now, don't misunderstand. I think Tony is a great guy and I'll never make fun of him. But, you had to actually see Tony fish to appreciate it. He did a little dance when the fish hit. He talked to it, his tackle, and yelled at anything that got in his way. If the fish ran under the motor, he sometimes said something in Italian that I didn't understand. To say Tony is an excitable fisherman is an understatement.

It was late when we finally gave up, but we had enough fish for Tony and all his neighbors.

It was a beautiful run back up the Bay that night. The stars were more vivid than usual because the air was so clear. Bloody Point Light winked at us as we went past. Car headlights on the Bay Bridge indicated heavy traffic.

I usually cut inside Sandy Point Light when I ran back from the Bay Bridge at night, though I advise others not to try it. It *is* shallow inshore of the light. The crab pot buoys were thick and hard to miss, though you can see them well when your eyes are accustomed to starlight.

The crab potters must have experienced some piracy of their crabs, because one night I stopped, lights on, to pick up something that had fallen in the boat. A big spotlight shone on me from inshore. The boat ran toward me at top speed. If it had been a police boat, there would have been flashing lights and loudspeakers. I easily outran the boat. It was probably an irate crab potter who thought I was a pot robber. That's the second good reason to run outside Sandy Point Light in the channel. No pots there.

I called Carole on the C.B. radio and she was at the dock with the wheelbarrow. I helped Tony load his station wagon with fish.

Tony DiBartolo with our catch.

A Honeycomb Plug Rack Saved My Dearest Body Parts

Over the years I developed a plugging "system" for rockfish and bluefish. My purpose was to keep my hands away from treble hooks and razor sharp bluefish teeth. If you've ever had a thrashing four pound rockfish on one treble hook and the plug's other hook firmly imbedded in one of your tenderest body parts, you'll know why.

The system begins with a spinning outfit of the angler's choice. I use an 8-foot rod with a medium spinning reel loaded with 14-pound test line. Once, I re-armed my popping plugs with two sharp stainless steel 2/0 treble hooks (most of my plugs now have a large single hook). Then, a 24-inch leader of 45-pound test braided wire is attached to the plug, and a loop is crimped in the other end of the leader that can be attached to the small snap swivel at the end of my running line.

Once hooked up with a bluefish, we bring it to the boat, grabbing the leader if it is a small blue, or gaffing the big ones. Then, the fish are deposited in a cooler, with the heavy leader protruding through the closed lid. Then, we safely unsnap the leader outside the cooler, grab another plug, and get back in business. We extract the lures later when the fishing slacks off and the blues are still.

Rockfish often frequent the same areas as blues, but rock are handled more carefully when they are to be released.

The main problem I had with this system was in keeping the lures from tangling. So, I built a plug rack from PVC electrical conduit of the proper inside diameter to accommodate my popping plugs. I made it like a honeycomb for strength, and it's been on one boat or another for 25 years. The bottom and mounting straps on the back are made from $\frac{1}{2}$-inch sheet PVC. Small holes were drilled in the bottom to drain the tubes. All parts were attached with standard PVC cement. Work in the open air with PVC cement for safety.

A plug holder can be made from any material available to the angler—schedule 40 PVC water pipe, plexiglas, wood, copper, or stainless steel.

I mounted the plug rack on the back of the Whaler's seat, and later inside the anchor locker door on my 20-foot Mako.

Honeycomb plug rack mounted on back of Whaler seat.

NASA Science and the Crab Floaters

Hugh Turnbull, a NASA satellite tracking engineer, was my guest on one of the rainiest rockfishing nights in history. It poured from the time we left the dock until sometime the next week.

Normally, I don't care about fishing in the rain, because of all the other nasty stuff that goes with it: Lightning, high winds, hail, and other things that can cause discomfort or death.

But, Hugh had driven quite a distance to fish with me, so I hated to call it off. We donned rain gear, and loaded our tackle and bait in the Whaler for a sloppy ride to the Bay Bridge.

We had been catching rockfish on the Eastern Shore side of the Bay Bridge, about piling 35 or so.

The tide was going out, and the wind was against the tide, which not only piled up bigger seas, but gave me some anchoring problems.

I anchored so the boat was under the bridge to provide us a bit of a rain shield. Not much, because it was raining horizontally. Rain that began to fall at the mouth of Chesapeake Bay was pelting us in the face.

We baited up and started fishing. It went slowly for a while. The rig we used was the same one I used when presenting pencil-sized eels to big stripers: Medium spinning gear with 12- to 15-pound test line ending with a small snap swivel. A two-foot leader of 30-pound test, looped at the swivel end, with a 2/0 stainless steel hook tied to the business end.

Soft crabs were cut into four or six pieces, depending on the size of the crab, and the size of the fish expected. A small pinch-on sinker was attached to the swivel end of the leader, with one bent-over ear through the loop in the leader to prevent sinker slide. Hugh and I each used a different sized weight for starters.

I don't remember who caught the first striper, but I bet it was only a nanosecond before the other angler changed to precisely the same sinker weight. Again, the stripers were feeding at a certain depth, and to get a bait in the strike zone, you had to either compute the speed of the tide in knots at all levels, plus set and drift, factor in the combined weight and drag of a sinker, hook, swivel, leader, and bait—or you could luck out, like we did.

Fighting stripers from a bouncing boat while a strong wind beats a horizontal rain into every facial pore and chink in your rain gear is miserable. But, it's better than not fighting stripers at all.

We fought fish. That old cliche about the excitement of screaming drags and singing line is true, even in gale force winds. There was a lot of happy screaming about, "Net this little 8-pounder for me," or "Get the gaff, this guy is a 15-pounder," and stuff like that.

Excitement, or adrenalin, or something, warms even the coldest, wettest fisherman. That old saw about fishermen having "a wet tail and a hungry gut" disappears when a 10-pound rockfish slams your bait and heads down the Bay. Circulation returns to hands and feet, and a smile lights up your frozen face. It's striper time!

Fortunately, the ride home was all "down hill" with the waves. And the rain was not in our faces, but behind our backs. Of course, when you are wet to the skin, a little more drenching doesn't make a big difference.

When all the gear was put away, Carole, marvelling at how some anglers torture themselves, spread some newspaper on the porch floor and took our picture with the catch. Hugh and I were as happy as two wet buzzards watching a road kill.

Later, Hugh called me with an exciting bit of scientific news. He had taken some of our sinkers home and calculated that a difference in sinker weight as small as $1/16$-ounce could keep a soft crab bait in or out of the striper's narrow strike zone.

It pays to carry a pair of sidecutter pliers or dikes along to snip unwanted ounces off your sinker. That applies to any bait fishing where the bait is suspended off the bottom.

As NASA engineer John Webb says, "Chisel THAT in a hunk of granite and tuck it in your wallet for future reference."

Once again, NASA space science had been applied to the needs of humanity. NASA Technology Transfer folks call it "spin-off."

Agnes Done Us Dirty

Hurricane Agnes spoiled a nice vacation for us in the summer of 1972. We had talked about a vacation trip that would include Mystic Seaport, Connecticut; Newport, Rhode Island; and Gloucester, Massachusetts. Maybe a little farther north along the coast if we had time.

Purely by luck, our 1970 Pontiac had a trunk large enough to carry two collapsed 9-foot fishing rods in case I happened to get a chance to make a cast or two at stripers on a beach somewhere. One has to be prepared for the worst. It was to be a beautiful marriage of sightseeing for Carole, and a coastal cast or two for me.

By the time I had arranged for vacation time from work, and Carole's Uncle Bruce and Aunt Naomi McDowell, came to stay with our Debbie, Hurricane Agnes was churning northward toward Maryland. The track promised to be inland. We were ready, so we left, anyway.

Mystic Seaport, Connecticut was beautiful in the rain. I made some good mood photographs of the old sailing vessels tied there. Newport, Rhode Island was interesting, particularly Ocean Drive. There we marvelled at the big, beautiful homes of the rich and famous perched on the ocean coast.

Two hardy souls were fishing from a jetty there. Agnes was pouring buckets of rain, but two guys were out there in yellow slickers, casting. Imagine that! O.K. in Maryland, maybe, where it was warmer, but it was cold here at Newport.

We parked and watched the anglers. Should I get out the rain gear and my fishing tackle and try a few casts? I gave it some serious thought. They didn't have any fish piled up on the jetty. If I had seen them catch a striper, or even get a bite, I would have been out of the car like a shot, middle of a hurricane or not. I settled for a photograph through the windshield. Warmth and comfort supersede cold and misery. Unless the fish are biting.

One of the classic striper spots I'd always read about was Sakonnet Point. It was a 40-mile drive from Newport around the Sakonnet River to a point of land we could almost see from Ocean Drive, but it was worth it. The roads to Sakonnet were not that good, and Agnes was pouring buckets

Newport anglers fish Brenton Point In the rain.

of water on us. Sakonnet Point was pretty, even in the rain. This was a striper fishing mecca I'd read about for years. Surprisingly, no one was fishing! I took a picture and we headed inland to escape Agnes instead of letting her follow us into Maine. No luck. Her spiral fringes engulfed us until we were nearly home.

Naomi, Bruce, and Debbie were surprised to see us. We had cut our trip a little short, but we saw some nice parts of New Hampshire and Vermont, plus Old Sturbridge Village in Massachusetts.

From our deck overlooking the Little Magothy River, we could also see the Bay across a marsh and the community beach. Everything imaginable was floating in the Bay. House roofs, uprooted trees, logs, timbers, everything that had been washed down the Susquehanna River or uprooted along the upper Bay shore. It was a mess.

I launched the boat from the new ramp we'd built in the front yard. Bruce and I toured the Bay from the Little Magothy inlet to the Bay Bridge. The new bridge was under construction. There was debris everywhere. I had to run the boat slowly to avoid it. The water was incredibly muddy, worse than the Mississippi at New Orleans, but with an oily, scummy look to it. The floods had washed uncountable nasty chemicals, sewage, and silt into the Bay. Recovery would take years. Many people blamed the striper decline on Agnes.

Debris from Hurricane Agnes clogged the bay.

Weeks later, I jumped in the Whaler with a fishing outfit to check out the bridge/s. The water was still as muddy as before but the debris had disappeared. It either sank or floated farther down the Bay. I cast a bucktail around the old bridge pilings, but no luck.

The second Cheaspeake Bay Bridge under construction.

The Bay still had an eerie, quiet feel to it. Like a graveyard. Out of this stillness arose a new monument, a second Bay Bridge. It looked a nautical Stonehenge, parts of the new bridge sticking up out of the water here and there, seemingly unconnected. Soon marine growth would cling to the new pilings, and little critters would cling to the growth. Bigger critters would eat them. The food chain ended in my favorite gamefish, striped bass.

And, this new bridge would at least double the number of pilings to catch rockfish around. Oh, happy day!

Belvidere Shoal: Bottom Bumping for Pan Rock

Although I'd rather catch one rockfish on light tackle than 100 on heavy gear, catching them on beefy trolling tackle was better than not catching them at all.

Wire line was not necessary for getting lures near the bottom in 20-plus feet of water, but I liked it better for that purpose than mono or dacron. I have used an old-time trolling outfit for a long time now, and I'm not about to change.

My old-timer's outfit: A 1950s True Temper beryllium-copper step-tapered trolling rod with roller tip, as sensitive as any modern graphite rod, was matched with a 1940s Pflueger Capitol #1989 star-drag reel loaded with 40-pound test monel single strand wire. Stranded wire line also works well.

A haywire twist connects a ball bearing snap swivel to the end of the wire. Next, hook the wire line's snap swivel into one eye of a three-way swivel. Many anglers secure the wire line directly to the three-way, but a snap swivel disconnect makes for easier storage. Use a dropper of 10-pound mono for the 12- to 20-ounce bell sinker tied to another eye of the three-way. Light mono line for the sinker dropper saves terminal tackle in case of a hang-up on bottom.

Sinker weight depends on water depth and how close I wanted to fish to the boat. It could take a 16-ounce sinker or heavier to keep the rig close to the boat if a lot of boats were crowded together. Once I had to fish nearly vertically with 24-ounces to keep from tangling with other boats fishing a small lump.

Finally, an 18-to 30-foot mono leader was tied to the remaining three-way eye, and a lure was tied to the end of the leader. Leader material ran from 15-pound test for leader-shy pan rock to 30-pound test for bigger animals.

Lures were either small spoons or 1/0 bucktails. John Taylor of Meredith Creek tied kip tail on his small trolling jigs. The short wavy hair covered his number 1 or 1/0 hooks nicely. He caught stripers up to 30 pounds trolling these tiny jigs in the fall.

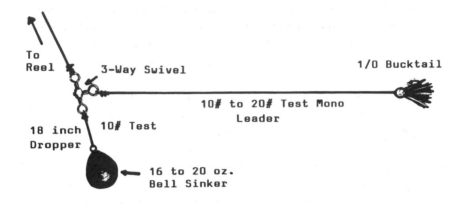

Bottom bumping trolling rig.

Some anglers add a short piece of pork rind that they neatly split up the middle to jigs or spoons. But, the ripple rind folks say "If you ain't got Ripple Rind, you ain't got spit."

Pork rind colors run from yellow to white or red as favorites, but you can't get me into that argument. I have heard that a strip of red flannel shirt tail is nice. Some swear a bull minnow decoration is tops for fall rockfishing. Others use nothing. I've caught stripers using all or none of the above, so I'll stay neutral.

Channel edges and lumps were my favorite places to bump the bottom when we lived in the Cape. Steering along a line directly between Sandy Point Light and Baltimore Light would put me along the edge of a drop-off about halfway between the two. That's near the sewer discharge pipe from the Sandy Point Sewer Plant now.

This area was always best in the fall. But, about November 1st, the entire area was suddenly blanketed with anchored gill nets. There were so many anchored gill nets in early November I had to stop fishing. You couldn't troll a straight line for a half-mile without tangling in a net. How a rockfish could swim from the Bay Bridge northward without getting gilled in those days is beyond me.

Other great areas were "lumps" on either side of the Craighill Channel north of Baltimore Light, which I assumed were dredge spoil. Once I found rockfish on a lump, I could catch several fish before they quit biting. Then, I moved to another lump.

Bottom bumping a small white bucktail jig with a green skirt was most productive. To bump bottom, I only fished one rod, holding it all the time. A rod in the holder got hung up too much because of the uneven bottom.

Once I found a lump on the depthfinder, I free-spooled enough wire line so the sinker bounced on bottom, and spun the reel handle to put it back in gear. Then I ran the Whaler slowly in a circle around the lump, holding the rod.

The trick in bottom bumping was to keep the lure slightly above bottom. To do that I constantly let out line or reeled it in, depending whether the depth changed, deeper or shallower. First, I raised the rod tip, then lowered it to bump the sinker on bottom a couple of times. If it didn't hit bottom, I let out more line. If the sinker bumped bottom continuously, I'd take in some line. It took some practice to keep the lure in the strike zone.

My old metal rod with the wire line made direct contact with the sinker as it touched bottom. I could feel whether I was over oyster shells, rocks, or on soft or hard bottom.

Trolling in a circle was productive in open water, too. Sometimes a school of fish was not huddled up around a lump or other structure. I immediately looked around for a set of marks as soon as the fish hit. If there was no one else fishing there, I'd drop a marker buoy. Then, I'd begin to troll in a circle.

A five-hour trolling trip with the rod in hand, bumping bottom with a 16-ounce sinker while dodging other boats, was guaranteed to make us sleep well that night. Particularly if we returned home late with a lot of fish to clean before hitting the sack.

Buckram Crabs Everywhere

One August evening in the early 1960s, surface-swimming crabs seemed thick enough to walk on from the mouth of the Magothy River to Sandy Point. There are annual August migrations of crabs, but never as many as that.

It was after a full moon, and there must have been a record slough of soft crabs in the Magothy. The surfacing crabs were not quite hard after their slough. Some call them "papershells," some call them "buckram."

What was most interesting about the crab swim was that rockfish were everywhere, feeding on the papery crustaceans. As the crabs swam along on the ebb tide toward Sandy Point, acres of breaking rockfish were gathered to slurp them up.

Through the summer we always carry a crab net. We scooped up a bushel of crabs from the surface and anchored the boat right there. We had so many crabs we used some for chum to keep the feeding rock interested. A half-crab on a 2/0 hook was the ticket to a hookup. No sinker was needed.

When we ran out of bait and chum, we scooped more crabs and anchored again in the middle of another feeding school of rock. The bait supply and the stripers seemed endless. Great fishing continued for several hours until sunset.

The next night, I couldn't wait to jump in the boat after work and repeat our previous night's fishing.

The fish and crabs were gone.

I have seen some incredible rockfishing, but never where the bait could be scooped up while fishing.

Pitts Creek: Stripers in the Stream

Omar Stoltzfus has some history as a kidder. It's sometimes hard to tell whether he is stretching a story with a straight face or telling the truth with a Cheshire cat smile. Only at his retirement party did his friends and relatives get back at him for his practical jokes over the years.

So, when Omar called about some strange rockfishing, I played it cool while I figured in the B.S. factor on this one, ho, ho.

Omar said his brother-in-law, Mitchell Adams, had caught some rockfish in a narrow stream so shallow it would barely float the boat. He said he would set up a trip. I thought I was the one being set up. When he said it was a tiny little creek off the Pocomoke River, the B.S. Bell clanged like a fire drill.

Carole and I had fished the lower Pocomoke not long after we got the Whaler. It was a beautiful trip on a river that hasn't changed since the Pocomoke Indians and pirates plied those waters. But, fishingwise, our trip was a flop.

Of course, it does take some time to get the hang of a new place, but Carole and I were "experienced" rock anglers when we tried the Pocomoke. I had a brand-new flasher depth finder, plus trolling and casting lures that were sure-fire striper baits. We couldn't miss. But, as pretty as the trip was, and as hard as we fished, miss we did. Omar's trip would flop, too.

Mitch launched his small outboard skiff at Shelltown. In a few minutes we motored up Pitts Creek, a stream so narrow and shallow I didn't know how we could get more than a few yards upstream. It seemed like we went pretty far, though. In a spot where the stream was not much wider than 20 feet, Mitch dropped anchor in two feet of water. Omar had bamboozled me this time, for sure.

"If there are rockfish in here," I probably said, "we chased them so far upstream they won't be back for a week."

Omar and Mitch smiled and baited with peeler crab. I followed suit to play along with the ruse, ho ho.

Pitts Creek was a pleasant place to be, even if there were no rockfish within miles of the place. The creek snaked through low marshland for miles. Not far across the marsh on either side, tall trees denoted higher ground. We had launched in Maryland and were fishing in Virginia, but not far upstream the creek meandered back into Maryland.

Omar grunted and lifted his rod tip as if he'd had a bite. I smiled. There were no rockfish in here. It was too shallow. We could touch the bottom. Omar was playing the game, alright.

Mitch set his hook into something big. It gave him quite a fight in those narrow waters. Finally, the fish was alongside the boat. Mitch called for the net. It was a two-pound rockfish!

Amazing. I began to fish in earnest, even gnashing my teeth.

We caught several more stripers in the two- and three-pound range, bigger rock than the 12-inchers we were catching up the Bay at that time. This, truly, was like catching rockfish in a bathtub.

"See?," Omar said, smiling, "Would I kid you?"

Omar had zapped me again.

Larry Huntington's Prototype Poppers

Larry Huntington, whose family has manufactured the Drone spoon since 1909, was one of the regulars we saw in our part of the Bay, plugging for rockfish. He saw the potential for another popping plug in the market, and set out to design one.

Larry handcarved several prototype wooden poppers, and weighted them all differently with a slug of lead in the underside of the lure. Each prototype was numbered. The one he gave me to test was either "6" or "9,"

I can't tell which. It is through-wired, has two treble hooks, and is painted white on the bottom and green on the top. Larry called periodically for a report on the number of fish I caught on the prototype.

Now, here is where Larry may have misread human nature. At least mine. I like handcarved stuff. I'll take a rough hand-carved duck decoy any day over a lathe-turned factory block. Once a decoy carver offered me one of two ducks. One was perfect, the other an early hatchet-hacked deke of some unidentifiable species. I grabbed the rough one in a heartbeat.

I have one of the first of Bob Pond's handcarved wooden Atom Plugs, and he signed it for me, "1 of the first 400, 1945, Bob Pond."

I have other handmade plugs like a beautiful one by Jack Stovall that he painted with an airbrush. That lure is just too pretty to let a bluefish chew on it. I treasure these handmades highly, because someone went to a lot of trouble to make them.

Jack Stovall with some of his handmade lures.

So, now you understand why I didn't give Larry's prototype a fair trial. I tossed it in the Little Magothy a few times (where I was sure nothing would grab it) to see how it worked, and it splashed along nicely. There was no way I could try out that lure anywhere a big striper or blue was likely to take it away from me.

Larry called for his report: "Catch anything on your number "6" (9?) this week," he'd say. "Nope, not this week," I'd answer. "How does it pop?" He'd ask. "Great!" I'd answer, which was true.

In January of 1977, long after Larry put the Huntington Drone popper into production, he called me and asked if I would talk to the Baltimore Anglers Club about surface plugging for rockfish. He had a conflict with the date. I told him I'd be happy to, and he said he'd bring me some of his slides that showed rockfish plugging to add to those I had.

When Larry brought the slides, we talked fishing for a while, then I showed him his old prototype. I had mounted it on a piece of driftwood with one of the production models. I asked him to sign the back of the plaque. He turned away from me, but when he turned back to sign my plaque, there was a tear in the corner of his eye. Tough 'ol hardcase rockfishermen are allowed to get emotional sometimes, too. I still have the plaque.

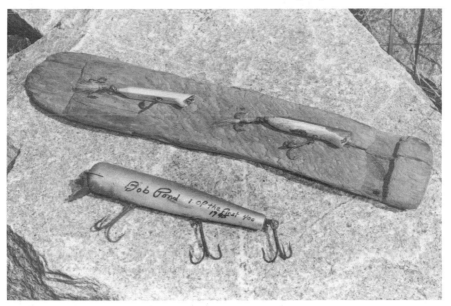

Larry Huntington's production and handcarved poppers on the driftwood plaque, and one of Bob Pond's original handcarved Atom plugs.

Many years later, I wrote a story about Larry's mother, Edna, who still runs the Huntington Drone lure company in her 80s.

Larry, his wife, Tish, and their son Larry are living in Costa Rica now, building Rybovich sportfishing boat hulls.

Not many years ago, I bought a slew of Huntington Drone poppers from a barrel in Angler's. They were marked down to $1. The new crop of fishermen just didn't know how good the plugs were.

Recently, Larry's brother, Lev, told me the the popping plug molds were lost.

Eel Dangling with Angie

Earlier, I mentioned that I used to buy live eels 200 at a time when Bay Bridge fishing was hot. Usually, eeling around bridge pilings got off to a slow start in late May or early June. Until things picked up a bit, I'd buy a few eels and keep them alive in a floating minnow bucket tied overboard at the dock.

From my original six eels in early May, my stock had dwindled to just one eel. No matter. Nothing was hitting anyway. I made several trips to try the bridge pilings, but no luck. Each time, when I finished fishing, I'd extract the hook from my one eel and put her back in the bucket. I got to be pretty fond of that eel. Even named her Angie, after the scientific name for the American eel, *Anguilla rostrata*.

If I didn't get out fishing for several days, the hole through her lips where she had been hooked would heal. Sounds cruel, doesn't it? I was getting real friendly with the little lady. Of course, I didn't know her/his gender, but she always behaved well on the hook, instead of tangling up in a ball around the hook as some energetic eels did. And, she did her best to wriggle and attract stripers around bridge pilings.

I fished her hard every time I went. Sometimes in the past I had hits by casting an eel between the double round pilings, and other times around the rock piles. Other times a striper would be suspended just a few feet down right next to a single piling, but in the slack water where there was no current to fight.

Stripers are not stupid. If they have to continually fight a current where there is little for them to feed on, there is a negative calorie balance. The fish will expend more calories swimming than he can replace feeding. That's why you can usually find stripers next to structure, out of the current, where they can dash out and grab food swept past in the tide. Those places are where you want to place your bait, lure, or in my case, Angie.

Of course, charter captains have found big fish in open water and presented eels to them with good success. But, most charterboat anglers lack the experience needed to fish eels around pilings in fast current. Six anglers on a big, hard to maneuver Chesapeake Bay charter boat will give the captain a fit around pilings if someone gets a fish or hangs up.

Outboard boats are more maneuverable around pilings, and two or three anglers can keep from getting tangled—usually. If Lady Luck sneers at you, and two anglers' eels get together, it is sometimes easier to cut all the lines and leaders and re-tie everything.

Sometimes, you can get lucky. Carole's uncle, Bruce McDowell, ("Unc" for short) and I were eel fishing around the bridge after dark. It was one of the few times I can truthfully say I caught stripers after seeing them on a depth finder. Usually, I find the structure stripers like with the flasher unit but rarely see the fish on it. I've been watching flasher depthfinders since 1964, and still charter captains point out a lot of things that I miss.

On the downtide side of a piling, the flasher lit up with big, solid blips at the 10-foot mark.

"Unc, drop your eel straight down 10 feet, close the bail, and hang on," I told Bruce. He did as told, and I dropped my eel, too. We both had hits and caught a fish each. Unc and I caught several big stripers before they moved away.

Stripers hit live eels like a ton of bricks. First, you might feel a strong jolt or two, then a solid tug, and the weight of a good fish. The strong jolts might be the striper smashing at the eel with its tail to stun it before turning around to take it headfirst. Other times, you just feel that awesome weight and the fish trying to empty the reel spool.

Anyway, Angie and I were alone one night. We were fishing a Bay Bridge piling in early May, when I got a strong strike. I fought the fish to the boat and netted it. It was an 8-pounder. Angie was still hanging out of the striper's mouth. I checked Angie over, and she had a lot of wiggle in her for someone who had been fishing hard all spring, and thumped pretty good by an 8-pound striper. I took her off the hook and released her. She swam quickly downward.

Angie was a good trouper. She deserved her freedom.

I told her to keep away from those bridge pilings.

Baby Blue Goes Hungry

Jim Lock and I spent many a happy hour chasing evening stripers. Jim lived two doors from us in the Cape, and he did love to fish.

Sometimes we'd head for the Dumping Ground with a peck of clams for bait, other times we'd plug the shoreline. In those days, there were plenty of rockfish. We rarely got skunked.

Jim and his wife, Helene, had a big 'ol Persian cat called Baby Blue because of the silver-blue color of her fur. The cat had a mean streak, if I'm permitted to say so. Baby Blue would lay across the back of Lock's sofa and dare anyone to sit there. One #%&@* cat tied up eight-feet of sofa! I often sat on the flagstone floor and glared at the cat.

Baby Blue particularly didn't like me. I guess because I always had cat smell on me from one or another feline we had around the house. Carole never was crazy about cats, except for a moose we called Inky, but I had grown up with them. When I was a kid, we had 14 cats, two rabbits, and a rabbit hound named Joey. Cats were good pets to have when Carole and I were both working because they were independent, often to the point of ignoring us when we came home. Later, we had dogs. Much more convivial pets.

I sometimes teased Baby Blue when she walked past and rubbed against my leg. I'd reach down and pull her tail. But, I had to be quick. She'd whip around, snarling and hissing, and take a swipe at me with claws bared. An altogether disagreeable cat.

Late one night Jim and I were cleaning rockfish in his garage sink. I had donated my share of our catch to Jim's freezer. Baby Blue was hanging around. You know how the smell of fresh fish draws cats. She even jumped up on the sink for a better look.

Jim's method of cleaning rockfish consisted of scaling them, then cutting off the tails and heads, then gutting them, and washing out the cavity in preparation for freezer wrap. Very labor intensive.

I suggested filleting the fish. Jim was aghast.

"Wastes too much fish meat," he said. Baby Blue, I swear, snarled maliciously at my suggestion. You see, she usually got left-over fish tails and heads nicely cooked by Helene.

"Hissss!!," was Baby Blue's reaction to my idea.

"Let me show you," I told Jim. "I'll filet a fish, then you can cut around on the carcass and see how much meat you can get off for Baby Blue. O.K.?" Jim agreed to the test, but I could see he thought I was going to miss a mess of meat.

I took Jim's razor-sharp filet knife and went to work. Compared to my filleting skill today, I was a rank hacker then. I made a cut down the rockfish's backbone on one side, then worked the knife carefully around the stomach cavity down to the tail. I got a nice piece of fillet with the skin still on, ready for frying. I did the same on the other side. Some anglers skin the fillet with a sharp knife. I left all the belly meat on the carcass because I think it tastes too strong. I handed Jim the knife.

"O.K.," I said, "you go around where I just filleted with the knife and trim off all the meat I missed for the cat. Jim started to wrestle with the carcass.

Baby Blue watched intently from her vantage point next to the faucet. Her tail twitched nervously. I think ol' Blue liked raw fish better than the cooked stuff anyway, though Helene would have had a hissy fit if she knew her precious cat actually ate raw fish flesh.

Jim finally finished his post-filleting salvage operation. He showed me a tiny mound of fish meat in the palm of his hand, maybe an ounce. He agreed that filleting didn't waste any useable meat, and I think I made a convert.

Jim held forth his tiny offering to Baby Blue. She ate it in one dainty slurp, and looked to Jim for more.

"That's all," he apologized to the cat. Baby Blue stalked off toward the house, glaring at me over her shoulder. I smiled.

Revenge is sweet.

4

THE MAKO YEARS (1974–1981)

Carole, We Really Need a New Boat

Wheatley Christianson brought a buddy with him to look at my 1964, 16-foot Nauset model Whaler. It had a 100-HP Johnson on it, and was in good shape. We walked across the yard to the dock, talking about how badly Wheatley wanted a Whaler. I knew the feeling. I'd felt the same way 10 years ago when I bought it. A lot of water had run under the boat since then, and a lot of cold spray had smashed me in the face.

I jumped down into my Whaler and put the drain plug back in.

"What did you do?" asked Wheatley Christianson's buddy.

"I put the drain plug back in," I answered, "Why?"

"Why doesn't the boat sink with the plug out?" buddy asked.

"This Whaler has enough flotation to keep the floor level above outside sea level with no one in it," I answered. The guy was amazed.

"I've got a Whaler like this one and I keep the plug in and use a bilge pump," the buddy said.

"Well, I take the plug out at the dock so rain water will drain out," I said. "I never had a bilge pump." Buddy just shook his head.

I pulled the console cover off. The mahogany console's brightwork shone like new. It had never been left uncovered since I bought the boat. That was it. The buddy nodded to Wheatley, who smiled and dug out his wallet.

It was Mako time!

Now, it was time to select a boat with a little more muscle and a drier ride. The 1974, 20-foot Mako was just the right length to trailer easily, and it was big enough to chase fish in rougher seas. There were times with the Whaler when I had to stay home because it was too rough. Makos have enough flare in the bow to ward off all kinds of spray. With the Mako, I could go fishing in all kinds of trashy weather.

I still have the Mako, and it has had its quota of six engines.

Unc and the Midnight Pluggers

One of the first trips in the new Mako started out a bust and wound up like gangbusters. Carole's Uncle Bruce "Unc" McDowell and I felt we deserved an August evening fishing trip. Rockfishing fever had been building up. Some people get grumpy if they don't get out rockfishing at least three times a week.

The live eel baits were aboard in a minute. We cleared the inlet and headed for the Bay Bridges before the ladies could object.

Running toward the bridges, I noticed a little knot of boats right next to the shore at Bay Head. Folks were just sitting in their boats like they were waiting for something. Unc asked what they were doing. I didn't know. Maybe a convention.

We swam eels around every piling on both bridges where I'd ever caught a rockfish. One or two fish was about it for the night.

Unc was a great guy to be around. Never complained. Ready to do whatever anyone else suggested. He was well-read. He could discuss just about any subject, and rarely argued about anything. Just one of those laid-back types that is quiet when you are, and there when you want to talk. He was one of those people I wish I'd spent more time with, but it's too late now.

It must have been after 10 p.m. when we left the bridge. I'd made the run so many times in the dark, I could do it blindfolded. It was pitch dark that night. Starlight didn't help.

When we were off Bay Head on the return trip, I noticed the light of a cigarette near shore. Someone took a puff which brightened the glowing tip. I slowed down. I'd never seen any boats in there before that night. They were inside the sandbar, almost touching the beach. I remembered they were there when we ran to the bridges. I turned in toward the beach.

Getting across the sandbar where I was swamped years before in my tin boat was slow going. It was really shallow. I had a new motor with an aluminum prop. I respected my new $150 prop too much to use it as a sand plow. Now, I use a stainless steel prop for my near-shore rock-banging forays.

There was a pocket of deeper water behind the bar. I vowed to keep an eye out for freighters going down the Bay, and if I saw one, I'd pull anchor and scoot before the breakers hit us. One capsizing at Bay Head was enough for this lifetime.

We pulled in some distance from the other boats. No one had lights on. I cut the motor. Then, we could hear what was happening. All around us, people were fighting fish. Drags screaming. Fish splashing hitting bait and surface lures. People laughing as they netted fish. Pandemonium. The old adrenalin started pumping. I go a little nuts when rockfish carry on like that.

"Unc" and the author with the midnight stripers.

I put a popping plug on Unc's line and told him to cast "over there." Now, casting lures in pitch blackness takes some doing. It's not a job for novices. Unc did just fine.

I don't know how those stripers could find our poppers in that pitch black night, but they did. The secret was to dance the plug on the water and keep it in one place, not easy with a heavy plug that wants to sink. By mastering that one trick we could fight fish after fish.

Everyone was fighting big stripers. The night was filled with happy laughter and giggling. Reel drags chattered and fish splashed. You could hear people remark about the big fish they just netted.

It was an evening like no other I'd ever experienced. I had a bushel basket in the boat, and it was jammed full of rockfish. Other fish lay on the deck. Unc and I used my plug/leader system, unhooking each leadered plug and snapping on another plug so we could keep casting. The fish kept the plugs until later.

"I'm tired," Unc said, "This is too much." He sat down for a smoke. I kept fishing. You only get into a blitz like this a few times in a lifetime. You don't quit until the fish do. Finally, they did. It was quiet around the boats. A few people listlessly continued to toss their plugs. Others were as tired as we were. Hits became less frequent. It was almost midnight. The blitz had lasted an hour and a half without letup.

I finally had time to look up at the shoreline. I could make out the very dock where my tin boat had been pulled up after my swamping years back. It made me feel uneasy, apprehensive. I wanted out of there, quick. The tide had dropped. Our return trip across the sandbar was a bottom-scraper. I looked for freighters. This was the exact spot where I was swamped. After what seemed like hours, but was only a few minutes, we finally cleared the sandbar and turned for home.

It was too late to clean fish that night. We iced them down and cleaned them on the dock the next morning. After pictures, of course.

We had enough fish to last Unc all winter in Florida.

Take a Lab Fishing, Take a Shovel

Christy was 75 pounds of loveable black Labrador retriever. Everywhere I went, Christy was there. She was obedient and well trained. She had to be to survive our "speedway."

Our place in the Cape was on a curve in Riverbay Road, a place where people seemed to accelerate in case there were some kids in the road. Like all dogs, Christy roamed in the yard, but she rarely left it. One day as she walked head down sniffing her way toward the street I heard a glasspack-mufflered cowboy coming, pedal to the metal, toward the curve on Riverbay.

"SIT!!" I yelled at Christy. Bless her heart, she sat. I'm sure her blind obedience saved her life. When people take me to task for sternly training our dogs, I tell that story.

Normally, after work I hopped in the boat to rockfish until after dark, or when they stopped biting. Then, and only then, it was time for dinner. Carole and I frequently discussed my fishing habits.

Christy and I played a sort of game when I got home from work. She would race from her pen, gulp her dinner, and try to jump in the boat before I could get away without her. Sometimes she made it, sometimes not.

Carole always had this ability to read Christy's mind. Later, I found out how she did it. When Christy had her pants full enough to look for a spot, the load seemed to pull her ears back. If you have a female Lab, watch her. It's true.

One evening, Christy made it into the Mako as it left the dock. She shed 20 pounds of black hair into the boat a day, but I enjoyed her company. Unless I was plugging the shoreline. Then she was a mess.

The first rule of Labrador retriever ownership is that you can never throw anything away. The dog always brings it back. Always.

The second rule is that Labs are water dogs. If you toss something away in or near the water, it doubles the dog's fun.

Surface plugs tossed for rockfish sent Christy into spasms of delight. She raced from one end of the boat to the other, watching the plug soar. She tried to get overboard to retrieve it. I yelled at her to "Stay!" She did. We replayed that scene every cast. She hung her front legs over the bow, rear end up in the air, and woofed at the plug.

Better yet, when the plug made its splashing way back to the boat she wanted to get overboard and grab it. In those days, I used two treble hooks on each plug. I didn't want to dig treble hooks out of any dog mouth that was also full of sharp teeth.

Anyway, she was excited, maybe had her ears back. I was more entranced with catching rockfish than with dog-watching. Christy came around the console from the front of the boat, looking guilty. I checked in front of the console. There was a neat little pile.

I had no shovel. We discussed her lack of manners all the way home.

She's gone now. I still see her out of the corner of my eye, a huge, snoring black dog sleeping on the shop floor at my feet.

Rock and Blues Along Kent Island

About the same time that our striper population began to crash, we noticed more, and larger, bluefish showing up in our catches. One autumn day in the late 1970s, I took one of our Goddard Photographic Section co-operative education students fishing. Not so much for fun, but for food.

Pat Izzo was living on a low budget between sessions at the Rochester Institute of Technology, where he later graduated with a BS in Photography. We planned to get him some fish to stretch his food budget. Did we get fish!

I had fished near Bloody Point for a week with good catches. Not trolling offshore as many do, but right up near the shoreline, casting popping plugs.

We quietly motored up close to a wooden bulkhead near "The Flag-pole" and cut the engine. A small anchor on a short line held the boat in place in the shallows. There were no fish showing on the surface. One cast changed all that. Big blues and stripers crashed our surface plugs in that shallow water. Mostly, they went straight up like a tarpon, though not quite as high into the air.

We caught blues weighing from 5 to 8 pounds, interspersed with stripers the same size until we had enough for Izzo to clean.

He looked a little peaked the next day at work. He had been up all night cleaning and freezing fish. He had enough fish fillets in his freezer to last him until he went back to school.

Bucktailing With Buddy

Lloyd "Buddy" Williams lived not far from us in the Cape, and we both worked at NASA Goddard. We had an easy-going sort of a carpool to work. Buddy was as laid-back as an Eastern Shoreman, and I was his understudy. If it was convenient for both of us, we'd ride together. If not, no problem. Most important here, Buddy was a rockfisherman.

Many mornings we left my dock before daybreak, got in a few hours of fishing at the Bay Bridges, cleaned fish, and made it to work late with an expenditure of an hour or so of annual leave.

One foggy November morning, we found our way to the Bay Bridges before sunup by compass and seat-of-the-pants navigation. Actually, I think the Mako would have found the way by itself, like a horse finding its way back to the stable. I had worn a groove in the water from the mouth of the Little Magothy to the Bay Bridges, and the boat simply got in that rut and followed it.

Our standard rig was a medium spinning rod and a 7/0 white bucktail with a piece of #240 Uncle Josh Striper Split Tail pork rind. Colors varied with whim and weather, but the technique was always the same.

We usually cast our lures from the downtide side of the bridge pilings. Rockfish were within a foot or so of the pilings, and a cast farther away would not draw a strike. My system was to cast the jig just past the piling

Buddy Williams at the Bay Bridges.

and let it sink as the tide brought it toward me. Depending on the speed of the tide, the weight of the lure, and the depth of the fish, a short cast might be better one time, and a long cast way past the piling would be best the next time. A slow retrieve was usually best.

I held the boat in place with the motor running as we went from piling to piling that morning. Buddy had heard that some stripers were caught near pilings on the eastern side of the new bridge. We worked our way eastward, piling to piling, a few casts near each one. The bow faced up the Bay that morning toward the round pilings of the new bridge. The tide was going out. Winds were light. We had a couple of fish, but no major action.

We were under one of those big overhead neon signs that tell drivers which lane they can use. The pilings below that sign we called "six-legged" because six (sometimes four) pilings held up one cross-brace for the roadway above. Pilings on the new bridge were concrete cylinders, driven into the bottom on a angle to support the bridge like multiple tripods.

The tide swirled between the six legs and made eddy currents the stripers liked. That was the place to cast a bucktail jig. The only problem was how to get a really mad striper out from between the pilings without cutting our line on barnacles.

Stripers always headed for an obstruction as soon as they decided they were in trouble. If that obstruction was barnacle-encrusted, you didn't stand a chance. Not with light 14- to 17-pound test line.

Some bridge regulars used 25- or 30-pound test line on a short spinning rod made from a pool cue, but it must been like casting baling wire with a crow bar, especially in cold weather. Not that you had to cast all that far. A 30-foot cast was enough.

This calm morning the fog soon lifted. A warming sun slanted across the water. And, we hit a pocket of stripers under our six-legged pilings. They turned us every which way but loose.

There is something about the strike of a broad-shouldered striper that jars you from wrist to shoulder. When they take a lure, they don't nibble. They yank. Then, they leave town.

That morning, Buddy and I had a real fire drill. As captain, I had the added joy of steering the boat, keeping it within casting distance of the pilings. In between, I netted fish for Buddy, and he netted fish for me. By that time the tide had taken us away from the pilings. It was cast, catch, fight, net, and return the boat to the pilings for a couple of hot (though the weather was cold) hours.

It was about as much rockfishing fun as anyone could have, bucktailing with Buddy that morning in November, 1978. It was the last time I got to fish with him. Not long after, before he reached retirement age, Buddy came down with a terminal cancer.

I'm glad we had a good rockfishing trip.

Dumping Ground Days

Chesapeake Bay charts show an area west of Kent Island above the Bay Bridges called the "Dumping Ground." In the mid-1970s so many boats were anchored there chumming for rockfish, people said you could walk from boat to boat without getting wet. Thousands of charter and private boats each caught hundreds of fish every day. We all thought there was no end to it.

Many boats had automatic grinders on the transom that intermittently released gobs of ground soft-shell Manninose clams into a moving tide to attract and hold huge schools of rockfish.

"You could spot the boat's captain," said Captain of the *Doghouse*, Mike Keene. "He was the one fishing right next to the chumming machine. And the mate was right next to him. They'd be *bailing* fish."

In a good chum line, stripers would come right up to the boat. It was like fishing in an aquarium, or shooting ducks over bait. Even novice anglers caught stripers when they were feeding heavily.

It was great fishing, and it could return someday when striper stocks recover. Light spinning gear was ideal for chumming as it allowed more fun per pound of fish than trolling with heavy tackle. Leaders of 30-pound test about 18 inches long were tipped with a 1/0 or 2/0 hook, and pinch-on weights were changed frequently depending on the strength of tidal flow. The trick was to get your bait to the proper depth and keep it there. Regulars found that you could entice hits by slowly lowering the bait at the speed of the tide to simulate the clams naturally falling in the water column.

There were many problems on the Dumping Ground, though. Greedy boatmen trolled through successful chum lines. Others anchored so close to other boats everyone's lines tangled when a big fish hit.

My wife's cousin, Billy Stewart, had his mother, Esther, and his father, Edgar, aboard one day. A charterboat anchored right next to them, so close they were in Billy's chum line. A big rockfish hit Esther's line. The striper swam under the charterboat and came up on the other side. The boat captain netted Esther's fish, cut her line, and put the striper in his own fishbox!

Billy said something to the charter captain about returning his mother's fish. The charterman answered it was his fish.

"If you don't move before I get ready to go," Billy promised, "I'll cut your #$%*&# anchor line when I leave." He would have, too.

Billy's adversary picked up anchor and left.

The Dumping Ground was one of the best places on the Bay to observe human hostility. Some people even dropped anchor in another's chum line! Many a sinker crashed through the party-crasher's windshield as a warning to keep one's distance. Many anchor lines were cut in anger. It was on the Dumping Ground that I learned the gentle art of Furtive Fishing.

Furtive Fishing as an Art Form

Carole and I hated the crowds on the Dumping Ground in those days. We usually dropped anchor outside the flotilla of boats where it was quiet. Not as many fish there, but we fished for fun, not to show aggression.

One day, I noticed the angler in a boat 100 feet away jam his entire spinning rod underwater and play his fish. His reel clicker had been disabled. Sitting low in his boat, he nonchalantly wound a rockfish alongside. He did not wave a net in the air, but he grasped his leader and slowly slid his striper in over the low transom while he looked straight ahead, like he was bored. I asked him why he did that.

"See that gang of boats over there?" he asked. I looked over at the fleet. Angry shouts and flying sinkers filled the air over there.

"Yup" I answered.

"Want them over here?" he asked.

"No." I got the point. I soon learned *not* to stand up while fishing, wave a net in the air, or play a fish with the rod tip up. I even disabled my drag click. Quiet and calm was the watchword. If we had stood up in the boat and waved a net in the air, we would be surrounded by our own little City of Hostility in short order.

It took some time to master the art of fighting a fish with the rod pointed down into the water, pour a cup of coffee, and stifle a yawn at the same time. We quickly learned to master Furtive Fishing techniques, and fished alone. Otherwise, we'd get unwanted company.

Devious Deception Improves Furtive Fishing

We hit upon a great deceptive ploy somewhat by accident. I had a peck of clams and my boss, Pat Kelly, aboard as we cleared the Little Magothy inlet jetty. We could see that the entire population of Anne Arundel County was anchored down shore off Podickory Point. Some fish showed on the depthfinder about halfway to Podickory, so we stopped to fish for them. We were all by ourselves. I wanted to keep it that way.

I began to school Pat in the fine art of feigning boredom while loading the cooler with 5- to 10-pound rockfish. He was a quick study, although as it turned out he might have overdone it a bit.

Every boat that came out of the big Magothy River would slow down and give us the once-over before joining the fleet a mile away. What they saw was two obviously bored fishermen sipping coffee. We gave them the universal palms up signal for "We ain't catchin' nothin".

One boater obviously didn't believe us. He slowly circled our boat, so close we could see the captain's unbelieving sneer. The boat was BIG. Menacing. The hull was painted black. A Darth Vader sort of boat. His mate stood ready to toss an anchor in our chumline if one of our rods so much as twitched. We had already reeled our clam baits up to the surface where only a truly treacherous and suicidal rockfish could get at our hooks and give us away.

Still he circled, unconvinced. I pointed out to Pat that the nearest boat in the main fleet was into fish. An angler stood at the transom, his bent rod tip a waving welcome sign to every avaricious angler in sight. His buddy compounded the idiocy by waving a huge net in the air. Other boats were already anchoring alongside him, close enough to shake hands.

Pat, a masterful and enthusiastic actor, stood up with all the attention-getting command that a 275-pound Irisher can muster and pointed at the hapless, about-to-be-surrounded angler.

"FAITH AND BEJESUS," Pat roared, "LOOKIT THE BIG FISH THAT GUY JUST GOT."

Darth Vader jammed both throttles to the firewall and disappeared in a cloud of blue smoke. Pat and I smiled at our deception and (nonchalantly) continued to catch rockfish.

Kaos the cat mooches Pat Kelly for some rockfish.

Furtive Charter Captains

Some Bay Bridge area charter boat captains practiced their own form of the "Don't Tell 'Em Nothin' School of Angling." Omar Stoltzfus and I had a chance to fill out two vacancies on a charterboat, chumming rockfish with grass shrimp.

"Hot Dang!", I had told Omar on the phone, "This guy really catches fish. Maybe we can catch some rock and learn something too."

Fat chance! As it turned out, he riveted his rear trouser pocket to the best corner of the stern as he and two of his regulars proceeded to catch one rockfish after another. I had naively assumed that a good captain would see that his clients were catching fish before picking up a rod himself. Omar and I caught nothing, were told nothing.

At the dock, our captain smiled pleasantly as he handed us each a rockfish and took our money. We had paid to watch him fish.

Now, get this. I don't blame that captain. Why? Read on.

Another charterboat captain told me later that he rarely takes out local anglers, preferring fishermen from out of state as clients. His reasoning is probably the same as that of the shrimper. Show a local angler what you are doing and he will soon be competing with you for the same fish—but from HIS boat.

Meushaw Jigs

"Oh, yes, I remember them. Catch all the rockfish you want with a Meushaw jig," said "Fishin' Charlie" Ebersberger of Angler's when I called to get Bob Meushaw's phone number, "I bought up the last jigs he had."

Bob Meushaw told me how he came to make his famous feathered jig, but first he told me a story about Bay Bridge eeling:

"I had six eels with me one morning," Meushaw said, "I decided to fish number 14, the first four-legged piling outside the launch ramps at Sandy Point Park. I had a 16-foot Whirlwind molded plywood boat with a 40-horse motor then."

"When I got out to the bridge at daybreak, I was disappointed. Someone was anchored at piling 14. I went to number 13 and caught a rockfish right away. I put on a fresh eel and caught another. Then, the guys at piling 14 moved to number 13 and anchored! They cast their eels. I moved to piling 14 and caught more fish. I only used ½-ounce or less pinch-on sinkers, but those guys were fishing right on bottom! They didn't know how to fish."

"I always kept my (spinning reel) bail open and let the fish run. He'd take off, then stop. Only then did I close my bail. Rockfish must want to get away from the other fish before they swallow an eel. They are competitive."

Meushaw jigs and Bay Bridge rockfishing were synonymous. Most of the anglers who fished the bridge made their own bucktail jigs. They either knocked all the paint off smashing them against the concrete bridge pilings or lost jigs on snags. It would have cost a fortune to buy that many lures.

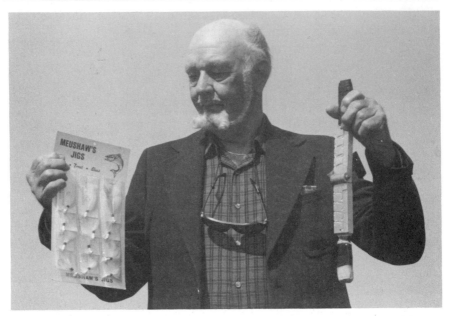

Bob Meushaw with a card of his famous jigs and the original jig mold.

That is how Bob Meushaw started, making his own. Next, he made them for friends. He had a mold made to pour four jigs at a time. Later, he added extended eyes to his jigs. Before long Meushaw was in the lure business.

Most people tied bucktail hair on their jigs. Meushaw used colored feathers instead. The feathered baits were dynamite on rockfish.

Someone once asked him how long it took to make a jig. "Two weeks," he said. One day to mold 500 jig heads, four more days at one coat of paint per day, etc. Two weeks, total. But, when he was done, he had 500 jigs.

Meushaw's first coat of paint was a flat white, then a gloss white, next pearl, then the final color coat. Then he painted the eyes, let them dry, and painted the pupils. He liked Herter's fluorescent lacquers and used their dyed feathers, too. Herter's went out of business long ago.

His favorite feather colors were yellow and white. "White for hazy days." Finally, he combined eight yellow and white feathers together on each jig. Only a third of the long neck hackle feather was used.

Meushaw used his jigs in tandem, one 18 inches above the other. He often caught two rockfish at a time on this gypsy rig. Other anglers cast single Meushaw jigs with ultralight spinning tackle in shallow water for "pan rockfish."

A retired Baltimore City Fire Captain (now 76), he once sold his rockfish catch to supplement his income.

And of course, to buy more jig materials.

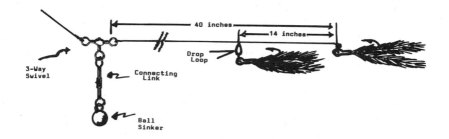

Bob Meushaw's favorite tandem jig rig.

5

EASTERN SHORE

We Cross the Bridge

When writers talk about bridges, they usually mean a bridge they build with words to connect two different thoughts, scenes or stories. When Carole and I crossed the Chesapeake Bay Bridges between Sandy Point and Kent Island on our way to a new home in Talbot County, it meant more than a simple move. It was a new way of life. We had been crossing the Chesapeake Bay Bridge/s ever since the first one was built, and we rode the old Matapeake Ferryboats before that. We honeymooned on the 'Shore in 1955.

It is ironic that the Bay Bridges that gave Carole and I so much rockfishing pleasure would provide us a bridge to a new life.

Hustle Versus Laid Back

Maybe others have noticed it when they cross the Bay Bridges, but as soon as our front wheels hit Eastern Shore soil, there is an immediate feeling of relaxation. On the western shore, there is always a sense of hustle and bustle. Dodging other cars in crowded traffic as I commuted between Cape St. Claire and NASA's Goddard Space Flight Center got worse every year. In 1960, my 28-mile commute took 40 minutes. By the time I retired in 1979, it was closer to an hour. More traffic sharing the same two-lane road. Drivers were more hostile, lane-changing and cutting others off to gain 10 seconds of time.

Contrast that with our Eastern Shore experience. Except for Route 50, where the prime concern on summer weekends is "reaching the beach," side roads are relatively uncrowded. One can drive slowly enough to see the beauty of the place, "stop and smell the flowers."

'Shore people seem more relaxed, more laid back. And, we never found that clannishness we were told Eastern Shoremen exhibited toward western shoremen. Everywhere we went, we were well received.

That may have been because we genuinely liked the 'Shoremen. We found them open and friendly. The bottom line is people with an attitude problem on the western shore will have an attitude problem on the Eastern Shore. 'Shoremen will sense it and shy away.

Retirement was the author's 49th birthday present. Carole baked him a fishing hat cake.

Other Bridges

Another bridge was being built in those days. It was a bridge between old and new ideas about striped bass. As our striper fishery took a nose dive, anglers became more interested in conservation.

Once, fishermen only wanted to know where and how to top off their coolers as fast as possible. And, their coolers were big. It was the accepted thing to do. Catch as many rockfish as possible.

Catches of 100 rockfish per day per boat were not unusual. Joe Habel once told me he saw garbage bags full of rockfish rotting in his dumpster outside Angler's every morning. People who parked their cars there to meet their captains would trash the fish that evening rather than clean them.

As stripers became scarcer, we noticed that anglers wanted to hear about the reasons for the decline. Some of the best attended meetings of our MSSA Talbot County Chapter were when DNR biologist, Ben Florence, or other rockfish experts were the featured speakers. I marvelled at the attention given by average fishermen to Ben's charts showing how accurately peaks and valleys in the Young-of-the-Year (YOY) juvenile index tracked the reported commercial catch three years later. A low YOY index one year indicated a low catch three years later, and vice versa.

Now, most striper fanatics understand conservation, hatcheries, tagging, YOY indexes, and catch-and-release mortality enough to talk intelligently about them.

One of the most important bridges we built in recent years is the one between our old fish-hoggery and our new striper conservation ethic. You see it everywhere. Maryland's recreational anglers have been releasing rockfish since January, 1985, and other coastal anglers have done the same. That ethic has extended to other species.

The "right of free plunder" that has existed in Chesapeake Bay waters ever since the first pirates and freebooters arrived has slowly faded, at least among recreational anglers. If the rockfish moratorium was the bridge between keeping every rockfish we could catch and conserving something for tomorrow, it was the best bridge we could build.

Mike, Poodle, and Otis

Soon after we moved to Bozman, I met some of the local anglers at the Bozman Store. The store is a gathering place for local folks, a social center where the bottom shelves in the center aisle are cleared of goods to become "liar's benches" where watermen can sit and swap stories. The heating grate is in the center of the aisle, so oystermen can regain some body heat after a cold morning of tonging. The crowd hasn't thinned out much since the Post Office moved out of the store, either.

Mike Haddaway told me how he and his dad had once caught rockfish from the bank on peeler crabs on the old Sutton Farm right in front of where our house now stands on Broad Creek. It was not unusual for the Haddaways to catch all they wanted for dinner, simply by casting their peeler crab baits to the outside edge of the grass.

Mike even marked my chart for me, and gave me local names for places long since eroded away, like "Ralston's," (local useage for long-gone Royston's Island off Island Creek). James Michener, who has a home on Broad Creek, may have combined Nelson, Royston, and Sharps Islands in his book, *Chesapeake*, as his fictional "Devon Island" that also eroded away.

Mike showed me some bars and lumps that historically held rockfish, and I fished them with a little success. Remember, I was new to the area, the fishery was beginning to crash, and rockfish were not plentiful there. Excuses, excuses.

John "Poodle" McQuay walked around my 20-foot Mako at the Bozman Store as I filled the boat's gas tank. He was giving it the once over. I said "hello," and did he like the boat? It turned out he had one exactly like it, but didn't use it much. We shook hands, and he said to call him "Poodle." His hands were about the size of hams, and he had worked on the water many years, fishing, oystering, and crabbing, so a funny remark about his nickname was uncalled for.

How did he get the nickname, "Poodle?"

"I don't know," Poodle said, "my father was called that, too."

Poodle and I went rockfishing in Broad Creek in my Mako. We trolled bucktails down the shoreline in about six-feet of water. Now comes the unbelievable part.

As Poodle steered my boat down the creek, he stayed in the same water depth, although the six-foot depth curved this way and that, sometimes as much a 90-degree turn! He didn't watch the depthfinder. He knew every inch of creek bottom like the back of his hand.

"We're coming to the 'ups and downs' now," Poodle said. Sure enough, the depth finder showed the undulating bottom going up and down. Amazing! I can't remember if we caught fish that day, but I sure learned a lesson about a waterman's ability to remember bottom.

Mike Haddaway showed how to fish—Eastern Shore style.

On our way perch fishing in later years, Carole and I often stopped by Poodle's crabbing "lay" in Broad Creek to mooch some peeler crabs for bait. He always had a few, and I always took him and his wife, Mary a mess of white perch in exchange if we got lucky.

Poodle McQuay looking for fishing peelers.

Norm's Tire Chain

In "amongst" the helpful striper fishing hints from Eastern Shoremen is this one I noted from Captain Norm Haddaway, who is never at a loss for words. Outdoor writers like to hunt and fish with Norm. He always has a good quote to add spice to a story.

"Drag an old tire chain tied to a rope across the bottom to find oyster bottom," said Norm, "You'll feel the oysters or stones grab the chain. If no one is around, set two or three buoys." (Once another waterman knows your spot, it becomes his spot, too).

Why would an old trick used by oyster tongers help a striper fisherman? Oyster or rocky bottom holds stripers.

The Way It Was

I also met Captain Otis Bridges at the Bozman Store. He was open and friendly. We talked a lot about rockfishing "the way it was," and I wrote a story from his quotes:

Captain Otis Bridges, now 87-years old, already had considerable experience on the Chesapeake Bay when he took out his first fishing party in 1919 at the tender age of 16. His 39 X 9-foot converted five-log canoe, the *Ghost*, was kept at Breezy Point, a summer boarding house on Harris Creek in Bozman. Originally built for sail before 1900 by Tommy Harrison of Tilghman Island, the *Ghost* had been converted to power with the addition of a 12-horsepower twin-cylinder Palmer gasoline engine.

Guests at Breezy Point in 1926 could go bottom fishing with Captain Otis for $1 each, and sometimes as many as 14 went along. In those days a $14 charter was a princely sum. Gasoline was cheap, and peeler crabs for bait were a penny each. Anglers used two-for-a-penny hooks on their handlines.

"We thought rods and reels were for sissies then," said Captain Otis, "No one had a fishin' pole when I first started. We used handlines. After you caught a few big rockfish or hardhead on a handline, you built up a pretty good callous on your hand. We trolled handlines with a spreader and two Drone spoons for rockfish. We bottom fished for hardhead (croakers) with handlines, too."

Hardhead running 3 to 3½ pounds were Captain Otis' mainstay in the 1920s because rockfish were scarce. In the 1930s rockfishing improved once the purse nets were outlawed.

"We chummed for rock with grass shrimp in the mid-1930s," Captain Otis said. "If you could afford to buy five gallons of shrimp for $25, and pay $25 for the charter. We set two anchors in a "Y" so the boat didn't swing. When we commenced to putting a few shrimp overboard at a time, rock would come up 25 to 50 feet from the boat. Fishing lines were marked at 25, 50, and 75 feet. In a strong tide, we let out 75 feet of line. With two shrimp on a hook you only got one chance to strike him. If you missed, he had your bait."

Later, Captain Otis trolled with home-brew rods made from pool cues, and a favorite Eastern Shore bait, the Chamberlain bucktail.

"Joe Chamberlain's bucktails were the best," Captain Otis said. "He had a patent on them. He'd only sell them to people he liked. His bucktails were the best because he took more pains with the paint. He baked his paint in the oven all night. He'd get up every two hours all night to give them another coat of paint. President Franklin D. Roosevelt used Chamberlain's bucktails."

"Fishermen were funny then," said Captain Otis, "they didn't really feel like they were fishing unless they could wet a line at dawn." That meant that guests at Breezy Point were ferried out to the *Ghost* in the pre-dawn darkness in rowboats after a very early breakfast. With a little starlight or a quarter-moon, he could see the minute differences in the water's surface that marked several tricky offsetting channels and over-

Captain Otis Bridges holds two Chamberlain bucktails.

lapping sandbars in Harris Creek. Cook's Point at the mouth of the Choptank River was his favorite fishing spot for seatrout, perch, rockfish, spot, and hardhead.

How does today's fishing compare? "Well," said Captain Otis, "It's probably off 80 percent from the best of times, but we had poor rockfishing in the 1920s, too. The purse netters about cleaned them all out. They were the worst nets going. When purse nets were outlawed, the rockfish came back."

"In 1935, it was hard to make a living on the water," lamented Captain Otis, "Oysters were only bringing 25 cents a bushel, and they were scarce. On a yacht, I could make $50 a month, plus clothes and meals. That was pretty good money then."

From 1935 to 1950, Bridges captained yachts between the Chesapeake Bay and Florida, working for the rich and famous like opera star John Charles Thomas and Howard Taylor of White Cloud Mattress.

In 1950, Captain Otis returned to Bozman, where he bought the Bozman General Store and a charterboat, and resumed fishing.

Captain Otis wanted to see if the stainless steel rods he sold in the store were any good. He set up some rods with spreaders and bucktails for a trolling trip. It was near dark and they hadn't caught anything on the rods.

The rock they did catch was on the deep sash-weighted "dummy lines" tied to a screen door spring so big fish wouldn't snap the line.

"I saw a swirl in the water ahead of the boat and headed for it," Captain Otis said. "Every line hooked a rockfish. A woman fishing behind us asked what she should do now. Everyone was busy. We didn't want to be bothered with her problems. She derricked her 15-pound rockfish right into the boat, ka-thump. 'Well, you said you were busy,' she said, 'I didn't want to bother you.'"

"That proved the stainless rods were O.K.," Captain Otis said, "but one of the fishermen noticed that most of our rockfish were caught on the deep dummy line. He asked why we brought all this fancy tackle when 20 of our 30 rock were caught on a door spring."

"Some people didn't want any rockfish less than 10 pounds then," recalls Captain Otis of the 1950s and 1960s.

"Once in 1961, we fished at Romancoke. I had both fish boxes full and was back at the dock at 10:30 a.m. We had over 700 pounds of rockfish." In 1962, Captain Otis averaged 100 rockfish and blues a day for 30 days straight.

"My fish boxes were too big all those years," Captain Otis complained, "If I'd had smaller boxes, I wouldn't have had to stay out as long."

And Captain Otis' favorite gamefish? "When you come right down to it, I guess rockfish, but the bluefish is the gamest saltwater fish that swims. I think what you don't have [rockfish] is what you want most."

"I've fished two Mayors of Baltimore," says Captain Otis, "and one of them—he's fished with me for 15 years—is Governor now," he adds with a twinkle in his eye. How is Maryland Governor William Donald Schaefer to fish with? "He's a regular guy, and he'll fish for about anything—but he wants to catch fish."

The Bozman General Store is still a gathering place for locals. Captain Otis' niece, Pat Haddaway, is in charge now. Captain Otis, wearing a long-billed big game fishing cap and flip-up sunglasses, can be found in the store most every morning talking with his old friends—when he's not out fishing with governors.

The First MSSA Chapter – Talbot County

Carole and I were on Captain Mike Pivec's charterboat as guests of Bob and Hannah Prince. Bob and I had both retired from NASA Goddard Space Flight Center, and we had fished with Bob and Hannah many times on their boat.

Pivec trolled northward up the Kent Island shore from his home port at Kentmorr Marina. Pickins' were less than slim that morning.

Conversation turned to Pivec's new Maryland Saltwater Sportsfishermen's Association (MSSA) that had just begun to make some waves in the Legislature about declaring a much-needed moratorium on the beleaguered rockfish.

In the late 1970s and early 1980s, populations of rock had crashed. Pivec hoped that the MSSA could gather enough political clout to protect the stripers.

"Ever think about forming MSSA chapters?" I asked Pivec. He said he had, but had been too busy.

"Why don't you start one," Pivec challenged. And, so with the help of Bill Perry, we started the first MSSA chapter, in Talbot County. It was great for me, as I learned a lot about fishing around my new Bozman home in chapter meetings. I also met a lot of great local folks to fish with.

Did we catch any rockfish that day with Pivec? Only one, about 14 inches. There is a drop-off west of Love Point with hard bottom. We were trolling the standard bottom-bumping sinker with 2/0 bucktails on 18-foot leaders when the little guy hit. We put it back.

When a knowledgeable charter captain could only catch one rockfish in previously productive striper waters, our trip was a clue to the fish's scarcity. The fish were in more trouble than we thought.

Striper Trolling from Prince's Living Room

Turn back your fishing clocks about 30 years to a time when Chesapeake Bay striped bass were plentiful and help us relive a classic trolling trip out of the past.

The time was really 1983, before Maryland's striper moratorium was declared, but we fished the same way Chesapeake Bay rockfish trollers had been fishing since the turn of the century.

Bob and Hannah Prince of South River had invited us along on their classic 1955 Matthews 42-foot Sport Fisherman, named the *Gillie II*. (A gillie is a fishing guide in the British Isles). This beautifully-kept relic from the halcyon days of sport fishing was really too pretty a boat to toss nasty fish into.

The Matthews' large cabin was as light, airy and comfortable as the living room in your home. A dining table folded out along one bulkhead, and a plush sofa faced forward with upholstered chairs along the other bulkhead. Bob pointed out one piece of solid ⁶/₄" mahogany on each bulkhead. It was

24 inches wide and ran 21 *feet* from inside the cabin to the transom. The cabin forward was divided into two "bedrooms." A galley and head separated the main cabin and sleeping quarters.

As we put our gear on board, Carole noticed that the Prince's snowball bush was in full bloom on this first week in May.

"We always catch big rockfish when the snowball bush blooms," Bob Prince said. A good omen? We hoped so.

The snowball bush and Carole with the Matthews in the background.

In the early 1980s, Maryland anglers could keep one striper over 32 inches per day, per person, beginning the 1st of May. In those days, the Bay was crowded with boats, trolling for trophy rockfish. Historically, the first week of May was the peak fishing time for big ocean-going stripers in the Bay for spring spawning.

Our trip down South River on that beautiful May morning gave us some time to admire the classic old Matthews, and imagine ourselves on such a trip taken by wealthy folks in the 1950s.

The Matthews had been kept in near-new condition by its meticulous owner. The varnish was bright, and a new coat of paint graced the hull. The foredeck wore a new coat of light green epoxy paint. The twin Chrysler "Hemi" engines were, to quote a Chesapeake waterman, "Clean enough to eat off of," and purred like kittens. Fine cabinetwork and monel fittings were everywhere.

In the main cabin's "living room" atmosphere, we relaxed while we trolled for hours, waiting for a strike. A glassed folding door separated the living room from the open cockpit area aft which was our fishing station. One might suppose that with 32 feet of boat devoted to comfort, and only 10 feet of fishing area we might be tempted to be 75 percent hedonistic and 25 percent fishermen, but such was not the case.

Hannah Prince and Carole relax in "the living room."

After countless years of bouncing across Chesapeake waves in an open center console boat, getting drenched and chilled in pursuit of stripers, comfortable fishing was new to me. Please don't think of me as a fink if I deserted the ranks of center-console all-weather striper nuts momentarily and permitted myself a small smile.

Clearing Thomas Point Light at the mouth of South River, Hannah steered a course toward Gum Thickets while Bob and I rigged the wire line trolling rods. (Carole prepared donuts and coffee in the galley). Bob's trolling rods were fitted with roller tips, and his Penn #49 reels were filled with single strand 40-pound test monel wire.

In the spring, we trolled near the surface with 4- to 8-ounce inline sinkers, attached between the reel's wire line and the leaders with ball-bearing snap swivels. Bob's leaders were 50-pound test, 30 feet long, with the lure tied directly to the business end. A second ball-bearing swivel was added halfway down the leader for lures that were likely to spin like surge tubing eels and spoons.

Bob liked to offer a smorgasbord of BIG lures on the five lines he trolled. He used #19, #21, and #23 Tony Acetta spoons in chrome or white. Other spoons included 11/0 Crippled Alewives, #34 Huntington Drones, and the #550 Hopkins hammered spoon. One line always got a 7/0 to 9/0 "banjo Eye" bucktail jig with two pieces of pork rind, one red/white and the other yellow/white. Buddy Harrison of Tilghman Island called this combination "Eastern Shore Fruit Salad."

Bucktail jigs must have *real hair* on them to catch fish. Plastic hair went untouched in numerous fishing trials (except for some really suicidal bluefish). Ben Florence, the DNR's Hatchery Chief, once told me biologists recorded the passage of a real hair bucktail through the water. It sounded like bacon frying. The combination of fruit salad and bacon frying! What a great way to call stripers to breakfast!

Bob ran a huge 18-inch long surgical hose red eel on the center trolling line, either with no weight or a small 4-ounce inline sinker. This is called the "floater" line by charter Captain Mike Pivec because it is nearly 200 feet behind the boat and on top. We left rods in their holders until clicking drags signalled a strike.

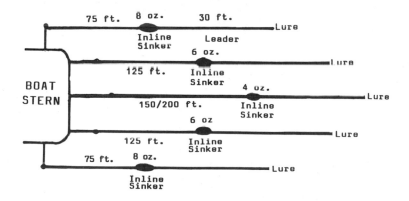

Spring trolling set-up.

Boat speed was set for maximum action from the spoons and hose. There is a secret to getting the proper twist in the hose lures, but I haven't mastered it yet. Some anglers bend the center of the hose around the finger a time or two, then let it loose to see how it looks. Dragging it behind the boat is the real test. It should swim like an eel from side to side, and not spin through the water like a dervish, say some captains. Mine spin anyway. And catch fish.

This day, one of Bob's motors was set to 800 RPM, with the second motor off. Bob had a certain pattern he trolled off Gum Thickets, and we relaxed in the living room with our coffee and doughnuts while he set his course by marks and depthfinder readings.

Old-time Bay anglers, and many still fish this way, found spots by lining up certain things like buoys with land-based objects like cupolas and house roofs. Two "marks" or lines of position (LOPs) are taken at each spot. In returning, when two LOPs crossed, the anglers would be within a few feet of their fishing spot. Today, for lazy folks like me, Loran-C does the same job.

Light tackle enthusiasts may be at my throat, but I still maintain that wire line trolling requires more attention to detail than the more forgiving spinfishing with monofilament line. In spinning, the stretch of the mono, a long whippy rod, and modern smooth drags, will allow a fair degree of angler error. Wire line stretches not at all, the rods used are stiff enough to control sinkers up to 24-ounces so they have the resilience of a crowbar, and the only thing left to yield to the fish is the reel's drag. An overly tight or jerky drag, plus a tiny kink in the wire line—and you could kiss a potential record rockfish goodbye! Also, $25 worth of terminal tackle.

Our relaxing spring day—a welcome respite after a cold winter—was punctuated with occasional screams from the reels when 15-pound to 18-pound bluefish grabbed our lures. Words and coffee cups would hang in midair as someone made a dash for the squealing reel.

Our blues hit hard and yanked line in pulsing tugs near the surface, while rockfish peeled line and fought deeper. "Aw, shucks" was the clue that a bluefish instead of a rock had hit, tangling lines and chewing up tackle with razor-sharp teeth.

Bob and I were relaxing in the living room, Hannah was below in the galley, and Carole was steering the boat, when a fish hit one of the baits and began to empty the reel spool. Bob was first to get the rod out of its holder, and the fight was on.

Rapid, tugging runs near the surface indicated it was a big blue. Carole steered the boat straight ahead to keep the lines from tangling. The boat's forward movement added strength to the fish's runs, but Bob soon had the fish coming toward us. Long, hard runs were interspersed with the same pump-and-reel tactics used when fighting any big fish.

Several times we saw color, but assuming it was a big blue, we only muttered about the fish's extra resistance to coming aboard, and its perceived lack of table quality. When it neared the boat, I saw stripes on the side of the fish! Rockfish! And, the size of it nearly took my breath away! As I nervously fumbled for the big net, Bob brought me back to reality:

"Miss this one, and you walk home!" Bob hollered. That helpful bit of advice steadied my shaking hands.

Bob Prince with a striper of a lifetime.

Getting a fish that big into a moving boat required teamwork. Carole steered, dodging other boats, Bob brought the sinker to the rod tip-top and walked backwards a few feet so I could grab the leader, then Bob took over leader duties so I could net the fish.

Netting was tricky, too. Many anglers lose fish when they try to net a fish tail-first. Touch a fish on its tail, and like many of us, it jumps ahead. Most likely it jumps ahead out of the net, and breaks the leader at the same time. As Bob eased up on the leader, the fish dove headfirst into my waiting net. Success!

When the big striper was finally in the net, it was too heavy for me to lift up over the high transom by myself. Bob lent a hand.

I had never seen a bigger rockfish caught, and it was the biggest Bob ever caught in 40 years of trolling the Bay. It weighed 42 pounds. The fish had struck on the big red hose. Big lure, big fish.

Bob's prediction about the snowball bush was right on in 1983!

6

LEARNING FROM THE LOCALS

Captain John Larrimore
... March 18, 1983

Bill Perry ran a Sportfishing Seminar at Chesapeake College in the early 1980s. It was a great place for a neophyte to learn about fishing, particularly a newcomer to the Eastern Shore. Speakers included Boyd Pfeiffer, Bill Burton, Bob Herder, Tom Goodspeed, Ben Florence, Betty Perry, plus charter Captains Ed Darwin, Harry Phillips, Bud Harrison, John Motovidlak, and John Larrimore.

Captain Larrimore's talk was on Friday night. He was acknowledged by locals as an expert rockfisherman. Rockfish! Hot dog! I riveted my attention on this fount of Eastern Shore rockfishing information. Speakers there didn't need to raise their voices because the seats were banked in a theater-like slope. Captain Larrimore began to talk in his low measured tone about rockfishing. He told it like it was, and you could tell he knew his subject. Wild horses couldn't have dragged me from that place on that night.

With the open and friendly attitude I have found all over the 'Shore, Captain Larrimore explained how and where he fished, and the types of bottom and areas to look for while rockfishing. He talked of trolling, which was his specialty, about shallow water and bottom-bumping. He told of oyster bottom, lumps, and "clay pans," large expanses of clay bottom that held stripers. He mentioned a productive clay pan off the "CIA House" on the Choptank River shoreline that I have looked for ever since and never found.

Captain Larrimore trolled the deeper Bay waters from Parker's Creek to the Bay Bridge from April 25th through May. He liked a 40-foot 50-pound test leader with a bead chain swivel near the drop sinker. He sometimes used two pieces of red, yellow, or white pork rind on his big bucktails. He started the season trolling all bucktails, and later added #19 Tonys to his rig.

Captain John Larrimore's spring trolling rig.

His July to November shallow water (3 to 4 feet) trolling rig was two swivels together for a little weight, a long 15-pound test leader and a small bucktail jig decorated with a "short yellow pork rind split all the way to the hole."

Captain Larrimore told us a story about two OLD fellows (he was 73 at the time) that he took rockfishing. They were anchored and had caught about 400 pounds of rockfish when Captain Larrimore pulled anchor. He made ready to "head for the barn."

One of the elderly anglers assumed they were getting ready to troll and started rooting round in his tackle box. Captain Larrimore emphasized to our fishing class, "They had *400 pounds* of fish, mind you!"

The elderly angler asked Captain Larrimore what kind of lure he should put on.

"You got anything in there that will catch a flying fish?" Captain Larrimore replied.

"I don't know. Are there any flying fish around here?" The angler innocently asked.

"Well, boys," Captain Larrimore said, "we're heading for the dock. Any fish you catch on the way in will *have* to be flying."

After his talk, I made my way down front and introduced myself. He could see I was fired up about learning to rockfish, Eastern Shore style. He mentioned some lumps I had found, and many I had not.

This was one likeable man. Sometimes you meet someone you feel comfortable with right away. Like maybe you knew them in a prior incarnation or something. John Larrimore was such a man.

On our way out of the auditorium that night, for I was still hanging on his every word, he said if I would bring my charts to his home at Tilghman, he would mark some rockfishing spots for me. Maybe he figured he would never get home to supper if he didn't tell me something, but I knew he meant it. He would have done what he said.

It is often said the road to hell is paved with good intentions. My good intentions to get down to see Captain John Larrimore were never carried out. I never did get down to see him, and he never got a chance to mark my chart.

He died not long after. A lot of great rockfishing information went with him.

Ben Florence on Rockfishing
... March, 1983

DNR biologist, Ben Florence, also talked about rockfishing at the Chesapeake College Sportfishing Seminar.

Ben is a kind of cult hero to those of us who were concerned early on about the striper's precipitous decline. He was one of the first DNR rockfish biologists to speak out about crashing rock populations. His bosses didn't want to hear about striper problems. Everything was O.K., they said.

Along with Joe Boone and Jim Uphoff, Ben was accused of talking to reporters. He didn't. Internal DNR gag memos were written. If ever a "Striped Bass Early Warning Award" is given, I nominate Ben, Joe, and Jim.

"I paid for it," Ben said many years later. "I don't talk striped bass politics any more." His career was sidelined for years because he had enough guts to warn about impending doom for Chesapeake striped bass. His boss at the time simply didn't know how to fire him, or he would have been gone. Ben is DNR Hatchery Chief now, out of the line of fire.

Ben's talk to the 1983 Sportfishing Seminar included information from his DNR field experience with stripers: He said that the Chesapeake Bay historically produced 90 percent of coastal stocks of stripers. He told of the 70,000 white perch x striped bass hybrids that were released in the Magothy River, and that the DNR also released some white bass x striped bass hybrids.

He estimated that recreational anglers got 15 percent of striper stocks in the early 1980s. He said a YOY index of 12 yields a 2 million pound total fishery, and a YOY index of 6 gives 1 million pounds.

Then Ben got to the good stuff. Striper fishing. Though Ben is mostly known as a striper biologist, he is also an expert striper angler.

Beginning May 1st, Ben trolled 8/0 bucktails on 40-foot 50-pound test leaders. He recommended ball bearing swivels for the leader and split bass strip pork rind. All of his trolled baits were the same. He used 12-pound class IGFA rods with 3/0 Penn reels.

"Troll slower to catch rock, faster for blues," Ben said, "I set the boat's speed so a #21 Tony wobbles. White #31½ Huntington Drone spoons work, too. The spoons should oscillate, not spin. In mid-May, troll small hose to duplicate May worms."

Through the summer, Ben trolled Choptank River edges and bars with 1/0 to 5/0 bucktails or sassy shads. For night fishing in the Choptank, Ben used a "popper and dropper" combination made from a hookless popping plug and an 18-inch mono leader with a small bucktail.

"When trolling a live eel on a 30-foot leader," Ben said, "If you feel the eel getting anxious, free spool to let the rockfish take the eel head first."

Ben talked about painting his own bucktail jigs. He used white RPS acrylic lacquer: Two undercoats, two coats of pearl white, and one coat of clear.

Shallow Water Trolling, Eastern Shore Style
... Summer, 1983

Shallow water trolling often paid off for me near Gibson Island, Bay Head, and Sandy Point. I even went so far as to install a flush-mount rod holder on each side of my Whaler console so I could fish rods horizontally from each holder, sort of "mini outriggers" for two eight- or nine-foot spinning rods. Later I installed a rod holder in each side of my Mako console. They worked great, too.

Trolling with no weight and a small spoon or jig was productive in two or three feet of water. Most of the fish we caught this way were "pan rock" from 12 to 15 inches. Sometimes a larger fish would hit in the shallows, but not in mid-summer.

When we moved to the 'Shore, Bill Perry and I got the Talbot Chapter of the MSSA into full swing. Bill invited Francis Howard of Tideland Sporting Goods to talk to the members about shallow water trolling. It was a wonderful revelation for me. Howard had learned his secrets from a very successful, but very quiet, shallow water expert, Gus Plutschak, who once caught enough rockfish to supply a local restaurant.

Francis Howard recommended trolling faster than usual in two or three feet of water right next to shore at high tide. His $1/16$- or $1/8$-ounce white bucktails had a green skirt and were adorned with a piece of Uncle Josh #210 white spin tail pork rind.

Howard said he favored the two hours before high tide until two hours after, mainly because that was the only time he could get his small skiff in over the rocks next to the shoreline. He let out 100 feet of 20-pound test line behind his boat, using a 5-foot leader joined to the line with a bead chain swivel. He marked his fishing line at 100', 125', and 150' with a black permanent marker. If he caught a fish at a certain length of line, he could return to that depth easily.

Howard also trolled right next to lighthouses, buoys, and other structure, bumping the bottom with the proper inline sinker.

We tried Howard's methods with good success. There is a lot of shallow water in the Choptank River that is suited to light tackle trolling in skinny water. Unfortunately, much of the shallow water near shore has a rock-strewn bottom. Good structure for rockfish, bad for propellers. Particularly aluminum ones. The only prop that will survive this environment is a stainless steel one. Susquehanna anglers weld pitchfork tines in front of the prop to protect it from the rock farm that grows there, but we use bigger motors to hustle the length and breadth of the Choptank. Pitchfork tines are not practical here.

Listening to local fishermen paid off, though it would take some time for me to be as proficient in the Choptank as I was around the Bay Bridges. It took me at least eight years to get really proficient at eeling and bucktailing around the bridges. It would take as long to get to know the Choptank half as well.

In September, 1983, I caught 21 small rock trolling the shallows near Chlora Point using Howard's methods. That was the good news. The bad? Only one was a 14-inch keeper.

Advice from Price

Sometimes, I think it would be nice to get a walk-around cuddy kind of a hull, so I could get out of the weather occasionally. But, then I consider the main drawback of a cabin boat. Casting room.

That's my favorite thing, casting to rockfish. Casting to bluefish. Casting tiny lures to white perch. Two experienced plug casters can work from the Mako without getting in each other's way or ripping the other guy's ear off.

Charter Captain Jim Price of Oxford has a hull just like mine, except his is a lot cleaner. In mid-summer, after fishing with peelers and other smelly baits, my Mako has established its own little colony of flies. Jim's boat is so clean, you hate to step into it with shoes on.

Jim keeps his Bimini top up all the time. Why? He occasionally takes out charter parties of inexperienced plug casters. When they get to flailing those treble-hooked plugs around in the air, he ducks under the Bimini top.

Price has fished the Choptank River all his life with nets or rod and reel. He takes his fishing parties from Oxford, which is within reach of a lot of rockfishing activity.

Price works hard to catch fish for his clients. In the course of a day's action, he may be found trolling with 16-ounce sinkers on the bottom, jigging with spinning tackle, trolling light tackle near shore, baitfishing near structure, or in Price's words, "any way they'll bite."

He may fish up river way past Cambridge, or as far out in the Bay as the Diamonds or Sharps Island Light. Price is a serious fisherman and spends most of his day with his eyes glued to his depthfinder. Ask him a question when he is communicating with his depthfinder and you will get a blank stare as if he just awoke.

Price believes that versatility is the key to catching fish. When an angler's favorite method does not work, many fishermen quit and go home, saying "they didn't bite today."

But Price says, "Work hard, work the rod, look for birds, and look for water movement."

"If one method does not pay off," he says "try something else."

"Although you might find rock in water from 8 to 60 feet deep in December, expect to find more fish in 40-foot depths."

"In the late winter, the fish in the lower river will be in 30 to 50 feet, whereas, in the upper river wintering rock will be in 15 to 30 feet of water."

He trolls through January, bumping the bottom with 1/0 bucktails and small spoons.

He also jigs with a multiple Japanese feather rig. I tried that rig with him one cold December day, and didn't catch anything. Jim swears by the rig, and I believe him. He once supplemented his income by commercial hook-and-line fishing in the Choptank for stripers, much of the time using the Japanese feather rig.

Jim Price with a possible striper hybrid he released.

Price once found fish on his depth finder, and began to jig for them. He noticed that the more fish he caught, the more thickly they schooled up beneath his boat. It seemed the more fish he caught, the more there were down there to catch.

I had the thought they may have been excited by the constant jigging action, and gathered to see what all the commotion was about. Fish can be curious, too.

Price will not get specific about spots that one can go directly to and catch fish. Although he has fished the Choptank all his life, he says, "As soon as you think you have the fish figured out, they'll go and do something else."

Captains Buddy and Bud Harrison
. . . April, 1983

Two of the first speakers to our new MSSA Talbot County Chapter were Captain "Buddy" Harrison of Chesapeake House on Tilghman Island, and his son, "Bud." They talked about trolling in the Bay for rock and blues and showed tackle they use every day on their 14 charterboats. The areas they covered were from Tilghman Island to Parker's Creek on the western shore, and included mid-Bay channel edges.

Almost standard on Harrison's charterboats is a fiberglass trolling rod with a roller tip top. Whether wire or monofilament line is used, the roller tip doesn't wear a groove in it like regular guides and surprise the angler with a cut line. Also, roller tips are low in maintenance.

Reels used by the Harrisons are Penn 309 level winders. The 309 is a moderately priced trolling reel, and parts are easily available. Better from the charterman's standpoint is the way the Harrison's use the level wind to detect the length of line out.

"Each traverse of the 309's level-wind guide is about 10 feet," Buddy Harrison said. Anglers are told to let out 14 traverses, which means 140 feet of line, or whatever. Line length varies with sinker size, water depth, and where the fish are located in the water column.

Wire line is springy and can cause a "bird's nest" of unbelievable proportions if the angler doesn't control his line. Some captains tell their anglers to keep the reel clicker on while letting line out to keep the slack out that causes over runs.

Lures used by the Harrisons run from Tony Acettas to Crippled Alewives and Huntington Drones in colors and sizes appropriate to the fishing. Buddy Harrison didn't use hose in the early May fishing. He used hose lures aplenty later in the summer for bluefish.

Buddy showed us a 7/0 white bucktail decorated with two pieces of pork rind, one red and one yellow. He called it "Eastern Shore fruit salad." He said rockfish loved that combination bait.

The interesting thing about Harrison's talk was that he "told his secrets" about fishing the Bay for rock and blues. He gave places, times, and tackle. Later, our MSSA chapter had our annual dinners at Harrison's Chesapeake House. Again Buddy and Bud gave us the latest methods and tackle to catch fish.

Having just migrated from the western shore, I wasn't used to that much openness, but we found other captains were willing to help us become better anglers, too.

Buddy and Bud Harrison sell oysters in the winter and go fishing in the summer.

Captain Henry Gootee Marks Charts
. . . December, 1983

Captain Henry Gootee of Golden Hill south of Cambridge spoke to our attentive MSSA group. He gave us the low-down on tackle he used:

"For bottom fishing, I never use anything but a regular two-hook bottom rig with beaded, snelled wide-gap hooks." All the fancy rigs others use didn't impress Captain Henry. He caught as many, or more, fish than anyone. He also told about some great oyster bottom "50 feet west of this buoy." After the meeting, he marked several charts for members. This was about as far from western shore "furtive fishing" as it is possible to get.

Captain Harry Phillips' Multiple Rock Rigs
... January, 1984

Charter Captain Harry Phillips talked to the Talbot MSSA group about rockfishing in the upper Bay. While much of his fishing was much the same as ours, he had developed some rigs that I never had the nerve to try. He used as many as five bucktails on a bottom bumping rig, plus a big sinker. I never wanted to risk that much tackle on treacherous oyster rocks, but I'm sure it worked for him.

Captain Phillips used 2/0 yellow bucktails tied with red thread and decorated with split #50 red pork rind. They were fished in tandem arrays that some call "gypsy rigs." But, he had two gypsy rigs and one single leadered jig on the same trolling rig! Five lures fished on one rod at the same time!

He gave us another tip I thought had merit; he cleaned his bucktails in Dawn dishwashing detergent.

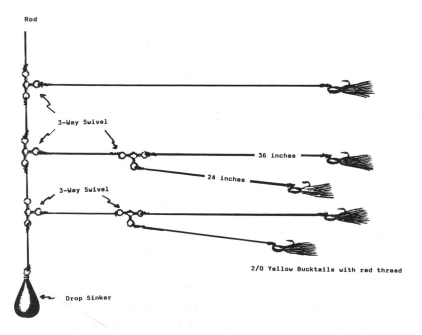

Captain Harry Phillips' multiple rockfish rig.

Chuck Prahl and the 14-Inch Choptank Stripers
... August, 1984

Chuck Prahl impishly peeked over the top of his glasses at me as he held a questionable rockfish up against the ruler on the gunwhale of my boat. "Think they'll grow up by September?" he asked.

I fervently hoped they would. Chuck's fish was 13¾ inches long, just a quarter inch shy of the 14-inch minimum that had been adopted by the DNR in 1983 to ease pressure on a dwindling rockfish population.

After taking a quick scale sample for the DNR biologists, we slipped it over the side. Of the 15 rockfish Chuck and I caught that evening, none were keepers.

We were anchored near Howell Point in the Choptank River in 14 feet of water next to a sharp drop-off. Tommy Hooper of Tommy's Sporting Goods in Cambridge, Maryland was anchored near us. He caught several rockfish, too. He and his two guests turned their boat upside down looking for a ruler. After borrowing an extra one from us, they were only able to put one fish in the cooler. Chuck and Tommy had fished the previous week, catching 10 and keeping five.

If one could ignore the newer boats and motors and our present location, it might seem that Chuck and I were repeating a trip from the past, when we both lived near Annapolis 20 years before. Chuck was a part-time charter-boat captain then, taking out parties in his 22-foot aluminum center-console boat. He called it a "tin can" and he was "Captain Tin Can" on the C.B. radio.

We recalled that long-ago night we fished Hackett's and Tolly's Points near Annapolis in the time honored way—peeler crab baits fished on the bottom. Bill Smith of NASA Goddard and his father were along that night.

Chuck recalled that the rockfish has a distinctive, strong tug when he hits a bottom bait, and the fish of 20 years ago were much larger. And not just because they seem to grow in the telling, either. Anglers of that day wouldn't go fishing unless Chuck would guarantee them five- to 10-pound rockfish. They wouldn't be bothered with the little ones that gave us such pleasure this evening on the Choptank.

Chuck and I had both moved to the Eastern shore since those golden days, and it was fun to reminisce as we fished for the undersized Choptank rockfish. We played the game of "Remember When?"

Remember when the boats fishing on the Dumping Ground above the Bay Bridge were so thick you could almost walk ashore on them? Remember all the rock we caught eeling and bucktailing the Bay Bridge pilings? Remember the 10- to 20-pounders we caught on shallow water plugs?

Chuck Prahl said "Can I borrow your striper stretcher?"

Remember the big rock I caught that October morning at the old wreck at Love Point?

I still remember Chuck's expression in the late morning of October 10, 1964. I sauntered into Chuck and Don's Tackle store in Annapolis as nonchalantly as one can saunter while dragging the largest rockfish I caught in my entire life. It's coal-shovel sized tail left a wide, wet, sticky swath on the tile floor. Chuck did a classic double-take when the size of the fish registered. Then and there he pronounced it the winner of the rockfish category in the then brand-new Maryland Sportfishing Tournament!

It turned out Chuck was right, too. The fish had weighed a respectable $32^{1}/_{2}$ pounds on his scale. Lucky for me that the tournament started in September, as the larger spawning fish caught in May surely would have beaten my humble 32-pound animal. We caught a lot of 20- and 30-pounders after that, but I could never top my October 1964 fish. No matter. Fish come and go, but Chuck's double-take will be with me a long while.

Our nostalgic conversation was punctuated with an occasional grunt from Chuck as he whipped his rod toward the sky to set his hook on yet another rockfish. My bottom rig was pretty much the same as his, though I used spinning tackle and he used revolving spool reels. Then why was he catching all the rock while I caught perch? This called for some investigation.

My terminal tackle consisted of a 2/0 stainless steel hook on a three-foot leader with a small drop sinker attached to the snap swivel at line's end. Chuck slipped an egg sinker on his line before tying on a swivel that served as a stop for the sliding sinker. Then he tied a three-foot leader to the swivel. At the business end of the leader he snelled a 1/0, number 65 claw-style hook with a turned-down eye. He maintained that a turned-down eye hook, properly snelled, suspends the bait in the current better. Chuck claimed, with over 30 years of rockfishing experience to back him up, a slip sinker lets the fish pick up the bait without feeling resistance.

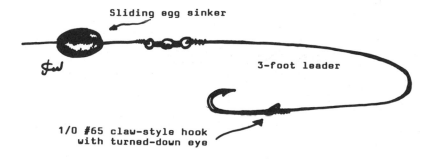

Chuck Prahl's sliding sinker rig.

He continued to grunt "Hnah!!" and set his hook with alarming regularity. I quickly and quietly changed my rig. He didn't have to slap me with a wet rockfish to get MY attention. Just catch more fish.

And catch fish he did. Nothing eluded Chuck's properly snelled hook that evening. I fully expected to see a rockfish stick his head up out of the water and ask me where Chuck's hook was.

"It's right over there, Mr. Rockfish," I'd say, "but you'll have to stand in line a while. And while you're waiting, send me over some more perch, will you?"

7

THE CRASH

Water Clarity: A Warning Signal

Many things have been blamed for the striper crash. The warning signals were up long ago. It didn't take a scientist to see that the water clarity in Bay waters was slowly changing.

I remember, as a kid, when we swam in the gin clear waters of Sawmill Branch at the railroad "Trestle Bridge" where Dorsey Road met Crain Highway near Glen Burnie. Two culverts under the Washington, Baltimore, and Annapolis (WB&A) railroad tracks had carved out a swimmin' hole as they cascaded creek water in a miniature waterfall.

We always stopped swimming in the waist-deep water when we heard the train coming. We stood in the thin water, buck naked, and waved at the WB&A "Toonerville Trolley" as it sped past on the raised bank above. We thought that the clear water hid our nether body parts from commuters. I expect the ice-cold water did more to make us insignificant than the water's ability to distort.

I recall shooting mallard ducks in a pristine marsh behind the "Ice House" on Crain Highway with my shirt-tail cousin, Edward Norris Creston "Cres" Bradley, Jr. We sat on the steep bank overlooking the clear stream flowing through skunk cabbage and other childish delights. We "froze" when ducks flew past to light in the stream. I was doubly careful with the old '97 Winchester Cres entrusted to me. That shotgun, with its tricky external hammer, would go off on a sniff or a sneeze.

Memories of one perfect shot stay with me. Cres turned to me with mouth agape when my mallard fell.

"You HIT it!," he said with some surprise.

"Sure, do it all the time." I shrugged off one of the best shots of a lifetime like it was nothing.

We got soaked to the waist wading through the marsh to retrieve our ducks. Who could afford hip boots then? Or retriever dogs?

Walking home across a field carrying what may have been a double limit of mallards, Cres asked me if I had my hunting license.

"Sure," I said, "think I'm a dummy?"

"Got your duck stamp attached and signed?" he asked.

"What's a duck stamp?" I replied. He blanched. Bad enough that we had counted our bag of mallards haphazardly. Now, this dumb-ball has no duck stamp, he likely thought.

Whathehell did I, a kid, know about duck stamps?

Our old duck hunting marsh is surrounded by development now.

I remember fishing, actually fishing, below Wagner's Pond in Sawmill Branch. I caught catfish from underhanging stream banks on handlines baited with garden worms, and took them home for Mom to cook. She laughed, and cooked the tiny creatures anyway.

I fished in Severn Run before those high bridges carried a zillion cars over it. The water was clear then.

We swam in Marley Creek in the 1940s. Many pleasant days were spent in clear, clean waters at the community beach at Margate. I remember diving off the bulkhead and swimming out to sun myself on an anchored raft. Grasses lined the shore.

I didn't know her then, but my future wife, Carole, lived in Margate at that time. She also remembers the clear water, and the waterside fun summer kids had in communities like Margate. I don't know if I'd swim there now.

When I met Carole much later, she lived on Brownshade Drive off Glen Burnie's Central Avenue. Her parent's property gently sloped down to Sawmill Branch. (Good thing she never saw me in the nearby swimmin' hole).

I recall camping at the Sand Caves on the Severn River in the summers of 1942 and 1943 with the Sears brothers, Wesley and Calvin, who lived across from me on Oak Lane in Glen Burnie. We camped near the Sand Caves until we ran out of food, sometimes as long as three weeks. We ate soft crabs fresh from the Severn for breakfast and lunch, and used leftover crab parts for bait for the perch we had for dinner. Glen Burnie's Boy Scout troop camped there, too. Authorities finally dynamited the Sand Caves after people got trapped inside them. There is a development there now.

We fished and crabbed the Severn from Granpa Sears' classic Chesapeake rowing skiff. Standing in the bow, we poled along in the shallows with a crab net for soft crabs. Severn River water was clear enough to see bottom six feet down.

We swam in the "sulphur pool" off River Road on Little Round Bay. I'd bet a sinker to a bobber there is a big waterfront mansion there now. Years later, Carole and I caught rockfish in crystal-clear water near the grass beds on Long Point between Round Bay and Little Round Bay.

Not many years after, Jimmy Tracey and I fished the Severn for chain pickerel. We tried every creek and cove off the main river, casting our Johnson Silver Minnows spoons with "female minners" attached. We worked upriver from the rowboat livery at Severn Inn on one side of the river to Round Bay, then downriver on the opposite side to home base. The water was still clear, and thick grass beds skirted the shoreline everywhere. Pike hung on the edge of the grass. One place I caught several pike was just inside the cove at Lindamoor. It was very deep just inside the inlet on the left with grass near the shoreline. I'm not sure I'd fish there now, even if there were pike to catch. The new Severn River Bridge has been widened to three lanes each way. I'd like to remember it the way it was.

Every place I swam, hunted, or fished as a kid is muddy, silted or polluted now.

We have spent centuries destroying the Bay. We trashed Bay waters with all manner of disgusting things: Everything from chicken guts to sewage to heavy metals. Developments silted in spawning streams. Folks who entreat us to "Save the Bay" have it wrong. Their bumper stickers should say, "Restore the Bay." Bring it back to what it was. Take away the silt, high fecal coliform counts, anoxia, dying fish. Bring back rockfish.

A Crashing Fishery

For years we allowed netting in striper spawning rivers. Purse nets surrounded great schools of stripers and wiped them out in the 1930s. Great shoals of sportfishing boats spanned the Dumping Ground, taking untold tons of rockfish, 100 pounds to 400 pounds per boat. We were all guilty. We thought there was no end to them.

I remember one day in 1983 at Hog Island on the Choptank River as Joe Boone, Jim Uphoff, and Don Cosden seined for Young-of-the-Year (YOY) stripers. We were talking about the crashing striper fishery. "Why doesn't someone do something?" I asked Joe. "Since when did fisheries managers respond to anything but a crisis?" Joe answered. He answered my question with a better question.

Why did managers let the striped bass resource crash to 10 percent of its former numbers before taking action? Politics! Money! And the watermen's long-standing belief—to quote one waterman: "God has been putting rockfish (oysters, crabs, clams, shad, herring, etc.) in the Bay for my family for hundreds of years. And he'll keep on putting them there." Couple that simple faith with something called "The Right of Free Plunder" that has existed in the Bay since the first settlers, and you can understand why commercials are reluctant to give up.

Illegal striper butchering "factories" were set up in the marsh near spawning rivers to process magnificent, huge spawning cow stripers that would be driven into nets by wet-suit clad "splashers." Observers said the "factories" were very efficient, cleaning tons of 40- to 60-pound cow fish in minutes, tossing them into waiting refrigerator trucks that travelled to out of state markets in hours.

Even since the 1985 moratorium, illegal 10-inch mesh nets have been found in the Nanticoke River in spawning season. Mesh that large is meant to catch big fish. Brood fish. No thought for tomorrow. Kill them today, and collect the cash.

Then, the crisis. As Joe Boone stated, fisheries managers react only to crisis. Striped bass were in great trouble before the moratorium was declared.

We were like a primitive civilization eating its seed corn. How many more cycles of striper boom-bust-moratorium do we have to go through before we learn to manage the fishery for the fish, not for the dollar?

I am reminded of a friend's quote:

"Today's disaster is tomorrow's archeology."

— Charles P. Boyle, NASA HQs

Storm Clouds Gather

Catches of striped bass began to fall off for most Chesapeake anglers in the late 1970s. It didn't affect those of us who fished mostly for big stripers around the Bay Bridges. Not concerned with catching big numbers of small rock, we concentrated on small numbers of large ones.

Paul Henley, one of the Bridge Gang mentioned earlier, lamented: "In the 1960s we had the Bridge to ourselves, then it got too crowded in the 1970s. By the late 1970s we had the Bridges to ourselves again."

A strange thing happened as the striper fishery declined. Once, the split of stripers between commercial and recreational fishermen was thought to be 50-50. But, when stripers became scarce, recreational anglers fished less. That very scarcity drove market prices up, and commercials fished harder until they drove the price down again.

Maryland's DNR estimated that commercials took 87 percent of all stripers in 1984, with 17 percent being caught by recreational anglers. Quite a difference from 50-50.

A piece of data that recreational anglers found unacceptable was the DNR's information that only 11 netters had caught 90 percent of the reported 1984 commercial take. Said another way, 11 netters caught 75 percent of ALL stripers caught in Maryland that year. If anything could make recreational anglers determined to have the striper declared a gamefish, three-quarters of all the rockfish going to 11 netters did it.

In the middle of the striper crash, Carole and I had other priorities. We sold our home in Cape St. Claire in 1981, and built another one on the Eastern Shore that year. Between my retirement in 1979 and finishing our home in 1982, my striper fishing dropped to somewhere between seldom and never.

Somebody, Please Do Something!!
...1983

By 1983 public sentiment in Maryland was strongly in favor of a striper moratorium. Recreational fishermen complained that rockfish had all but disappeared. Maryland's reported commercial catch had dropped over 90 percent, from a high of 5 million pounds in 1973 to 445,000 pounds in 1983. Some commercials complained that the DNR was using catch report figures against them. A few netters said they would no longer report their catch.

Striped bass were not reproducing. The Young-of-the-Year (YOY) index had dropped drastically below the long term average of 8 and it stayed there for a decade, except for 1982's index of 8.4. The 1982 year class would have to be protected as tomorrow's spawners.

Dr. Phil Goodyear of the U.S. Fish & Wildlife Service (USFWS) and Dr. John Boreman of the National Marine Fisheries Service (NMFS) recommended a 55-percent cut in striper fishing mortality in the 15 coastal states that belong to the Atlantic States Marine Fisheries Commission (ASMFC).

Maryland placed additional restrictions on commercial fishermen. A 14-inch minimum was in place, and a sport creel limit of 10 fish per day.

In February, 1983, MSSA members holding a candlelight march on the State House in Annapolis were told by a DNR official that there would be a rockfish moratorium if the 1983 YOY index was low. It *was* low at 1.4, almost the lowest in history. No moratorium was declared then.

Pressured by commercials in the famous "midnight meeting" of October 14, 1983 that charter Captain Bob Spore reported in his *Arundel Sunpaper* column, DNR officials backed down on tougher regulations for commercials, but cut the sport creel limit to five per day. Spore wrote that he was the only non-commercial fisherman present at the meeting.

Editorial writers had a field day with the "midnight meeting" information, and Captain Mike Pivec wrote about the results of the meeting in MSSA's *Tidelines*:

"Let me dispel the rumor about a shut down or a moratorium on striped bass," Pivec wrote, "those are words out of the mouth of a fool. You would think after all the work that has gone into the plan and all the publicity it's received, that someone would stop playing games with our striped bass. But, ladies and gentlemen, it's business as usual." Pivec also said, "we must start right now to stop this useless proposal. This fishery can not afford to have this type of fishing pressure."

Gilbert Radonski of the Sport Fishing Institute was one of those who wrote Governor Harry Hughes. He objected to the "midnight meeting" and urged the Governor and DNR Secretary Dr. Torrey C. Brown to listen to the professionals—the DNR biologists—to reduce the harvest of stripers no less than 80 percent in Maryland waters. Radonski called for the closure of spawning rivers to fishing in January instead of April, no anchored nets above the Bay Bridges and no additional sport restrictions beyond the 10-fish creel limit and one fish over 32 inches per day.

Bill Burton wrote in *The Evening Sun*, "We have been promised moratoriums, only to learn later of changes to accommodate the short term welfare of watermen at the expense of the long-range welfare of of a species admitted to be in trouble, even by Dr. Brown." Burton pointed out another problem: "No one with a scientific background in fisheries is any higher within DNR than the mid-department level. It is becoming increasingly evident to me that many decisions are made more on a political, rather than a scientific, basis."

Ed Dentry, outdoors columnist for the *News American*, humorously nominated several Maryland DNR officials for 1983 outdoorsmen "Oscars" on January 1, 1984. After castigating several DNR managers for backing down on a rockfish ban, Dentry gave himself The Journalistic Blunder Award for writing in October, 1983 that the DNR would soon recommend "tough new rockfish regulations," The Famous Last Words Award went to the Tidewater Administration (DNR), for issuing a statement saying there would be no new rockfishing regulations on the very day a new 14-inch minimum cleared the General Assembly. Dentry gave the

Rockfish Management Award to Captain Jim Price of the Maryland Charterboat Association, who "nursed his 14-inch limit bill through the Senate's final hours without DNR help."

A Moratorium Bill for Maryland

Maryland Senator Gerald Winegrad, at a striped bass meeting in Annapolis on November 28, 1983, stated he had prefiled an Emergency Bill, S.B. 47, that would prohibit the sale or possession of striped bass. The legislation would expire December 31, 1984 or before that if the YOY index reached 15. Senator Winegrad cited, among others, a seafood dealer who said a total moratorium was necessary.

Response to the moratorium was predictable: Recreational anglers for, commercials against, legislators choosing sides, the DNR caught in the middle while they furiously tried to muzzle their more conscientious biologists. The fish were losing ground fast.

Commercials and their legislators complained: A moratorium would put them out of business; stripers were just recovering from Hurricane Agnes; conservation was not desperate based on last year's [1982] index; bluefish were eating spawned rockfish; the DNR was incompetent to regulate the fishery; hatcheries can make up the difference; and—go right on fishing, we are all on the same team.

Recreational fishing interests and biologists supported S.B. 47. MSSA President, Mike Pivec said the moratorium was a dire necessity to protect the 1982 year class. "If overfishing occurs," Pivec said, "striped bass will be wiped out." He offered to support the DNR in "any protective measure."

Past President of the Maryland Charterboat Association, Bob Lord, said, "What happens after the 1982 year class is fished up?" and "Hatcheries can not produce the 15 million fingerlings needed to support a commercial fishery."

Lobbying for the Maryland Charterboat Association, Captain Jim Price said, "It would take years and millions of dollars" to set up a hatchery program. He cited Joe Boone's forecast that the striped bass fishery had been reduced to one year class, 1982. Price also hinted about his endangered species petition that would "Give Dr. Brown the authority to close the fishery: It puts the responsibility where it belongs, with Dr. Brown."

A Threatened Species Petition

With all of the public and recreational angler pressure on to close the striper fishery, one of the most significant aids to the beleaguered rockfish came from two private citizens.

Maryland Charter Captains James E. Price of Oxford and Robert F. Lord, Jr. of Linthicum filed a "PETITION FOR THE DECLARATION OF STRIPED BASS AS AN ENDANGERED OR THREATENED SPECIES" on November 23, 1983. The petition was directed to Maryland DNR Secretary Brown. It said that the 1982 year class would be fished up by 1986 under present regulations. It called for endangered or threatened species classification for striped bass in Maryland, saying that "with the 1983 YOY index at 1.4, the critical nature of the situation is even more evident."

Part of the basis for the Price/Lord petition was found in a paper written by Joe Boone who was in charge of the DNR's YOY survey. Boone's "1983 Tidewater Fishing Forecast & Homily" stated: "Continued dependence on nature to compensate for flagrant overfishing is to gamble with the very existence of this magnificent fish (striped bass)." Boone's "homily" also pointed out that although the 1982 striped bass YOY index was an improvement over the 1979, 1980, and 1981 averages of 4.2, 1.9, and 1.2 (the DNR now says the indexes were 4.0, 2.0, and 1.2) respectively, this is still below the past 25-year average of 10."

Striper Protection Gathers National Momentum

"We are seeing much greater interest now," said Andrew Schwartz, aide to U.S. Representative Gerry E. Studds (MA). It was January, 1984. "People who have never spoken on fishing issues are speaking out now. People are seeing this as an environmental issue." Representative Studds and Senator Edward M. Kennedy awaited the February release of Dr. Boreman's report and recommendations before introducing legislation to protect the striper.

The National Wildlife Federation's Lynn Greenwalt said, "The striped bass is the aquatic equivalent to the American bald eagle."

The National Audubon Society (NAS) said they hoped to make their considerable legislative and lobbying expertise available for new striper laws. Donal C. O'Brien, Jr., of the NAS said about his Nantucket fishing, "I think we are seeing an educational process here. Five years ago I couldn't have imagined releasing a [striped] bass. Then my son started throwing them back. Now I couldn't imagine killing one. That's a pretty fast education."

"All sorts of organizations are now beginning to realize just how major the problem is," said Dick Russell of the Boston-based Striped Bass Emergency Council in January, 1984. Russell said a national effort was needed. Russell had endeared himself to Maryland DNR officials the previous month at an Atlantic States Marine Fisheries Commission (ASMFC) meeting near Baltimore by quoting Maryland DNR biologists who said the DNR's official proposed cuts in fishing mortality would amount to less than the required 55 percent.

Russell later quoted Ralph Abele of Pennsylvania, then Chairman of the ASMFC's Striped Bass Management Board. Abele: "You'd better get your s—together, otherwise the Feds will take over, and I wouldn't blame them. The striped bass is a migratory fish. Let's not lose year class after year class while we fight this out among ourselves."

Claudine Schneider and Gerry Studds to the Rescue

Congresswoman Claudine Schneider (RI) introduced an East Coast Striper Moratorium bill in Congress (H.R. 4884) on February 21, 1984. It called for a three-year moratorium in all coastal states north of South Carolina. This moved the focus of the striper fight from Maryland to the Hallowed Halls of Congress. It was the same fight as before, just more visible nationally. Maryland Representative Mike Barnes had co-sponsored the bill as of March, 1984. Maryland Representative Roy Dyson did not. Dyson said the striper problem was caused by pollution that was being cleaned up, and that a fishing cutback was not required. (In 1986, Dyson urged a *coastal* striper moratorium. Congressman Studds argued against, and noted that Dyson had opposed federal regulation of stripers two years before. "In a sense, I got religion," said Dyson, "I admit positions I took in the past may have been a mistake.")

Schneider's bill had support from many commercials and recreationals along the ocean coast who momentarily stopped fighting each other long enough to back her bill. Others did not back the bill. NOAA Administrator, Dr. John Byrne, testified on March 20, 1984 that a Federal moratorium on striped bass fishing was premature.

The ASMFC's striper plan to reduce fishing mortality 55 percent had not been fully implemented then, but a new federal hammer was about to descend on recalcitrant states.

The National Wildlife Federation and others suggested a compromise, basically a mandatory federal moratorium in states that did not implement the ASMFC plan.

Representative Studds introduced a bill, H.R. 5492, which did not demand a complete moratorium. The Studds bill authorized the Department of Commerce to close fishing in any state that did not implement and enforce the recommended ASMFC plan by June, 1985. Studds' measure won approval in October, 1984.

Ripe Cows and Tiny Larvae Were Hard to Find
... April, 1984

I watched Maryland DNR biologist, Jim Uphoff, as he separated tiny striped bass larvae from white perch larvae and debris in a petri dish. He had dragged an otter trawl in one of the Choptank River's prime spawning areas for several hours to capture these tiny critters that could help predict the spawning success of the 1984 year class. He found only 11 larvae.

Asked about the low numbers of larvae, Uphoff said that at that point the larvae were of secondary concern—he and other researchers had not seen enough spawning fish in the river to support "any kind of fishery."

I agreed because I had spent the previous two days net fishing with William "Skip" Bason, a biologist under contract to the Maryland DNR to gather and fertilize eggs for hatchery work and Bill Price, a Choptank commercial fisherman. In a day and a half we had only caught 5 fish—all males in the 3- to 5-pound range. Bason said he fished for two weeks without catching one cow due to the scarcity of large fish.

At lunch on our second day of fishing, Bill Price was depressed.

"Fish all day at Ganeys Wharf in spawning season and only catch five rock," Bill mumbled, "*somebody* better have a moratorium."

Near the end of the second day we moved to a different part of the river. Price enlisted the aid of Harold Christopher, a commercial fisherman from Tanyard who had fished that part of the river for 50 years.

At Christopher's direction we set the net across a tidal flat in what Choptank commercials call a "retch" (reach). In one short drift of the 180-yard long 7-inch mesh net, we caught 19 rockfish weighing from 40 to 65 pounds each. None of these was a "ripe" spawner. Bason thought these fish were from the "dominant" 1970 year class. Bason also voiced his concern that there were almost no rockfish between the 1970 year class and the 1982 year class.

Researchers estimated the 1984 spawning population was composed of 20 percent big 1970 fish, and 80 percent 1982 fish—small male rockfish just reaching sexual maturity.

Bill Price brings in gill net as Harold Christopher prepares to release a cow striper.

In an interesting aside, Bason noted that our male stripers stayed with their noses in the corner of the boat's live tank.

"All someone would have to do is build an underwater structure with a corner in it," Bason kidded, "and come once a day to collect the fish."

In the April 23, 1984 issue of *Sports Illustrated* magazine, author Robert H. Boyle offered the hypothesis that "acid rain is significantly responsible for the decline of striped bass reproductive success." The article stated that the precipitation that falls on Maryland can have a pH of 4.45 to 3.5, or 15 to 110 times more acid than normal. (The May 8, 1984 tornado-spawning storm that wreaked havoc in parts of Dorchester County brought with it acid rain that was measured at pH 3.2).

Striped bass larvae have difficulty surviving pH levels below 7, according to Dr. Serge Doroshov of the University of California at Davis, where they raise stripers at a pH of 8.

Captain Jim Price of the Chesapeake Bay Acid Rain Foundation felt that the acid rain theory gained support because of tests run by Johns Hopkins University at Vienna, Maryland. Johns Hopkins researchers brought healthy North Carolina striped bass eggs with them and fertilized the eggs on the spot with Nanticoke River male stripers. Tests were conducted on the resulting striped bass larvae by immersing the larvae in mixtures of tap water and acidic Nanticoke River water, lowering the pH of the water by adding Nanticoke water. Survivability was high with large percentages of tap water. What happened when pure Nanticoke River water was used?

"Why, it killed all of them," Price said.

At the time the tests were done, the river water had a pH of 6.5. Also present in the Nanticoke were amounts of aluminum that scientists believe could have been toxic to striper larvae.

In June, 1984 Uphoff towed again for striper larvae. He caught 1,000 striper larvae in one week. Then heavy rains fell. Nanticoke River pH fell to 3.2 overnight. Uphoff noticed a die-off. He only caught 60 larvae the following week.

Where Was the 1983 Year Class?

In 1984, Wayne Gatling, at the ripe old age of 32, was already a seasoned charterboat captain. Son Brian at age 11 was his dad's mate.

Captain Gatling ran the last active charterboat out of Rock Hall—a port that once supported a fleet of more that 50 charter fishing boats. In the 1960s and early '70s, tons of rockfish were caught every day by Rock Hall charter boats. Their anglers came mostly from Pennsylvania, according to Gatling. When rockfish populations dropped 90 percent, the death knell sounded for the once-great Rock Hall charter fleet.

Gatling told me he thought that those who predicted doom and gloom for the rockfish were wrong. He saw large schools of small rockfish playing [breaking] on Hodge's Bar above Rock Hall on summer evenings. He said the large numbers of small rock indicated the DNR biologists Young-of-the-Year (YOY) surveys were wrong. He hoped the small 8-inch to 10-inch fish could be from the unsuccessful 1983 year class, not the moderately successful 1982 year class.

Captain Gatling invited me and my wife, Carole, to go along with him on his *Lara Lynn III*, to see these small fish "play" and collect some scale samples from the smaller fish. Fish scales have rings like the cross section of a tree trunk. Biologists can tell how old the fish are by examining these growth rings.

But first to collect some scale samples. How we suffered for science!!

Tiny eighth-ounce bucktails and #13 Tonys on 15-foot leaders behind 4 to 6 ounce in-line sinkers did the trick in 10 to 18 feet of water on Hodge's Bar. Captain Gatling used flexible medium spinning instead of stiff bay rods, to better telegraph a "fish-on."

He trolled in a circular pattern. Each time we crossed a 10-foot high "lump" one or two of the three rods in their holders would bend. One of us reeled the fish in until the sinker was near the transom, then walked back a few steps. Our mate grabbed the leader and swung the fish aboard.

I took accurate measurements and scale samples from the fish under 11 inches—those that might be assumed to be from the 1983 year class. I photographed the smallest, an 8-incher. All stripers were examined for the freeze-brand that marked hatchery-raised fish. I detected no marks.

We caught 35 rockfish before we anchored to bottom fish with soft crab for white perch. Only four of our rockfish were keepers over 14 inches. We also caught 122 white perch and 58 large catfish.

DNR biologist, John Foster, later examined my scale samples. He said only the smallest rock, an 8-inch fish, was from the 1983 class. The other small rock, from 9 to 11 inches, were from the successful 1982 year class. Biologists explained the range of sizes for the 1982 year class—from 9 to 15 inches—as being due to a long spawning season, some fish found more food than others, and for the same reason many of us are different sizes —"genes."

Our admittedly unscientific sampling off Rock Hall seemed to support warnings from biologists that the 1982 year class was the only one left.

Captain Wayne Gatling and son Brian with a Hodge's Bar Striper

When the 1982 year class entered the net fishery in the fall and winter of 1984 at high prices, large numbers of them showed up in fish markets. Soon markets were glutted with the last stripers that could be caught before the January 1, 1985 moratorium went into effect. The price soon dropped to 35 cents a pound.

8

A MORATORIUM

The Pressure Builds

The MSSA and other fishing groups, the outdoor press, and private citizens were putting pressure on Maryland Governor Harry Hughes and the DNR for a complete moratorium on rockfish in 1984. Tugging on the other end of that rope were those who stood to lose money. But, even many commercials privately admitted a closure was necessary.

In July, 1984 the DNR proposed further cuts in the sport creel limit. Instead of five rock per day for all hook-and-liners, the new rules would still allow five per day for charterboat anglers, but only TWO per day for anglers in private boats.

A brand new Chesapeake Bay Sport Fishing License (CBSFL) was poised to go into effect in January, 1985. The new DNR cuts would still allow charter anglers to keep five rock a day, though they could be from out of state and didn't have to buy a CBSFL. Maryland recreational anglers who pay license fees out the gazoo were being cut from five rock to two a day. That went over like a lead fishing float. At this point, a moratorium had not yet been declared.

My letter to DNR Secretary Brown in early August also appeared in the Easton *Star-Democrat*. I stated the new two and five rock proposal was discriminatory, and that I felt a two rockfish creel limit was a concrete admission by the DNR there was no longer a viable fishery for striped bass—and how could a prudent manager do anything but completly shut down the striped bass fishery?

Dr. Brown replied, ". . . while everyone likes to be treated equal, their [charter and private anglers] impact on the resource is very unequal." He stated private boats took 85 percent of the sport catch of rockfish, while charterboat parties harvested only 9.75 percent. (That same 2 and 5 fish rationale later surfaced in proposed regulations when the fishery reopens).

127

Secondly, and this should have been some kind of a clue, Dr. Brown wrote that he had already "determined that the striped bass is deemed in need of conservation." The classification "In Need of Conservation" is the lowest of three classifications in Maryland's Endangered and Threatened Species Act.

Dr. Brown was walking a tightrope between a crashing fishery, politicians who could cut his agency budget, conservationists bent on a closure, and commercial interests. He had found a perfect solution in the Endangered & Threatened Species Act, but no one had noticed.

Yet.

A New Career, Writing About Rockfish

My interest in rockfish goes back a long way. My articles about stripers appeared in *Tidelines*, because MSSA members supported striped bass conservation and wanted to read what was going on with stripers. Another outlet for my striper conservation pieces was Louise Hawkins' Talbot County paper, *Attraction*. Some of my articles appeared in *The Fisherman*, *Salt Water Sportsman*, *Striper*, and others. I joined the Mason-Dixon Outdoor Writers Association (M-DOWA), and was steadily building published credits to qualify as an Active Member of the Outdoor Writers Association of America (OWAA).

This new career let me learn more about my favorite subject, stripers. It also brought me in contact with some really great people in the striped bass field.

The following chapters on tagging, acid rain, enforcement, YOY, hatchery work, White Paper Committee, catch and release, pollution, gamefish, etc. resulted from this interest. Everyone won't agree with what I write. I make no apologies. I call it the way I see it. If you disagree, write your own book.

Scientists Turn Up the Heat

Dr. George Krantz, then Tidewater Administrator, was very candid on September 6, 1984:

"This is the first time in history that the watermen have said, 'We know we have to do it'," Dr. Krantz told me about the possibility of a moratorium.

"Tell Mike Pivec the MSSA has to get in touch with Torrey [Secretary Brown] before the 13th if they believe a moratorium is better than a 55 percent cut. Boreman and Goodyear [Drs. Boreman and Goodyear had recommended a 55-percent cut in fishing mortality] met with the Governor on Saturday. I think 55 percent is a human estimate about what Mother Nature is going to do."

Dr. Brown asked Dr. Krantz for his evaluation of the situation.

Dr. Krantz told Dr. Brown: "We may have already passed the breaking point."

Dr. George Krantz points to a photograph of a freeze-branded hatchery striper. From left to right: Skip Bason, Jim Price, Dr. Krantz, Charlotte Merryweather, and Bob Lunsford.

Reality on the Choptank
... September, 1984

"I'd say the health of the species is declining rapidly," Joe Boone said on his 27th Young-of-the-Year (YOY) survey on the Choptank River. "I'm not saying we have a terminal patient yet, but it's not good."

Boone's partner on the survey, Jim Uphoff, said, "The 1982 year class is getting ready to be destroyed like the 1978 year class."

Boone had already released his "1984 Tidewater Fishing Forecast & Homily," in which he deplored the rapidly declining striped bass stocks while "divergent factions vigorously promote a plethora of viewpoints spanning the range from 'fishing as usual' to an immediate moratorium

... skepticism (about official pronouncements) will continue until emphasis is clearly directed toward restoration of the species rather than prolongation of moribund [dying] fisheries."

Boone also stated the remaining Chesapeake population consisted predominantly of two-year old members of the fair 1982 hatch. Younger and older year classes were scarce, Boone added. A low 1984 index "should be the alarm that mobilizes immediate protection of the Chesapeake strain."

On September 10, 1984 at one of the Choptank River YOY seining sites, I asked Boone his opinion.

"If the three-year average index is 5 or less, they should declare a moratorium," Boone said.

"Is that based on the Goodyear/Boreman computer model?" I asked.

"No," Boone said, as he measured a tiny juvenile striper, "This is the real world."

Other conscientious DNR scientists who had been too vocal in talking to the press about striped bass problems were reprimanded by middle managers. Although these biologists survived the gag memos and the internal storms, they would rather forget about it. Some of them are still wary about talking stripers.

The 1984 index was only 4.2

Surprise!!!

Bill Perry, in his position as outdoor columnist for the Easton *Star-Democrat*, was invited by the DNR to hear the new striped bass regulations on September 11, 1984. He arranged for me, a fledgling outdoor writer, to attend. We expected to hear that we would be cut to two stripers, with some small adjustment for commercial fishermen.

DNR Secretary, Dr. Torrey C. Brown presided. His remarks took us by surprise:

"I am today taking steps to declare the striped bass a Threatened Species and am proposing a moratorium on commercial and recreational taking and fishing for striped bass January 1, 1985."

Dr. Brown outlined his reasons for the closure, which included an analysis of spawning stock, larvae survival, and a low YOY index. He said the ASMFC planned cuts of 55 percent would not provide enough protection. Evidence of a worsening situation prompted the decision for the moratorium, which was supported by Governor Hughes. Dr. Brown said he would ask the ASMFC to recommend other states take conservation measures more stringent than the 55-percent plan, including moratoria where necessary. He mentioned a Watermen's Compensation Program at between $1 and $2 million.

One of the first questions was how long would it last?

"Until we get acceptable levels of reproduction. Best guess is at least four years before we could clearly demonstrate a response."

How about hybrids? "If its mother is a rockfish or its father is a rockfish, it's a rockfish," Dr. Brown said.

Bill Burton: "Is a lawsuit possible?"

Dr. Brown: "Don't even suggest that!!"

"This is clearly in advance of the Studds bill," Dr. Brown said, "This is a leadership position for Maryland."

Sportfishermen and conservationists along the entire east coast thought Dr. Brown took a courageous stand when he declared the moratorium. The word never got out that many commercials supported the ban, too.

I wanted to ask Dr. Brown if his Threatened Species classification resulted from Jim Price's petition, but didn't. I was the new boy on the block, surrounded by legendary outdoor writers like Burton, Perry, Kreh, and Dentry. It was my first press conference. I kept quiet then. Not now.

9

RESTORATION

Restoration, Sadly

Writing the word "restoration" in reference to striped bass is saddening. Why the hell should we have to "restore" *anything*?

Letting natural resources deteriorate to the point where crisis management is necessary is unthinkable. But, it happened.

Maybe the rockfish will come back. There have been wild cycles in rockfish populations before. Looking back at some 1989 quotes, it is interesting to see just how surprised some people were by the 1989 YOY index:

Verna Harrison, then Maryland DNR Assistant Secretary, told me in an interview for *Salt Water Sportsman* in January 1989: "We have discovered that only 42 percent of the 1982 year class returned to spawn this year instead of the expected 95 percent."

Steve Early, DNR Striped Bass Project Leader told me in early 1989 for *Salt Water Sportsman*: "We have had about a threefold increase in wintering fish in the Bay. But here is the catch   they are small fish, not the adult female spawners we need. There is a tenfold increase on the spawning grounds," he continued, "but the positive effects of this have not been seen yet."

To my question about opening the striped bass fishery in Maryland any time soon: "We only have one year class—1982. No business would hang their hat on one year class. That is not a stable thing to do. We can't depend on the 1982s for a complete recovery" Early said.

These statements were from the best knowledge available at the time, perfectly reasonable.

Shortly after, the announcement was made to reopen in October 1990. What happened in the interval between the hundreds of interviews like those above and the anouncement to reopen?

Part of the problem of fisheries management, the way I see it, is that present scientists and managers are mostly young people or non-fishermen.

When they say, "The [rock] fishery is restored," they don't know how good it was in the halcyon days.

"Old Timers" remember running from one school of breaking rockfish to another until they found the size fish they wanted to catch. In autumn, I remember seeing breaking stripers from the Magothy River to the Bay Bridge over to Love Point and back to Bodkin Creek, and I'm sure rockfish were breaking many miles up and down the Bay from the meager range just described.

Now, the youngsters see a school of breaking fish a mile wide and three miles long, and declare: "There are plenty of rockfish."

Fooey. Let me see it again: A solid school of stripers breaking from Cambridge down the Choptank and all the way across the Bay. Then, I'll believe the youngsters. They are looking at numbers on a computer printout.

Ask us 'ol gray-beards if the rockfish are back.

Rocky Road to Recovery

Maryland's moratorium, plus more stringent fishing regulations in other coastal states, met the ASMFC's plan for a 55-percent cut in striper fishing mortality.

The Atlantic States Marine Fisheries Commission (ASMFC) was chartered as a coastal interstate compact by the U.S. Congress in 1942. It included all Atlantic states from Maine to Florida. The ASMFC has no regulatory powers. Member states meet and form a consensus, then recommend fishery management regulations to those states. Then it is up to the states to pass those regulations. Sometimes in the past, they didn't.

Congressman Studds' 1984 Atlantic Striped Bass Conservation Act (called "Act" or "Studds" for short) was a federal Sword of Damocles hanging over the heads of coastal states that didn't fall into line on striper regulations. Under Studds, recalcitrant states would have a federal striper moratorium declared until they instituted ASMFC's recommendations. Virginia and the Potomac River Fisheries Commission were about to have their striper fisheries closed down under Studds when they declared their own moratoriums in 1989.

Few striper regulations were recommended by the ASMFC between 1942 and the 1970s. It was fishing as usual, which is to say, considerable and rapacious. When the striper fishery crashed, the ASMFC oiled up its rusty striped bass gears and went to work.

In 1981 the ASMFC published the Interstate Fisheries Management Plan for Striped Bass ("Plan" for short). Size limits and spawning period closures were some of their first conservation measures. Most recently, the 38-inch coastal limit under the Plan's Amendment #3 would have protected the 1982 year class until 90 percent of its females could spawn at least once. The demise of Amendment #3 would be triggered by a Maryland YOY "running index of 8 for three years."

One thing you can say about bureaucratic management. Properly motivated (and obscenely funded), it can respond to crisis. More data has been gathered about striped bass in the last decade than in the previous century.

Not that bureaucrats are allowed to manage stripers any better. Stripers are still political footballs. But now, we know a lot more about what we're doing wrong.

I sincerely hope that a quote I remember from my days at NASA will also apply in the future to striper management:

"It is possible to make the right mistake."

— Charles P. Boyle
NASA HQs

10

STRIPED BASS AND THE HATCHERY

Rocky and the Hatchery

"The job of a hatchery is to put itself out of business," said Maryland DNR Hatchery Chief, Ben Florence. Florence meant, if striped bass spawning populations were successfully rebuilt, the hatchery had done its job. It would be out of business. If hatchery restoration of spawning stocks was unsuccessful, they were also out of business.

A decision was made to attempt to rebuild Chesapeake Bay spawning stocks of stripers by raising and releasing them in their parents' rivers of origin. There had been no large year class since 1970 to supply brood fish, spawning success had plummeted, and big mature female brood fish were scarce on the spawning grounds.

The U.S. Fish and Wildlife Service (USFWS), the Maryland DNR, Virginia's Department of Game and Inland Fisheries, and two large electric power companies would cooperate. The cooperative program began in 1985. It was preceded by pilot programs like the August, 1983 Nanticoke River release of 17,000 freeze-marked fingerlings hatched and grown by Skip Bason under contract to USFWS, DNR, the Baltimore Gas & Electric Company, and Delaware Power & Light.

Joe Boone of the DNR released a study in February, 1984 called "Augmenting Natural Striped Bass Populations through stocking." He evaluated the possibility of adding to striper stocks, based on monitoring of 101,000 white bass x striped bass hybrids released into the Patuxent River. He got a hybrid YOY index of 1.3, and estimated each 1.0 index of pure stripers would require stocking 150,000 fingerlings. He said it would take 6 million fingerlings to raise all of the spawning areas statewide only 1.0. Multiply 6 million by the required index (i.e., 8) to find out how many hatchery fingerlings would be needed annually to rebuild the striper fishery, in this case—48 million.

Spring 1984

Ben Florence stood by a 500-gallon tank on the Nanticoke River at the old Vienna Coast Guard Station watching some captured rockfish he would spawn out. He told me his bosses, Dr. Brown and Verna Harrison, had asked if there was a hatchery plan ready. Ben told them no. Why? No one had even set the goals yet, he replied.

Ben was upset that day because a local commercial fisherman saw a dead rockfish in the tank and called a Cambridge reporter, who wrote a negative story about one dead fish instead of the DNR's efforts to make thousands of hatchery stripers.

"Investigating Feasibility"
...June, 1984

Could a new $5 million hatchery rebuild striper stocks? The Maryland DNR hosted a two-day meeting to investigate the question. Originally, a new hatchery was planned near the head of the Bay, but production by the Manning Hatchery in southern Maryland later proved adequate.

Dr. John Boreman of NMFS suggested ways to head off a crash. Increase egg abundance through better survival of brood fish, or stock hatchery fish.

"The most effective way to insure more striped bass eggs is to close the fishery," Dr. Boreman said. "The way to guarantee survival is to have a clean environment. The way to stock fish is to have a hatchery."

Dr. Reggie Harrell, then of South Carolina, said hatcheries are not a panacea. If contaminants kill natural fish, they will kill hatchery fish, too.

Federal officials warned that hatcheries could not provide for a put-and-take fishery.

"The best way to implement a hatchery program," said Harrell Johnson of North Carolina, "is to cut off all fishing."

"We shouldn't sit around waiting for that great year class in the sky," said Robert Stevens of the USFWS, who had raised stripers for 30 years, "There is little evidence we'll quickly clean up the problems of heavy metals or acid rain. To not have striped bass in the Chesapeake Bay is a national disgrace."

On the Choptank
...Spring, 1987

A strange two-boat procession made its way down the Choptank River near Highbanks. The lead boat would frighten you if you met it on the river in the dark of night: it looked like a giant marine praying mantis with its forelegs hanging down into the water. It was 20 feet long, made of aluminum, with metal booms extending from each side of the bow. Two parka-clad men, one in the bow, and one amidships, waved giant four-foot diameter nets in the air. The boat's operator, seated behind an instru-mented console, wore earmuffs to shut out the noise of a generator. Compared to this vessel, the second boat was pretty normal, if you discount the 500-gallon water tank amidships, and a gauge-festooned oxygen bottle standing next to it.

Imagine the puzzled reaction of a family group on their pier as these strange-looking craft putted their way along in the shallow water near shore. The second boat's occupants frantically dipped large stunned striped bass that floated to the surface.

As 40- to 50-pound stripers were gingerly swung aboard the second boat, one man hurriedly checked each fish's vent for signs of ripe eggs. Some fish were returned to the water, others were placed in the big holding tank amidships. Some smaller stripers were kept, too, mostly males with running milt (sperm). Unselected fish, lying on the surface belly up, soon revived and swam away.

With a Maryland striper moratorium—on a river where striper fishing with net and hook has existed for decades—well, any striper catching (or keeping) activity generated a lot of interest. Shoreside residents protected "their" fish by calling the DNR police if they saw nets go overboard or bass anglers that might be tempted to keep a rockfish. Marine police made constant checks of anglers on the spawning rivers when the stripers were in, and DNR press releases indicated the officers and courts were tougher on rockfish moratorium violators each year.

But relax, sportfishing fans. These boats were fishing legally, catching spawning striped bass to strip them of their eggs and sperm to produce more striped bass in Maryland's hatcheries. Ben Florence, the Maryland DNR's Chief of Hatcheries, said their goal in 1987 was to produce 500,000 striped bass fingerlings that would be 5 to 6 inches long by release time in October.

As the aluminum boat passed the pier, the shorebound spectators could see "U.S. Fish & Wildlife Service Electroshocking Boat" written on it's side. At the ends of the two arms extending from the boat's bow, four antenna-like wands pointed downward into the water. Jerry Stivers of the Maryland DNR, wearing insulated rubber gloves and shoes to protect him from getting shocked, wielded a dipnet from the bow.

DNR biologist Steve Early was amidships with another net, scanning the water surface for stunned floating stripers that Stivers missed. Behind the boat's control console, Charlie Wooley, Chesapeake Bay Fisheries Coordinator for the USFWS, sat peering at a depthfinder that clearly showed large fish under the surface. Other instrumentation told him that 340 volts of pulsed direct current was flowing through the wands off the bow into the water at 60 to 10 amperes, depending on changes in water salinity.

The "chase boat" was a 25 x 9 foot open fiberglass outboard-powered workboat driven by DNR Hatchery Chief Ben Florence. Dr. Reggie Harrell of the University of Maryland wielded the net in the chase boat. It was quite a procession, indeed.

Harrell dipped a 5-pound striper and held it up for Florence's inspection. "This one's been hooked," Harrell said, showing Florence a small blood-caked hole near the fish's mouth. Harrell slipped the fish back overboard, just as a bass angler had done after catching that striper on a bass lure by mistake, perhaps that same morning.

It went well. The electroshocking team found good numbers of spawning cow stripers in the 40 to 50 pound range. Florence would rather spawn the big females because they produce many more eggs, and healthier ones.

A cow striper will cast 1 million eggs for each 10 pounds of body weight. Of the dozen or so big cows captured and examined that day, Florence kept only four—those fish that would spawn in the next 10 hours or less. Florence has it down to a science—he can accurately tell how many hours before a cow's eggs will be ripe by examining a pipette of eggs taken from her vent.

Ben Florence checks a pipette of striper eggs as Dr. Reggie Harrell and Charlie Wooley prepare to put the cow striper in the holding tank.

"We're getting smarter every year," Ben Florence said about the DNR's efforts to propagate striped bass. Fish mortality dropped in the hatchery program as fisheries biologists learned new techniques, including the addition of salt to the holding tank water.

"We believe that the fish's electrolyte system is unbalanced by stress, and the addition of salt to the water restores that balance," Florence said.

Tranquilizers were added to the tank water to ease stress, too. "If I start behaving strangely," Florence said, distastefully smacking his lips after an active striper in the holding tank gave us all a good bath, "just blame it on the tranquilizer."

"They should spawn for several weeks yet," Florence said, noting the 57.4 F temperature reading on his depthfinder. "They'll spawn until river water temperature reaches 64 to 68 degrees."

First, the fish arrive in mid-Bay rivers like the Choptank. Other big stripers wait in mid-Bay until the upper Bay waters warm to their liking before moving northward.

After spawning, the big Choptank River cows (few male stripers exceed 15 pounds) leave the Bay for the ocean. Tagging studies, Florence said, have showed striped bass are river-specific; they return to the rivers of their birth. Next, the upper Bay's big cows spawn. At almost the same time, smaller stripers are moving into mid-Bay rivers to spawn, and following the pattern of the larger fish, smaller ones spawn later in the upper Bay.

A lowering afternoon sun cooled the strong breeze, and the two boats headed for a rendezvous with the tank truck at Martinak State Park. There was quite a crowd of well-informed campers waiting to see what the biologists had caught.

"What are you doing?" is a question bystanders did not ask. They knew. Camera enthusiasts crowded around to get photographs of big striped bass. They were not disappointed. Florence and Harrell carefully netted the fish in their boat's holding tank and held them captive in stretcher-like slings as they passed the fish up to Jerry Stivers on the DNR's tank truck for a ride to the Joseph Manning Hatchery at Cedarville in southern Maryland.

At the Hatchery, Ordered Chaos

Hatchery workers often toil around the clock when the stripers are spawning. During the frenetic hatchery-induced "spawning" process, female stripers are stripped of their eggs and those eggs are fertilized with

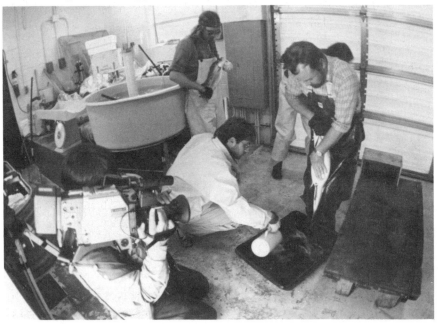

Jim Van Tassel (on right) strips the eggs from a cow striper as Manning hatchery worker (top left) brings another male striper to fertilize the eggs. Steve Dobert shoots the "Striper" video for National Fish & Wildlife Foundation.

the milt, or sperm, from male stripers. Six people or more, each with an assigned duty, are moving around quickly at the same time when a cow is spawned. It only takes two minutes or so. Then, the fertilized eggs are deposited in small circular tanks to grow into larvae. Finally, the tired striper parents are released into their natal rivers.

To preserve genetic purity, fish eggs and sperm from different river systems are not mixed together in this artificial spawning process. When the resulting larvae have grown into fry it they are placed into rearing ponds. In October, 5- to 6-inch long fingerlings will be returned to the hatchery to be tagged and released into their rivers of origin.

Tiny micro-encoded wire tags are placed into the cheek of each hatchery-raised striper. Data about the fish's natal river, age, and date of release are coded into a piece of wire that anglers will not detect. Biologists use sensitive metal detectors in the field to discriminate between wild and hatchery stripers.

Every hatchery striper gets a tiny wire tag in its cheek.

Hopefully, these fish will return to spawn themselves as Age IV or V stripers. Ben Florence may catch them again to repeat the hatchery cycle.

Will hatchery-raised stripers replenish this troubled species? It is looking better all the time.

Dr. Torrey C. Brown, Maryland DNR Secretary, watches as Charlie Wooley demonstrates a device that will detect the wire tag in a hatchery striper's cheek.

One Million Released
... November, 1987

"O.K., little guys, now you're on your own," Hatchery Chief Ben Florence said as Jerry Stivers opened the valve on the tank truck to release 12,500 tagged hatchery-raised striped bass fingerlings into the Choptank River at Oxford, Maryland.

"They've really had it made all summer," Florence said of the 6- to 8-inch long stripers, "they've been fed three times a day in their hatchery pond, no predators, now they're going to find out what the real world is like."

Florence must have felt like a proud parent when he released the fish, because starting the previous spring, he was instrumental in their production. He had gathered their parents in the upper Choptank River when they showed up to spawn. After spawning the parent fish, most of the resulting striper fry were shipped to federal hatcheries as far away as Ohio and North Carolina to be raised.

The 12,500 fish that Florence released at Oxford in late November were spawned from Choptank River parents in May and raised in the USFWS Harrison Lake Hatchery, Virginia, through the summer. In autumn, it was time to bring the fingerlings back to the Manning Hatchery in southern Maryland to be tagged.

"Every hatchery fish we released was tagged," said Florence. Fishermen won't see the tiny wire cheek tag, but DNR biologists with magnetic detectors determined ratios of wild to hatchery fish during their winter net surveys. A sub-sample of 10,000 fish also got the visible "spaghetti" tags.

In 1987, the expected total of more than 600,000 hatchery stripers, added to the 1985 and 1986 production of 186,000 and 361,000 respectively, ran the three-year total to well over 1 million that have been released.

Nine extra workers were hired at the hatchery to maintain a daily tagging production of 20,000 stripers.

Hatchery fish are released in the fall for several reasons: First, predators like bluefish have left the Bay. Second, larger fingerlings have a better chance of survival. And third, the annual young-of-the-year (YOY) index seining surveys are over, and recently released hatchery fish won't affect the index.

Raising hatchery striped bass simply to release them and have them swim into nets or onto a hook would not allow the species to reestablish itself. The fish must continue to be protected until today's hatchery stripers can come back to their rivers of origin to spawn. The striper hatchery effort is not a put-and-take fishery like that of fresh water trout. It is to rebuild spawning stocks.

"We are making an impact," Florence said, "for each 100,000 fish we release, we raise the YOY index in that river by one point." In one summer survey in the Patuxent River, hatchery fish accounted for 73 percent of all stripers!!

DNR Conservation Associates Jerry Stivers and Sid Compton dipped the last few remaining hatchery stripers out of the big tank on the truck and passed them to Hatchery Chief Ben Florence standing on the Choptank River shoreline. Florence gently dipped the net and turned it over to release the last few fish. Groggy from the tranquilizer, the fish wandered around, clearly visible against the white oyster shell bottom, getting their bearings before swimming away to an uncertain future. Sea gulls were swooping and diving farther out in the river.

"Good luck, little guys," Florence repeated, "you're on your own now.

Left to right: Jerry Stivers, Sid Compton, and Ben Florence.

Ben Florence releases hatchery fingerling stripers into the Choptank River.

11

STRIPER TAGGING

The Importance of Striper Tagging

Thousands of fishermen along the Atlantic coast have helped in the restoration of striped bass by returning striped bass tag information, according to Jorgen Skjeveland, Chesapeake Bay Coordinator for the USFWS.

Between 1985 and 1989, more than 100,000 hatchery and wild striped bass had received an external anchor, or "spaghetti" tag. By the end of 1989, fishermen had returned more than 10,000 of those tags. Tag return data is now helping fisheries managers make decisions about the recovering striper fishery.

The cooperative coastal striper tagging program, begun in 1985, now involves Maryland, Massachusetts, New Jersey, New York, North Carolina, Rhode Island, Virginia, and the District of Columbia, plus the National Marine Fisheries Service (NMFS), and the USFWS.

Anglers are asked to be on the lookout for the bright orange streamer tags, called "spaghetti" tags. They can either snip the tag off with nail clippers or scissors if the fish is not legal to keep in their area, or record the numbers on the tag. Fish should be handled as little as possible. Avoid touching the gills and return the fish to the water carefully. Tags bear the message:

USFWS—IF UNDERSIZED, CUT OFF TAG—RELEASE FISH
REWARD PH. 301-269-5448 CALL COLLECT (on old tags) or,
REWARD PH. 1-800-448-8322 (on recent tags)

Callers with tag information are asked to provide as much data as possible about the location of capture, approximate length, and condition of the fish. All tag returns are answered with a letter, a fishing cap bearing the logo, "Participant, Striped Bass Restoration," and the latest information about the tagging program.

Multiple tag returns (over four) are rewarded $5 per tag.

A standard anchor tag rests on the brim of a reward cap for tag returns.

Rewards are provided by the non-profit National Fish and Wildlife Foundation, Room 2725, 18th & C Streets, NW, Washington, D.C. 20240. The Foundation also donated two state-of-the-art electrofishing boats to be used in capturing adult spawning stripers for the hatchery. The Foundation accepts grants and donations to be used in cooperative efforts between the public and private sectors in high-priority wildlife conservation programs like the Striped Bass Restoration Project. Their award-winning 28-minute video, "STRIPER," can be ordered for a $20 donation to the Foundation at the above address.

Anglers generally ask two questions about the striper tagging program: What do we expect to learn from tagging? And, what have we found out so far?

Of the 3+ million hatchery stripers raised and released since 1985 in the Maryland/Virginia/USFWS cooperative program, 46,000 have external anchor, or "spaghetti" tags. By early 1990, more than 1125 hatchery striper tag returns were recorded. Most of these fish were released. Tag returns will help fisheries managers and scientists determine the effectiveness of hatchery stocking, age and growth, migration rates, fishing and natural mortality rates, and stock size.

Until 1987 it was assumed that one and two year old stripers remained in the Chesapeake Bay and did not migrate out of the bay until their third, fourth, or fifth year, and that is still largely true. But, tag returns now indicate that some stripers from 9-months to one-year old leave the Chesapeake Bay and start to forage along the Atlantic coast as far as New Jersey. Two year old fish have moved as far north as New York, Connecticut, and Massachusetts.

Hatchery fish that were raised and stocked together may travel in schools. In fact, two stripers, released on succeeding days, November 19 and 20, 1985 into Maryland's Patuxent River, were caught on succeeding days in Connecticut's Pawcatuck River in June 1987!

Biologists also found that hatchery-raised striped bass were becoming anadromous. They spent time in the ocean, and were expected to return to Chesapeake rivers to spawn. Also, one and two year olds had entered the Atlantic coast fishery.

A complete analysis will continue for some time, according to Dr. Paul Rago of the USFWS National Fishery Research Center (NFRC) in Kearneysville, West Virginia. But, a quick look at the data now available is interesting to anglers.

"Tag returns are helping us understand migratory patterns better," said Dr. Rago. "One striper swam 500 miles at an average of 16 miles per day before recapture. That fish had a very strong migratory urge!"

Migratory striped bass are found from the St. Lawrence River to North Carolina, and stripers thought to be non-migratory may be found in rivers from South Carolina to the Gulf of Mexico.

Most of Dr. Rago's data analysis so far has been concentrated on striper mortality. Tagging data shows that 20 to 40 percent of adult wild stripers in the ocean and tributaries may die naturally every year, and there is a disconcerting 70 percent annual natural mortality of juvenile hatchery stripers. But, the size and age of these populations are not comparable, said Dr. Rago. There may be similar comparisons between adult hatchery fish and juvenile wild stripers. More tags must be returned, and more data analyzed.

Tagging data also showed that hatchery stripers can make a large contribution to wild stocks. In Maryland's Patuxent River, hatchery stripers comprised 50 percent of the stock in 1988, when there was low natural reproduction. Tagging helped biologists estimate that between 10 and 15 percent of Choptank River stripers were hatchery fish in 1989.

One of the most practical future applications of tag return data might be in the area of stock size estimates. Maryland DNR Hatchery Chief, Ben

Florence, said DNR biologists have used the ratio of wild to hatchery fish (knowing how many tagged hatchery fish were released) to estimate the total number of striped bass in a river. With more data, and more analysis, this could be expanded to estimate the coastal striped bass population.

The coastal striped bass tagging program is providing valuable results right now, and will give us a better understanding of the troubled striped bass as more tag information comes in. That's where anglers can help. Return those tags.

Private Tagging in the Choptank
... Winter, 1984

Private citizens often ask, "What can I do to help the striper?" And then having made that minimal effort, settle back and "let George do it." For some guidelines about what can be done by committing private money and time, they need to talk to Jim Price of Oxford, Maryland. He has probably spent more of his own time and money on striped bass conservation than any other private citizen except Bob Pond of Atom Fishing Lures.

Jim Price set up the Chesapeake Bay Acid Rain Foundation, Inc. (CBARF) to focus public attention on the effects of acid deposition on stripers.

He also bought 2,500 stripers in the winter of 1984 from his commercial fisherman brother, Bill Price, who netted the fish in the Choptank River. In cooperation with Steve Early of the DNR, those fish were measured, tagged, and released.

"This may have been the last chance for years to save a large number of fish before the moratorium," Price said at the time. He saved 2,500 stripers for future brood stock while adding information about the migration of those Choptank fish in following years.

Several of Price's tagged stripers were later recovered as far north as the Kennebec and Penobscot Rivers in Maine. He has had over 100 tag returns to date.

Winter Striper Tagging Off North Carolina
... January, 1988

"It was bitter cold, the surf was running pretty high, and part of the time the boat was iced over," said Charlie Wooley of the USFWS about the danger of mid-January, 1988 trawls along wave-tossed North Carolina beaches.

The mission was to capture wintering striped bass and tag them as part of a program to determine their movements when they return to their rivers of origin to spawn in the spring.

"We were as close to the beach as we dared get, in as little as five fathoms of water (30 feet), because that's where the stripers were. Also, bringing fish up from greater depths farther offshore is more traumatic to the fish. We ran three shifts around the clock for 10 days. The farthest we sampled from shore was a mile-and-a-half."

During the survey, 10 biologists captured and tagged 1,335 adult striped bass from seven to 65 pounds. Three had been tagged before: one in the Hudson River by the Hudson River Foundation; one bearing an American Littoral Society (ALS) tag from New Jersey waters; and one that was tagged in the Chesapeake Bay by the Maryland DNR.

The cooperative tagging program involved the 18-person crew of the 170-foot long National Oceanic and Atmospheric Administration (NOAA) trawler-design research ship, *Oregon II*; plus 10 biologists from the USFWS, the Maryland DNR, and North Carolina's Division of Marine Fisheries.

Sampling was conducted using two 65-foot stern trawls fished simultaneously for periods that varied from 15 to 30 minutes, 24 hours a day. Although the main target species was striped bass, flounder and sturgeon which appeared healthy were also marked with internal anchor, or "spaghetti" tags. All fish were released. Trawl mortality on stripers was less than one percent, but several stripers were kept for sex ratio and genetics studies.

The *Oregon II* worked the Atlantic coast between Corolla, North Carolina and Cape Lookout, North Carolina. Wooley said no stripers were caught south of Cape Hatteras.

Ripening eggs in female striped bass off North Carolina in January triggered their March migration toward their spawning areas. Large "cow" stripers were met in spawning rivers like Maryland's Choptank and Potomac by smaller male fish who cast their milt, or sperm, and mixed it with ripe eggs cast by the cow stripers.

On the spawning grounds, biologists used gill nets to catch stripers and determine sex ratios, year classes, and population density. The biologists also looked for the orange spaghetti tags.

"The objective of the winter tagging program off North Carolina was to obtain biological data on the wintering stripers as they disperse to their spawning rivers," said Wooley.

"And my gut feeling is that most of them will wind up in the Chesapeake Bay."

Where is Striper Number 22747 Now?
. . . May, 1988

Charlie Wooley was casting plugs for bluefish in Maryland's Choptank River when he caught a striped bass bearing USFWS tag number 22747.

To the casual observer, Charlie's catch was no big deal, but the odds were against him—of all people—catching a tagged striper.

First, Charlie only had time for hook and line fishing a day or two each year. Second, he was the Chesapeake Bay Fisheries Coordinator for the USFWS at the time he caught the striper. Along with dozens of state and federal biologists, he had worked day and night in the coastal striped bass tagging and hatchery programs since they began. He saw millions of stripers tagged. Wooley was the focal point for tag return data. (Charlie has since been promoted. His replacement is Jorgen Skjeveland)

By catching #22747, Charlie was transformed into a recreational angler who returned a tag number in the very program he coordinated!

Wooley was active in cooperative programs between the USFWS and the Maryland DNR ever since the agencies agreed to rebuild spawning stocks of coastal striped bass by raising hatchery stripers.

Charlie coordinated the cooperative Atlantic Coastal states tagging program, where more than 45,000 wild fish got external anchor tags identical to the one found in his fish, #22747.

What did we learn from Charlie's striper tag #22747, and what will #22747 tell us in the future? Well, #22747 was 540-mm long (21¹/₄ inches) when it returned to spawn in the Choptank River. Steve Early of the Maryland DNR caught the wild striper and tagged it on April 4, 1988. By reading a scale taken from #22747 later under a microscope, Early found the fish was born in 1984.

Then, more data was provided on May 7, 1988 when #22747 decided that Charlie's single-hooked surface lure was something good to eat.

Charlie and I were fishing the Choptank River with Jim Price, plugging for shallow water bluefish.

"Well, look at this," Charlie said, gently holding up #22747.

"This guy has been tagged." Charlie did not clip the tag. He recorded the tag number and released the fish.

The reason Charlie did not clip off 22747's tag was to obtain even more data from the fish in the future. There are two places on anchor tags that carry numbers—one on the external piece of tubing, and on the flat piece that anchors the tag under the fish's skin.

Charlie Wooley prepares to release his tagged striper.

The first data point was recorded when #22747 was tagged. Then, Charlie caught the fish and recorded the tag number for data point number two.

The next person to catch #22747 may clip the tag (and report the number and catch location). That will be a third data point.

The fourth report on #22747 might come from a fish market, consumer, or a private angler who spots the internal anchor of the tag inside its belly when the fish is cleaned.

Then, there will be four data points to tell us where #22747 has been, and when.

Added to other tag return data, migratory patterns can be studied in the same way as the USFWS's successful migratory waterfowl banding program.

"Striped bass are making a comeback now," Wooley said after he caught #22747, "but, we need a lot of tag returns and several years of data before we can complete the puzzle."

It is fun to speculate where #22747 might be now. Did it return to the Choptank River to spawn in 1990? Is it swimming along the coast, or will it summer in the Chesapeake? Who will catch it next?

Did Charlie reward himself a "Participant, Striped Bass Conservation" cap for catching (and releasing) striper #22747?

"You bet," he said.

Why not? He certainly earned it.

Hatchery Striper Travels to Canada
... June, 1989

Les Foldi's alarm went off in the wee hours. Even in St. John, New Brunswick, Canada, there are striped bass addicts who fish odd hours. Not many of them, to be sure, but they make up in enthusiasm what they lack in numbers.

Only those with striper fever will know that Foldi jumped quickly out of bed trembling with anticipation. His wife of 12 years was used to the comings and goings of a husband who has adjusted his waking hours to peak tides.

Les was to meet his fishing buddies, Grant and Dave, at their "secret spot" in time for slack tide just before dawn. They would fish only the first 1½ hours of the flood tide. Soon after that, 30 feet of water would cover the shore where they stood to cast.

Les grabbed an 11½ foot surf rod mounting a big spinning reel loaded with 14-pound test line, a pocketful of 2-ounce white bucktail jigs and some pork rind. Occasionally, he tossed silver-sided swimming plugs with an 8-foot spinning rod, but only on slack tide when the fish were on the surface "finning out" like swordfish. Foldi's secret spot is only 5 minutes from home. When Carole and I were in New Brunswick, we drove right past it in 1989 (sob!), probably when Foldi was bailing in stripers! Talk about ships passing in the night!

Fish were finning at slack tide when Les met Grant and Dave. The three of them comprise most of a five-member group of New Brunswick striper addicts who call themselves the "Die-Hards." They fish every productive tide from June to October. The place they fish is tough, too. Only the young can stand that much fishing, from that rugged a place. Foldi is 32. His buddies are about the same age.

"We cast uptide, and retrieve our bumpers (bucktail jigs) with the tide, eh?" Les said, adding a typical Canadian "eh?" to the end of each sentence.

On one of his first casts, Les hooked and landed a 5-pound striper and laid it on the rocky bank to keep, although they release many stripers. There are almost no regulations on striped bass in New Brunswick, as they are not a major species there. In fact, any fish not a salmon or trout is sometimes considered a "trash fish." That also includes the plentiful smallmouth bass, which crowd lakes that are notably lacking in anglers.

Foldi continued casting. Later, Grant noticed something that looked like an orange "wire" hanging from Foldi's first fish. It was a U.S. Fish and Wildlife Service (USFWS) tag bearing the number 45888 and a message to call a telephone number in Maryland, collect. Les later gave the USFWS his catch information, and was rewarded with a fishing cap bearing the logo, "Participant Striped Bass Conservation," a letter of thanks, and a packet of information about stripers. His tag return information added something valuable to our knowledge of striped bass.

Les Foldi's catch was a first in fishdom. Number 45888 was the first Chesapeake Bay hatchery striper to gain international traveller status, according to USFWS Chesapeake Bay Fisheries Coordinator, Jorgen Skjeveland.

Foldi captured his international hatchery striper as a three year old in the St. John River in New Brunswick, Canada on June 29, 1989. The Chesapeake Bay hatchery striper had migrated northward along the coast for more than 1,000 miles to reach its capture site.

Wild striped bass have migrated along the Atlantic coast since time immemorial, but the USFWS tagging program has proved that hatchery stripers travel as far along the coast as stripers born in the wild.

Foldi's tagged hatchery striper was a product of parent fish captured in Maryland's Patuxent River in the spring of 1986 and taken to the Manning Hatchery in Cedarville, Maryland to be spawned artificially.

Striper #45888 grew to 8 inches in the USFWS Harrison Lake Hatchery, Virginia, during its first summer. It was returned to the Maryland DNR's Manning Hatchery for tagging and release into the Patuxent River on December 3, 1986.

Generally, Chesapeake stripers spend their first two years in their natal rivers. Historically, most stripers were caught before they could leave Chesapeake Bay. Since the Maryland 1985 striper moratorium, tag returns now show a large percentage of one- and two-year old hatchery stripers are caught (and released) in Maryland waters. Then, at 18 inches in their third year, many leave the Chesapeake Bay to migrate northward along the Atlantic coast. In 1989 the minimum size for stripers on the ocean coast was 36 inches so most of the hatchery fish caught were released, being undersized.

The "Die-Hards" of New Brunswick, Canada make their own bumpers all winter, waiting for the June run of stripers. And, they probably eat more salt pork than the average angler. Why? Because they make their own pork rind from the thick salt pork skin.

"When we lose a dozen bumpers (and pork rind) at $3-plus each, it pays to make your own, eh?" says Foldi, who pours 150 jig heads at a time. He uses 7/0 hooks when he molds his 2-ounce banana jigs. He paints them white, and ties white bucktail hair on with red thread. Except for the banana jig head, his jigs are just like the ones I make for Chesapeake stripers. "I've been fishing stripers steady for 5 years now, eh?" Foldi says, "but my dad fished them for as long as I can remember—in the same exact place. I didn't know how much fun he was having until now!"

Foldi is a Die-Hard striper addict to the exclusion of most other species: "I fish trout opening day, but that's about it. Then I go for stripers, eh?"

The reason the Die-Hards don't get too specific about their "secret spot" is that only a few anglers can fish it at a time. It can't stand a lot of pressure. The entire St. John River holds stripers all the way up to the Mactaquac Dam at Fredricton, and even upriver past that, because 30-pounders have been hoisted up the dam's fish-lift. In that entire river, not many people fish for them.

Interestingly, the Die-Hards have caught 12-inch stripers, indicating there could be a resident, or spawning stock in the St. John River.

Once, a local newsman wrote about the Die-Hards and their striper spot. "It was so crowded for a couple of weeks, we couldn't fish there, eh?," Foldi told me.

But the newcomers didn't know how to fish their bumpers. They lost dozens of $3 jigs without catching any stripers, and soon gave up.

You don't have to travel to New Brunswick, Canada to catch a tagged striper like Foldi's international gadabout #45888. You might catch a tagged striped bass anywhere along the Atlantic coast.

Watch for those tags, eh?

Hoke's Radio-Tagged Stripers Come Home
...April, 1990

Dr. Charles "Hoke" Hocutt was on cloud nine. He had surgically implanted radio transmitters in seven female striped bass in April, 1989. Now, three of that seven had returned to the Nanticoke River to spawn in April, 1990.

"This proved our technology was valid," Dr. Hocutt said, "and getting nearly a 50-percent return *in one year* is unheard of in tagging programs." In conventional tagging programs, a return of four to five percent over several years is considered good.

From a cost standpoint, Dr. Hocutt's radio tags cost the same as 500 internal anchor, or "spaghetti" tags used by the USFWS, $150. Spaghetti tags only give scientists two or three data points: When the fish was

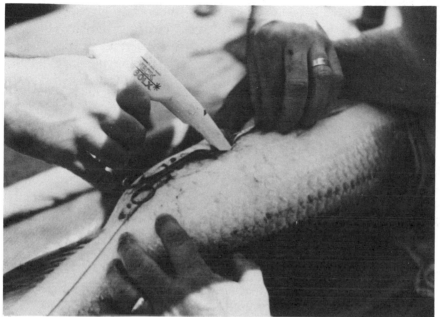

A radio tag is surgically implanted in a Nanticoke River cow striper. Photo courtesy of Dr. Charles Hocutt.

tagged, perhaps when and where it was caught and released, or caught and kept.

Hoke's radio tags can give spawning ground data on a daily, or hourly basis. Remote reading stations could record when the stripers arrived, how many times they passed the station, how long the fish was in the river, and when it left.

Going one step beyond radio or anchor tagging systems, Dr. Hocutt suggested that combination radio/ultrasonic tags could provide more data points by tracking a striper's entire migration from Chesapeake Bay along the Atlantic Coast, and back to its Chesapeake spawning grounds.

Radio tags vs. anchor tags in fish can be compared to the different methods used in the successful USFWS waterfowl banding program. For years, waterfowl were leg banded, giving scientists two data points per bird: When it was banded and when it was killed.

Then, new easy-to-read neck bands on Canada geese allowed multiple sightings as the birds migrated from wintering grounds to their breeding grounds in Canada and back. Compare Hoke's radio tags with neck bands on Canada geese that give more data points per animal. Leg bands on waterfowl and anchor tags in stripers provide similar and useful, but different, data.

Most people don't know that the 1989 striper radio tagging program was run out of Hoke's hip pocket. It was not funded by any government agency. A professor of ichthyology at both the University of Maryland's Horn Point Lab near Cambridge and their Eastern Shore campus at Princess Anne, Dr. Hocutt already had the radio tags. Then he worked with Skip Bason and Bob Johnson of Delmarva Ecological Labs on Nanticoke stripers at Delmarva Power and Light's Vienna plant.

"Skip started all this, you know," Hoke said, referring to Bason's early work with striper hatcheries and the freeze-brand marked fingerlings Skip released into the Nanticoke. Recaptures of branded stripers told the percentage of wild to hatchery fish in the river, like tagged stripers do today.

Hoke, graduate student Scott Seibold, and associate, Dr. Roman Jessien, tracked the fish in the river day and night, through the 1989 spawning season.

His greatest elation came when they heard the radio signals that told them one striper had returned on April 13, 1990 to spawn. Twin antennas on a small plane allowed them to detect the radio signals from the air. They tracked that first returned fish for nine straight days.

Hoke and his crew also spent some hairy evenings on the Nanticoke in a 14-foot aluminum boat with his radio receiver, chasing the striper from far below Vienna on the Nanticoke to Marshyhope Creek, past the Eldorado bridge to the Route 392 bridge near Hurlock, then back downriver.

Then, the second striper came back. "To get one fish back was great, two fish fabulous," Hoke said. "Now I'm getting greedy. I want to see three or four!"

Fish number three arrived April 22, 1990. "I was so excited I nearly jumped out of the plane," he said. That's when Hoke climbed up on cloud nine. He hasn't come back down.

"This is exciting," he said. "Think about what those fish, and the transmitters, had to survive both in the Bay and ocean. First, the stress of the implant operation; then, battery or transmitter failure, sharks, killer whales, plus commercial and sport fishermen."

"My original interest was spawning ground behavior," Hoke said, "and we are getting a better handle on that since these fish came back. Now we can extend our efforts to migration patterns if we can get funding."

The MSSA voted to donate $2,700 for a remote "data locker" to track several transmitters as they pass a fixed point in the Nanticoke. But, more funding is needed.

Dr. Hocutt will meet with the Emergency Striped Bass Board soon. Perhaps he can get funding even though the striped bass is no longer

Dr. Charles Hocutt with his tracking receiver and antenna.

considered to be under emergency management, and federal striped bass funding will slowly evaporate.

Dr. Hocutt hopes the long range applications of his work will answer important questions. Do stripers come back annually or every other year to spawn? Radio tags work in fresh water, but not in salt. Ultrasonic tags work in salt water. Could combination radio/ultrasonic tags be used to remotely track striper migrations, from the salty ocean water to fresh water on the spawning grounds? Would submersible receivers planted along the striper's migration routes be practical? Do stripers operate on tidal or time clocks? Do spawning stripers go back to the same rivers every year? If so, should that affect striper management?

As with any science, one question answered asks hundreds more.

A footnote: "One of our three of seven fish—we saw her last on April 19, 1990 in the Nanticoke River—was caught off Block Island, Rhode Island on June 20, 1990," Hoke said. "She was in excellent health, and measured 41 inches. She was caught at 7 a.m. on cut mackerel bait at Southwest Point, Block Island. Unfortunately, she had swallowed the bait, and was likely to die, so the angler, Mark DuChambre, had to keep her. They usually release all the stripers they catch," Hoke said.

Bob LaPlant, who fished that morning, said, "We thought we could release her, but she had the hook too deep." She weighed 37 pounds: "A small striper here," LaPlant said.

Small? LaPlant said "they usually catch, and release—we're sport fishermen here—stripers between 50 and 70 pounds most of the summer."

When they cleaned the big striper they found Hoke's transmitter in her gut, bearing his name and phone number.

Hoke's radio-tagged striper swam over 600 miles in two months, roughly 10 miles a day, not counting stops for lunch and dinner.

Hoke said, "She showed females come back to spawn in consecutive years in the same river [the Nanticoke]. She also gave us travel time between the spawning ground [Nanticoke River] and the foraging ground [Block Island]."

He sounded like a proud parent: "This fish gave us all she could," he said.

Tagging Hits Home
. . . May 12, 1990

"I've got something pretty big on here," Carole hollered as we trolled slowly down Broad Creek toward the Choptank River. "It feels like a horse on this light tackle."

We were out on a windy, cold day "just messing" looking for some early spring blues, when something messed with Carole's bucktail.

I turned the Mako sideways so Carole could fight the fish broadside to, and still remain seated. The boat rocked crazily in the wave troughs. It was too rough to stand up and fight the fish over top of the motor. The fish slugged it out underwater, and we couldn't see "color" until it was near the boat.

I went for the net. The fish put up a great battle. It didn't appear that big in the water. I guessed it was 12 inches long.

When the fish was alongside, I could see it was a small striper. I netted it for Carole. I was about to release the fish, when I noticed something sticking out of its stomach wall.

"This fish is tagged," I told Carole. "Let's get a picture." Carole wrote the tag number, 117404, on the back of a lure box. I got the camera out.

We didn't want to stress the striper, so I worked fast. Have you ever tried to get good pictures when your hands are freezing, the wind tears every lightweight thing right out of your hands, and the boat is rocking in three-foot seas? Takes the fun right out of it.

No matter where you try to walk, a wave will rock the boat and you stomp a wet foot right into your open camera case.

When you get the exposure set, the horizon straight in the finder, and get your subject to hold up the fish and smile, the boat lurches. Suddenly your nice, even horizon tilts downhill just as you squeeze the shutter button.

Carole holds her tagged striper.

The striper was 16 inches long, and fat. It either had plenty to eat, or was a male spawner full of milt, but I didn't squeeze it to check. The poor striper had already coped with fish hooks and a photographer.

Carole was elated. She has helped me organize and edit the material for this book. She remembered the tons of material I wrote about striper tagging. Now she was taking part in the "field work." Sort of hands-on participation. She was very concerned that "her" fish would be released before it was stressed. When she released it and saw it swim away, she smiled and breathed a sigh.

Since it was too rough and cold to continue fishing, we headed back to the house for a warm cup of coffee and some homemade apple pie.

I had some material on tagged hatchery stripers given me by the USFWS because of my striper writing. It was easy to look up "Carole's fish," tag number 117404.

Striper 117404 was spawned of upper Chesapeake Bay parents in the spring of 1988. Then, the fish and its tiny brothers and sisters were raised in ponds in Senecaville, Ohio until autumn.

Carole's 117404 was tagged with the tiny wire cheek tags that we couldn't detect, and was given anchor tag #117404 at Manning Hatchery in southern Maryland.

On October 27, 1988, Carole's #117404, along with thousands of other hatchery stripers, was released into Fairlee Creek in the upper Bay. So were 999 of the 117,000 series anchor-tagged stripers that included #117404.

Carole looked over the USFWS data sheets on the kitchen table as we warmed ourselves with steaming coffee.

"Look how far some of the 117,000 series swam before they were caught," she said, "Here's one that was caught, hook & line, in the Delaware River near Philadelphia. Several in New Jersey. Some in the Patapsco near Baltimore. Here's one tag return from the Nanticoke."

It was really amazing how far these two-year-old 1988 stripers had disbursed already. Shortly, most of them would leave the Bay and travel northward along the coast as far as Maine. Later, they might summer as far north as Canada.

The recaptured fish from the 117,000 "graduating class" were still undersized or illegal, and were reported as released. Most had only been captured once.

Carole's striper might be reported several times if anglers do as she did. She only recorded the (collect) telephone number and fish's serial number on the moss-covered tag. She left the tag in the fish. Clipping the tag is O.K., too.

"Reading a lot of dull numbers and data about the importance of striper tagging is one thing," Carole (my editor) says, "but, when you catch your very own tagged fish, it means a lot more. It kind of brings it right home."

12

YOUNG-OF-THE-YEAR INDEX

YOY History

Maryland's juvenile striped bass survey, sometimes called the Young-of-the-Year, or YOY Index, has long been an accurate barometer of future rockfish production. In the past, peaks and valleys in the YOY chart would match peaks and valleys in the reported commercial catch three years later. In the past when the Chesapeake Bay contributed an estimated 90 percent of coastal striper stocks, fishermen looked to the Maryland YOY index to predict their future catches.

YOY data has been so reliable that the Scientific and Statistical (S&S) Committee of the Atlantic States Marine Fisheries Commission (ASMFC) bases a large part of its coastal striped bass management recommendations on Maryland's YOY index.

Started in 1954 and managed by DNR biologist and striper expert, Joe Boone, from the early 1960s until his retirement in 1986, the YOY index had only been questioned once before the controversial 1989 index.

A group of watermen said they could catch many more YOY stripers than the survey showed. The DNR folks just didn't go where the fish were, they said. Boone showed them how to sample, and a Citizen's Seining Survey (CSS) was established. "The 1984 CSS caught less YOY fish than we did," Boone said later. The CSS was quietly dropped.

How They Get the YOY Numbers

The YOY survey is taken in spawning areas in Maryland's part of Chesapeake Bay. Each of 22 sites is sampled twice at one-month intervals in July, August, and September. So, 22 sites x two seine hauls x three months = 132 hauls. In addition, 18 auxiliary sites have been added since the the mid-1970s, but that data is not added into the YOY index.

At each sampling site, a 100-foot seine is held at one end by a DNR biologist while another biologist wades out into the water with the free end until the net is fully extended. Then, the free end is brought in a semicircle back to the beach. The seine is pulled ashore, and everything in it is counted, including menhaden, minnows, silversides, crabs, and YOY stripers. The number of YOY stripers caught in the entire survey is divided by the total number of seine hauls (132), and that final number becomes the index. Auxiliary site fish are not counted in the index. Historically, Joe Boone would not even discuss the numbers of fish caught until he analyzed the data. The final index was always released by the DNR Secretary at the end of September.

YOY stripers.

To give the reader some of the flavor of the YOY field work and the concern of those involved through the crash, recovery period, and reopening, following are excerpts from three of my manuscripts published in: MSSA's *Tidelines* in September, 1983; the *Fisherman* in November, 1987; and *Salt Water Sportsman* in March, 1990. (The stories here are included as I sent them, before editing by the publications. New material or explanatory information is enclosed in brackets, "[]").

"Preliminary Young of Year Survey Bleak"
. . . September, 1983

It came as no surprise to any Chesapeake Bay fisherman in the early 1980s; the rockfish was in trouble. As I watched DNR biologists, Joe Boone, Jim Uphoff, and Don Cosden haul their sampling seine in the

Joe Boone records data as Don Cosden and Jim Uphoff measure and count YOY stripers.

Choptank River on July 14 and August 10, 1983, it became crystal clear that things were getting worse each year.

"Striped bass spawning was a near failure two out of the last three years," Boone said, "and now possibly three out of four. That's why there is intense concern among all of us."

Boone added that the 1982 index was 8.4 and this 1983 index was likely to be less than 3, among the worst in the 29-year history of the survey.

In the July and August, 1983 Choptank River surveys I watched, it was unusual to see even one striped bass fingerling. Boone said that they had averaged 17 to 20 fingerlings per haul of the seine in the "dominant" years, and he considered 7 to 10 fingerlings "successful."

In August, two hauls of the seine at Hambrooks Bar netted only one fingerling. Two hauls near Secretary produced only three fingerlings. The previous 1982 Choptank River *average* was 13.

As the biologists continued their surveys, moving up the Bay, Boone did not expect things to look any better. He predicted that 1983 would be the third year out of the previous four that would be "really grim."

The 1983 YOY survey was completed in late September and the index, as expected, *was* one of the lowest in history at 1.4, putting a lot of pressure on the DNR to make good its promises to restrict or ban rockfishing.

"YOY Index Up Slightly"
. . . November, 1987

Maryland's striped bass YOY index was up slightly in 1987, to 4.8, the best index of the 1980s, except for the 1982 index of 8.4. Remember the great rockfishing we had in the mid-1970s? That was the result of the record year class of 1970, with an index of 30.4! The 1987 index of 4.8 is only half the 1954 to 1986 average of 8.8.

Maryland DNR Secretary, Dr. Brown said a three year running average of 8.0 or better would be necessary before the moratorium would be lifted. One DNR biologist estimated that it might be five years or more before the rockfish recover enough to support a fishery.

And don't forget House Bill 1300, passed in 1985: It says when the fishery is opened, it shall be opened for all. The commercial fishermen zinged that bill through with no opposition because recreational fishermen relaxed after the moratorium was declared.

In August, 1987 we accompanied DNR Striped Bass Project Leader Steve Early; Don Cosden, who is in charge of the YOY surveys; and biologist Allyn Altomare, on the second of three rounds in the Choptank River.

The first sweep of the seine at Castle Haven downriver produced 1,946 menhaden, one halfbeak, one spot, 189 silversides, some anchovies, and no stripers. The second sweep, a half-hour later in the same location, was the same—no rockfish.

Don Cosden, Allyn Altomare, and Steve Early at Castle Haven.

And so it went, working upriver, site by site. Three YOY rock at the second location, Hambrooks Bar; and one at the third site, Warwick River, were recorded by Steve Early. Two rock at the fourth site and five at the fifth (both auxiliary sites) would not be averaged into the index.

Way upriver, at the mouth of the Tuckahoe, the catch improved. Seven tiny YOY rock were taken in each sweep of the seine. Downriver, the sea nettles were thick, and the young biologists wore protective clothing when they waded out with one end of the seine to make a sweep. Upriver, they could wade in swimsuits.

"Is this why you went to school?" I kidded Allyn Altomare, a recent graduate in marine biology, as she sat on the beach, covered with sea nettles and sand, picking tiny fish out of the stinging nettles in the seine.

"Oh, yes, I love it," she said, wrinkling her nose.

Bob Pond of Massachusetts, manufacturer of the Atom plug (a popular rockfishing lure since 1945), was along.

"We have to know first-hand what is happening to the resource," Pond said, "to make our manufacturing decisions." It was not only manufacturing decisions that concerned Pond. He loves the striped bass. I fished with Pond in October, 1962. We caught 20- and 30-pound rockfish at the old wreck on Love Point on his Atom plugs. The fervency and zeal he exhibited for catching stripers then is matched by his concern for the resource.

Pond spent most of the spawning season at the Manning Hatchery—at his own expense—examining striped bass eggs, looking for clues as to why the striped bass is not reproducing. He has also spent time in Nova Scotia each summer working with the Canadian stripers. You've seen Bob Pond at most fishing shows. His organization, Stripers Unlimited, has raised money for striped bass research for years.

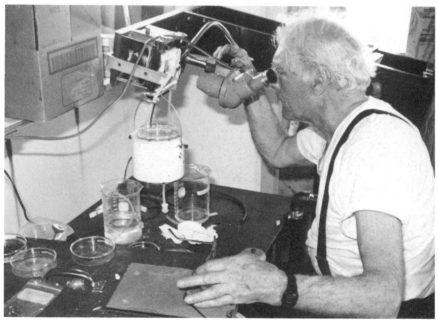

Bob Pond examines striper eggs.

This was only the second month of a three-month survey, so DNR biologists were understandably jumpy about putting index numbers on what we saw that day, but I witnessed a grim situation. If the auxiliary sites were factored in, the Choptank index, from what I saw, would be 2.1, about as low as it has ever been. Not including the auxiliary sites, I got an index of 2.25—still dismal.

As it turned out after the other two rounds in the survey, and all the numbers were totalled, the Choptank index was a whopping 12.1, well above the long-term Choptank average of 7.4! The Potomac River held its own with a 6.4, only slightly below its long-term average of 6.6. The Nanticoke River and the upper Bay fared the worst. The Nanticoke's 2.5 was way below its average of 6.6. The upper Bay, once the greatest producer of striped bass with a long-term average of 12.9, fell to a 0.3!

Comments from DNR personnel after the 4.8 index was released were positive:

"We are encouraged by the slightly increasing index," said DNR Striped Bass Project Leader, Steve Early. "We are also seeing increasing numbers of small spawners."

Another encouraging fact that the DNR biologists noted was that there were equal numbers of fish caught at most of the sites in the two major rivers, the Potomac and the Choptank. In other words, the fingerlings were equally distributed from upriver (nearly fresh water) to downriver (more saline water) sites. "That is more important than finding a large amount of fish at one place," Early said, "We'd rather see the fish distributed over the entire river."

"We are seeing the signs of a continuing trend of recovery," said DNR Secretary Dr. Torrey C. Brown, "and all of the evidence points to it—the juvenile index, and measures of relative adult abundance."

Although many upbeat comments surfaced after the 4.8 index was announced at the end of September, 1987, it was still a subdued group of biologists and observers that motored back to the launching ramp that August day. We had found only a few striper fingerlings in the Choptank. The mood was glum.

Bob Pond summed up the great rockfishing we all had in the 1960s and 1970s, and predicted a pretty dismal outlook for the future: "We had the best of it, you and I," he told me, sadly.

Perhaps we did.

"What Happened at Hambrooks Bar?"

A firestorm of protest erupted among mid-Atlantic recreational anglers in August, 1989 when it was announced that Maryland's juvenile striper index was high enough to reopen a "limited fishery" on striped bass.

The Atlantic States Marine Fisheries Commission (ASMFC) had protected the 1982 year class until 90 percent of them had spawned, with Amendment #3 stating the "trigger" to reopen would be met when Maryland's YOY index reached a "three year running average of 8." Until then, the coastal minimum size would increase to protect the 1982 brood fish. The 1987 index of 4.8, added to 1988's 2.7, and subtracted from the trigger of 24, meant the 1989 index had to be 16.5 or better to reopen the fishery. There was no reason to believe the three year running average of 8 would be reached any time soon.

An index of 25.2 was announced in August, 1989 *before* the third round of the YOY survey. The DNR and Governor Schaefer announced the ASMFC's guidelines had been met and a "limited fishery" would be opened, some people rejoiced. DNR officials were quoted as saying the fishery was restored. The Governor urged caution.

The announcement to reopen met with resistance: Conservationists, anglers, and some fishery scientists said the reopening was premature.

I asked to go along and report on the third round of the YOY survey on the Choptank River. Bob Pond, Avis Boyd, and Jim Price were the other "civilians" on the trek. Since there were too many people for the DNR's boat, I had permission to take my own boat. I was not to disturb the seining sites, so we stayed well out of the way of the DNR biologists.

A problem had arisen in the summer of 1989—the long established survey site on the Choptank River side of Hambrooks Bar had eroded badly. It was too deep for a man to wade out with the seine. After pre-seining several nearby sites prior to the survey, a new site on the back of Hambrooks

Several interested parties watched Don Cosden and Rick Schaefer bring in the seine on Hambrooks in September, 1989.

Historic YOY site is shown on outside of Hambrooks Bar in this 1972 aerial view.

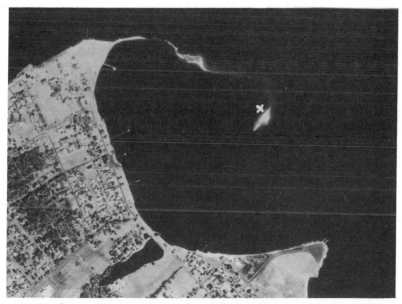

The 1989 YOY seining site is marked on this 1989 aerial view. What was once the end of Hambrooks Bar is now an island.

Bar in shallower water was selected as a substitute.

I have interviewed and worked with numerous state and federal biologists, and there is one thing I must repeat: The Maryland DNR's biologists are the most conscientious and dedicated group you could find anywhere. They are scientists, not emotionally involved with stripers the way fishermen are. If they find something in their seine, they count it.

Joe Boone later said: "My worst nightmare when I was conducting the survey was if everything was going good, and I was getting good data, and I suddenly scooped up 1,000 fish. That really haunted me." Joe's worst dream came true—luckily for him, after he retired.

The DNR biologists found plenty to count at Hambrooks.

On the first round in July, 1989 at the new Hambrooks Bar site, the biologists had caught 265 juvenile stripers. On the second round in August, they caught an astounding 1162! On the third round, we saw them catch 60 YOY stripers. When all the juvenile fish in the entire survey were totalled (3,327), 44.7 percent (1,487 fish) were caught at Hambrooks, only one of the 22 Bay-wide sites!

Joe Boone jumped into the fray. He said the large number of fish from Hambrooks Bar should be discounted as an anomaly as he had discounted unusually large catches in the past. [By deducting the Hambrooks fish the 1989 YOY index would be 14.6, not enough to meet the ASMFC 16.5 trigger to reopen the fishery]. Boone also said the 1989 juveniles could not be considered a "dominant year class" because they were not evenly distributed around the Bay. Also, the 1989 Hambrooks data was taken at an entirely new site, so it should not be included.

"If this is not an anomaly," said Boone, "I never saw one."

Boone outlined two major problems:

1. Using suspect numbers as a trigger mechanism.

2. Opening on the 1982 breeders. "You should open the fishery on excess fish [the 1989 year class]."

Steve Early of the Maryland DNR was responsible for the YOY survey: "Scientists on the Emergency Striped Bass Study (ESBS) supported the index," said Early in defense of the 1989 YOY numbers.

ASMFC Striped Bass Management Board members meeting on August 23–24, 1989 expressed concern about juvenile abundance triggers. Their meeting minutes indicated that concern: ". . . one good index could occur adjacent to two extremely poor years (e.g., 24, 0, 0) and reach the trigger but not be representative of a healthy stock." Next, they added a "coefficient of variation" (CV) as a "parameter for trigger values of future indices but not to add it to the the current (1989) Maryland index." They also said under the new guidelines, "the 1989 index would not have met the trigger requirements."

In October, 1989 the ASMFC superseded Amendment #3 (that protected the 1982 brood fish) with Amendment #4, calling for a limited fishery. They approved an 80 percent reduction from historic harvest, a one fish (recreational) limit, a 28" minimum in coastal waters, and an 18" minimum in inland waters; e.g., Chesapeake Bay, Roanoke Sound, and the Hudson River. The fishery would not reopen before July, 1990.

Anglers expressed concern about the numbers of 1982 brood fish that would no longer be protected because they were longer than the 28" coastal minimum. They worried about hook-and-release mortality rates in parts of the upper Bay, where 79.8 percent of all hooked stripers later die. The conservation ethic built up around striped bass evaporated when anglers read in their local papers: "It's pretty clear that the populations of rockfish (stripers) have recovered."

Delaware, Maryland, and Virginia anglers (with moratoriums in force) voiced their concern about reopening their striper fisheries:

Hoss Cochran was on the Rockfish Committee of Delaware's Finfish Advisory Council: "I'd like to see a few more numbers before it's opened," Cochran said, "and keep it closed until it's restored. But, I think the best solution is to make it a gamefish."

Izaak Walton League Maryland Chapter President, Bill Roulette III, said "The moratorium should not be lifted so soon. The DNR should let the population multiply to make sure that the level doesn't recede."

"I think this is strictly politics," said Jim Price of Oxford, "The Governor [Schaefer] making this statement is nothing but a political show. It has nothing to do with good management from a biological or scientific point of view."

Price asked the ASMFC for an investigation of the Hambrooks situation. He pored over stacks of computer printouts of the juvenile survey. He said the Choptank (and Baywide) index was skewed by the Hambrooks site results, and there would not be as many "keeper" stripers in the river in three years as the DNR thinks. "The DNR might have fooled the people," Price said, "but they can't fool Mother Nature."

MSSA members voted in chapter meetings to keep the moratorium, but the MSSA Board voted to accept the DNR's explanation of the YOY data, which was tantamount to agreeing with the reopening. The MSSA Board also knew they should support Governor Schaefer in the reopening. The Governor had promised support for gamefish status for Maryland stripers, but not in 1990, an election year.

The Atlantic Coastal Conservation Association of Virginia (ACCA/VA) voted to support continuation of the moratorium for two more years.

Their Executive Director, Eric Burnley, said angling clubs in New York and New Jersey were opposed to the opening, too. "The trigger has been pulled," said Burnley, "but we believe it's a misfire."

Jim Walker of Bozman summed it up for many Chesapeake Bay recreational anglers: "I don't care if the moratorium is not lifted in my lifetime," he said, "I'd rather be conservative, so future generations can experience the great rockfishing I've had."

YOY in the Future: What If?

If succeeding year classes of stripers crash, then what? At the present time, there is no criteria in place to close down the fishery. The "Ready!—Fire!—Aim!" mentality evidenced in the headlong rush to reopen the striper fishery has not been replaced with a logical plan to completely close the fishery if the YOY index crashes again.

Steve Early, now promoted to DNR Stock Assessment Coordinator, was asked at the February, 1990 meeting of the Mason-Dixon Outdoor Writers Association (M-DOWA), "What is the criteria for closing the fishery?"

"It will never be closed again," he told M-DOWA members. Where did he get that policy? In DNR meetings with his bosses? From the ASMFC? Did this indicate Early's faith in the striper's ability to restore its stocks, or in the DNR's management ability?

Outdoor writer, Gary Diamond, asked the DNR's Pete Jensen about the "shutdown trigger" in a press conference on April 17, 1990.

"I don't know if we want to talk about a moratorium now," Jensen said, hedging. His boss, Assistant DNR Secretary, Jim Peck, was not so bashful: "We *will* close it if necessary." Peck did not state the "if necessary" criteria.

Diamond later wrote in *The Fisherman*: ". . . many other questions concerning the rockfish will not be known until 1996 when these fish [the 1989s] return to the rivers of the Chesapeake to spawn. If they don't, biologists and fisheries administrators will have made a big mistake by reopening the fishery. If they arrive in large numbers [in 1996] and successfully spawn, the scientific community deserves a medal. Only time will tell."

Now: What If? What if the 1990 YOY index crashes? We will know the 1990 index before the fishery opens in October, 1990.

If there is a low index, detractors would say, "I toldja so!"

DNR folks would say, as they have in the past, "Fish swim."

But, if the ASMFC based its reopening criteria on the 1989 YOY index, and the 1990 index crashes, what then?

Will DNR managers go back to the ASMFC and say, "We were wrong—close it again!"

MARYLAND STRIPED BASS JUVENILE INDEX, 1954–1989

Year	Head of Bay	Potomac River	Choptank River	Nanticoke River	Overall Average
1954	0.9	5.2	1.2	25.1	5.2
1955	4.4	5.7	12.5	5.9	5.5
1956	33.9	6.2	9.8	8.2	15.2
1957	5.4	2.5	2.1	1.3	2.9
1958	28.2	8.4	19.5	22.5	19.3
1959	1.9	1.6	0.1	1.8	1.4
1960	9.3	4.3	9.0	4.7	7.1
1961	22.1	25.8	6.0	1.5	17.0
1962	11.4	19.7	6.1	6.6	12.2
1963	6.1	1.1	5.4	4.1	4.0
1964	31.0	29.1	10.6	13.3	23.5
1965	2.2	3.4	9.5	21.6	7.4
1966	32.3	10.5	13.6	3.3	16.7
1967	17.4	1.9	5.3	4.1	7.8
1968	13.1	0.7	6.3	9.0	7.2
1969	26.6	0.2	4.8	6.2	10.5
1970	33.1	20.1	57.2	17.1	30.4
1971	23.7	8.5	6.3	2.0	11.8
1972	12.1	1.9	11.0	25.0	11.0
1973	24.7	2.1	1.0	1.1	8.9
1974	19.9	1.5	15.3	3.9	10.1
1975	7.0	7.8	4.7	5.2	6.7
1976	9.8	3.2	2.4	1.7	4.9
1977	12.1	1.9	1.2	1.0	4.8
1978	12.5	7.9	6.0	4.8	8.5
1979	8.3	2.2	2.8	0.9	4.0
1980	2.3	2.2	1.0	1.8	2.0
1981	0.3	1.4	1.3	2.4	1.2
1982	5.5	10.0	13.0	6.2	8.4
1983	1.2	2.0	0.9	1.0	1.4
1984	6.1	4.7	2.8	1.5	4.2
1985	0.3	5.6	3.7	2.1	2.9
1986	1.6	9.9	0.5	2.2	4.1
1987	0.3	6.4	12.1	2.5	4.8
1988	7.3	0.4	0.7	0.4	2.7
1989	19.4	2.2	97.8	2.9	25.2
Average (1954-89)	12.6	6.3	10.1	6.3	8.9
Standard Error	1.8	1.2	3.0	1.2	1.2

Maryland DNR data, corrected in April, 1988. Older tables include several incorrect numbers.

13

FRESH WATER STRIPERS

After hearing all of the data about the Chesapeake striper crash, moratorium, and restoration, the reader of this book probably feels the same way we did in the middle of all the bad news about our rockfish. It was time to find some legal striper fishing. Where? In fresh water lakes or ponds where striper populations are thriving.

Lake Lanier Stripers

Fishing guide and outdoor writer, Bill Vanderford is a Lake Lanier, Georgia expert. In his book about bass fishing in this lake near Atlanta, he wrote about stripers.

"For many fishermen," Vanderford wrote, "the striper is a fish that lives along the Atlantic coast, and is chased by fanatics with telephone pole sized rods and reels who believe that being half drowned by the cold surf of autumn is fun." (He sure found US out!)

"However more and more fishermen are discovering that the stripers have been born again in big fresh water impoundments like Lanier, and fishermen in ever-increasing numbers are learning that these big line-sided bass can be as much fun as black bass."

Bill tells about crappie fishermen who had their poles shattered by big stripers, and bass anglers who had tackle ripped up by some huge fish wearing stripey pajamas.

He also said he and his guides had better striper fishing at night, and near dawn and dusk. Just like home on the Chesapeake. Though Bill recommends minnow plugs instead of our more familiar bucktails, live eels, and crabs, we won't hold that against him. On some of our trips, we tried salt water techniques in fresh water. Did they work? Some did.

What could we lose? We went sweetwater striper fishing, though we didn't get a chance to accept Bill's invitation to fish with him on Lake Lanier because of a hurricane. One day, we will.

Smith Mountain Lake
... November, 1985

We stood on a floating pier, Carole and I, and watched in horrified amazement as our Smith Mountain Lake, Virginia striper fishing guide launched his buzz-bomb of a bass boat. The boat trailer disappeared underwater, the bed of his pickup truck looked like a swimming pool filling up, and the truck's rear wheels were submerged!

"You wouldn't get away with THAT where I come from," I told this Kenny Rogers look-alike in farmer's overalls. "Salt water would eat up your trailer in no time—and the rear third of your pickup would dissolve, too." He just shrugged his shoulders. Do it all the time.

I heard about the fabulous striped bass fishing in the inland lakes for several years and couldn't wait to try it. The October, 1984 issue of *Sports Afield* clinched it. The writer and his guide caught 34 stripers in a day and a half.

My first clue that things were not as advertised was in the Virginia Fishing Regulations that came with our licenses. There was a two rockfish creel limit on Smith Mountain Lake. In the aggregate. That meant you could fish for a week and still only have two stripers in your cooler. Local game wardens would be happy to count them for you. If YOU counted wrong you got a look at their nice new jail.

Our second clue dawned more slowly as the day went on. We cast bucktails continuously to one "Hot Spot" after another with the guide saying over and over, "You Gotta Believe"—a country record saying if I ever heard one. We got nary a tap.

"There they are," the guide said, looking at some random blips on the finder. We renewed our casting in earnest.

"How do you know they're not shad, or even a school of crabs or something?"

"You gotta believe."

One of the most entertaining parts of our afternoon consisted of several lightning-quick trips between "Hot Spots." A bass boat only slightly bigger than a skateboard powered by a 150 HP outboard can get a considerable grip on the water. We seemed to pull 6 G's. Our noses were flattened against our faces. Doing a skillion miles per in an open boat in November with our ears pinned back flat against our heads, our first thoughts were about survival. It was like the white knuckle flight in a stunt plane. Hang on to something or get blasted out of the cockpit.

I wondered if the wind chill charts were calculated up to 6 jillion miles per hour, because I was losing body heat faster than a naked astronaut. The result of all this frantic activity?

"We" caught a single 21-inch rockfish. The guide hooked it. Why did "we" catch it? He handed the rod to me so I could wind in what was probably the last rockfish in the lake. The striper had a tired and harried look. No wonder. We had chased him from one end of the lake to the other all day with our jet-propelled skateboard.

During lulls in the activity, which were considerable, the guide regaled us with stories about hunting and fishing. He told us he had taken three deer (allowed two), 20 turkeys (allowed two), and he had been offered $5 per pound for rockfish. Whoa!

The thought occurred to me—would anyone who would take over the legal limit of game be likely to set a little piece of net for $5 rockfish? I dared not ask.

To reverse the usual story about pollution being a bad thing, the Smith Mountain Lake Improvement Association put unrelenting pressure on the Virginia State Water Control Board because the City of Roanoke dumped raw sewage into the river that fed into the lake. Roanoke built a $30 million sewage disposal plant, and the lake cleaned up.

Cleaning up the lake, though, adversely affected the striper population. Before, nutrients in the sewage fed plankton. Great shoals of shad fed on the plankton. Rockfish populations exploded with plenty of shad on their menu.

As the sewage nutrient level dropped, forage fish did, too. So did rockfish populations. With less forage fish, Virginia stocked less stripers.

I still read stories about great striper fishing at Smith Mountain Lake. "I gotta believe!"

Lake Cumberland: Legal Rockfish

"Cast this Redfin plug right over there," Joe Hughes said in the pre-dawn darkness at Lake Cumberland, Kentucky. Morning mists swirled up off the lake surface.

"A big striper has been rolling right off this point the last few mornings. Retrieve it slowly on the surface so it makes a V-shaped wake and wiggles a little." The lure was a strange pinkish color.

"That lure looks like a rainbow trout, doesn't it?" Hughes explained: "Stripers love to eat rainbows."

First cast, first fish. A big striper followed the Redfin in the V-shaped wake, knocking the bejabbers out of the plug. I tried a little Chesapeake Bay magic from the old days, slowing the retrieve, then speeding it up.

"There's no law that says you can't experiment with the retrieve," Hughes said as the lure disappeared in a shower of spray.

The striper had finally tired of messing around and engulfed the lure. It put up a good fight, reminiscent of many others on chilly Chesapeake mornings when 10- and 20-pounders slammed my surface plugs. I didn't feel the slightest bit guilty about catching a Lake Cumberland striped bass, either. They are not a threatened species in lakes throughout the south.

"Net? I don't have a net," Hughes said as the fish neared the boat, "you'll have to grab it by the mouth."

"Like jolly blue heck I will," I yelled, "Not when that sucker's got a mouthful of plug decorated with those needle-sharp treble hooks you just honed." Hughes grabbed a foot-long lure and used it as a gaff, hooking the plug's huge tail treble hook in the striper's mouth to swing the fish aboard.

I admired the big striper flopping on the deck, the first I'd caught since the Maryland striper moratorium took effect in 1985.

My 10-pound striper took the award for the biggest fish caught by an outdoor writer in the striper tournament. I won a Ryobi V-Mag reel and a Zebco casting rod. (Outdoor writers and manufacturers fished with local guides, but were not entered in the tournament).

The author with his 10-pound Lake Cumberland striper.

Bill Vanderford won a similar fishing outfit for catching the smallest outdoor writer's fish, a .04-pound Kentucky spotted bass.

Those sweetwater stripers were basically the same fish that inhabits the rocky coastline of the northeast Atlantic and the sandy bottoms of the Chesapeake Bay. Biologists say stripers are salt water animals, with a chemical balance more suited to living in the salt. Stripers are more easily stressed in fresh water, they say. But this Lake Cumberland, Kentucky striped bass put up a fight equal to any coastal striper.

Since Atlantic coastal striped bass populations declined, many striper anglers transferred their attention to fresh water lakes. Stripers are similar, no matter where you find them. But, striped bass behave differently in Lake Cumberland than in other freshwater lakes throughout the south, according to master guide Tim Tarter. He and his nine guides fish Lake Cumberland for monster stripers 12 months a year.

Tarter had plenty of room in his oversized bass boat that afternoon for Sammy Lee (Fishin' Fever radio shows), Joe Kuti (then a Ryobi Vice President), myself, and enough tackle to last the average angler six lifetimes. Average angler? Tim is not average when it comes to wearing out tackle. He fishes night and day all year.

Tim Tarter and Sammy Lee cast for Lake Cumberland stripers.

Sammy Lee picked up one of my Chesapeake Bay-sized striper lures.

"I've seen times in bass tournaments when I could have weighed in some of these baits—and won!"

Sammy opted for medium bass gear and caught a 3-pound plus small-mouth bass that went into the livewell. Later, Sammy promised, he was going to hold it under the nose of a hard-partying, late-sleeping outdoor writer.

We continued to cast our surface baits at the wooded shoreline with no (striper) hits. "Eighty percent of the stripers caught in this lake are caught on Redfins and Dog Walkers, but in mid-summer we have to use live bait," Tarter said.

Tarter discussed the differences between salt and fresh water stripers when we fished Lake Cumberland that night:

"This is mainly a night-fishing lake," Tarter said, "70 to 80 percent of the really big fish are taken at night. Stripers chase shad up on the muddy banks after dark and we cast Redfins and Little Macs at them. You often see big fish rolling on the surface at night. I can't forget this—the lake record striper weighed 58 pounds, 4 ounces, caught on a surface lure on December 7, 1985."

I asked if some Chesapeake Bay striper technology could be transferred to Tarter's Lake Cumberland fishing. Did they troll lures along the bottom as we do?

"No, there are too many stumps and rocks on the bottom at Cumberland, but we do cast bucktails toward the bank in 15 feet or less of water from November through April." Tarter uses a slow retrieve in cold weather, sometimes with a momentary stop.

Wait! They fish all winter? Yep, you heard right. It is a 12-month fishery. The lake doesn't freeze over.

Back to the differences between coastal and Lake Cumberland stripers. While casting popping plugs for stripers is popular along the Atlantic Coast, Lake Cumberland fish don't respond to surface lures the way they do in other southern lakes, Tarter said.

"Cumberland is a nontypical lake. To run and gun, and throw into breaking fish is rare on Cumberland. But, there are a lot of single fish feeding on top. We busted their tail last February on surface swimming lures," he said.

"Live bait is most dependable," Tarter said. Many of his anglers are not experienced plug casters, and live shad fished deep is more productive for the novice. The fish hold in the main channel. When they decide to feed, they herd shad up against the bank in about 60 feet of water, 20 feet below the boat. Then they only feed for 5 minutes to a half-hour.

If Tarter took the time to find fish on his depth finder, the bite would be over by the time he located the fish.

"It's a hit-and-run situation," Tarter said, "If I don't get bites right away, I move to another spot."

How about the favorite Atlantic coast bait for big stripers—live eels? They have been tried. What happened? "They ate 'em all up," Tarter said. Catch fish on them? You bet. Ever try them again? No, too hard to get live eels inland.

I told Tarter about casting poppers at night-feeding stripers along a Chesapeake Bay shoreline many years ago, when the fish were right against the bank in two feet of water. How my wife's uncle, Bruce, caught big stripers until he tired and sat down, but I continued casting into the pitch-black night.

But, night fishing with Tarter, casting treble-hooked swimming plugs toward a wooded bank and retrieving them in the darkest Kentucky night of the century was frustrating. That night, we not only didn't find any willing stripers, but somehow my lure found itself in the trees a good bit of the time. Too polite to make fun of my lack of night-casting prowess, Tarter spent much of his time retrieving plugs from treetops. He made no comment about me trying for "tree fish," but I bet his fishing guide buddies got an earful later.

Like Chesapeake Bay and coastal stripers, Lake Cumberland fish may stay all day in shallow water on overcast days. Stripers are light sensitive. "Bites" in salt or fresh water stop when the sun comes up.

The biggest difference between Lake Cumberland and Atlantic coast stripers is that Cumberland fish are less attracted to structure. Where coastal stripers can be found next to rocks, bridge pilings, and jetties more often than not, Cumberland Lake fish are found more frequently in open water or near cuts, points, or breaks.

"I'm sure glad our stripers don't hang around tree stumps," said Tarter, "I don't want anything in my way when I hook a big fish." He added that most of his stripers run from 10 pounds to 40 pounds plus, and the average is 15 pounds. He releases most stripers under 10 pounds.

Tarter of Nancy, Kentucky sounds like a Lake Cumberland press agent when he talks about the size of his striped bass: "Most of our stripers are too big for the structure, anyway."

Penrod's Potomac Stripers
... November, 1987

The Potomac looks like any other great largemouth bass river in the early morning, when mist shrouds the shoreline and blots out all traces of civilization. One can also imagine huge stripers tearing up the surface here. Because in these waters big stripers and bucketmouths live in harmony, sharing a lot of the same things for lunch and dinner.

On a foggy November morning, bass fishing guide Ken Penrod operated the bow-mounted electric motor on his 20-foot bass boat and cast his Fire Tiger 7A Bomber with the constant cast-and-reel of a seasoned pro, hour after hour. I tried a chartreuse Deep Wee-R, having often heard about tidal water bass fishing: "If it ain't chartreuse, it ain't no use."

Above the morning fog, the jet engines of airliners in-bound for Washington International Airport whined as pilots eased back on their throttles on the landing approach. "One plane a minute," Penrod said. The huge airliners were out of sight above, but not out of hearing.

As much as we would have liked to be left in peace along wooded banks where George Washington once fished, the fog soon lifted and our nation's Capitol materialized out of the mist. The wooded Maryland shoreline was replaced by downtown District of Columbia cityscape as we moved upriver. I wondered what 'ol George would have thought of all this "new" development.

"This point is always good for a few fish," said Penrod, as we moved under the Woodrow Wilson Bridge. "And, don't be surprised if you hook a big striper here," he added. The point was lacking in willing bass or stripers that morning. Two other bass boats ahead had already worked the shoreline with worms and crankbaits.

The Potomac River cleanup started in the mid-1960s, Penrod explained. When President Lyndon B. Johnson announced a nationwide clean water program, reporters reminded—and embarrassed—him about the hometown river, the Potomac. Since that time there has been a gradual clean-up of the river and aquatic vegetation has returned.

Penrod said that largemouth bass are reproducing naturally in the Potomac now: "The hydrilla provides cover and oxygen, and it's also a good channel marker, because it grows in relatively shallow water." By avoiding the grassy areas, you can generally stay in the channel, he said, but newcomers should use navigation charts to avoid problems.

The cleanup and the return of largemouth and striped bass to the upper Potomac was good for the recreational fishing business, too. Penrod has built a sizeable following of clients for his guide business because of the plentiful supply of fish. His 15 guides take 1,500 parties a year fishing, mostly on the Potomac. If anglers can catch 40 fish a day here, why would they want to fish other rivers and lakes where the average is 15 or less bass per day?

Several bass boat anglers were casting to the rotted pilings of an old ferry dock that juts several hundred feet into the Potomac. Some of the fishermen worked hard at it, but others were just out for a relaxing morning in the sun.

Penrod pointed out: "Those [relaxed] fellows are on the wrong side. Uptide. They are bound to get hung up in the submerged pilings." They did, constantly.

"That guy knows what he's doing," Penrod said about a wormer who cast from the downtide side of the pilings. He had several hits, but didn't connect. We fished the Chesapeake Bay Bridges the same way in the old days—from the downtide side.

I pulled a yellow Hawg Boss Super Toad past a piling, retrieving it downtide. Three feet from the piling, a bass slammed the tiny crankbait. Ten-pound test line and a lightly set drag made for a longer fight than competition anglers might tolerate, but this was fun fishing. The bass was 14 inches long, about the size of most of the bass caught that day.

"All of the piers and pilings along the Potomac are bass and striper habitat," said Penrod as we motored past the Naval Research Station and Bolling Air Force Base.

Farther upriver, the three bridges that cross the Potomac near the Pentagon hold stripers next to their pilings, where bucktail jigs decorated with pork rind will take both largemouth bass and stripers. Penrod mentioned that stripers can also be found over some lumps just downstream of the 14th Street railroad bridge near Washington International Airport.

The scenic George Washington Memorial Parkway winds along the Potomac through Virginia in a parklike setting for several miles, passing over a picturesque stone bridge near the Pentagon. Commuters on the parkway above often see bass boats fishing the lagoon below. The lagoon is not only scenic from the water, it is bassy and striped bassy looking too. Both shorelines are rip-rapped with stone. A great spot to cast crankbaits. Pier pilings inside the lagoon at the Pentagon Marina hold bass for worm fishermen. Poppers or jigs tossed near stone riprap always produced stripers for me in Chesapeake Bay waters, so why not here?

This part of the river alone would take weeks to fish properly, even if the angler could ignore the scenic beauty of the place. Coming out of the

Ken Penrod catches stripers and largemouth bass within sight of the Washington Monument.

Lagoon, the Jefferson Memorial and the Washington Monument across the Potomac are framed by the same arched stone bridge.

"Stripers are caught upriver as far as Fletcher's Boathouse," Penrod said. "Cut herring or crab baits are best in May."

Tidal water extends upriver to the Key Bridge, but Penrod headed downriver past the peninsula that forms East Potomac Park, then he U-turned around Hains Point to check out the Washington Channel.

Joggers in the park there sometimes walk-troll crankbaits along the seawall to get in some exercise and fishing at the same time. They catch both stripers and bass.

Penrod trolled up the Washington Channel along the Fort McNair seawall with the same crankbait that he had been casting all morning.

"Washington Channel is textbook striper country," Penrod said. He fishes stripers here along drop-offs. His 7A Bombers in Fire-Tiger paint probe the lumps at the seven- or eight-feet depth.

Penrod also trolls a gypsy rig of two jigs for stripers here. A gypsy rig is composed of a twin leader with each leg a different length. On the short leader (the leading jig) he uses a ³/₈-ounce jig with a four-inch pearl swimmertail. On the longer leader, the trailing jig is ³/₈ ounces with a three-inch white swimmertail.

Stripers showed on the chart recorder, stacked up like cordwood over deep holes and bottom lumps. No strikes from the unpredictable stripers disturbed our quiet, scenic journey.

Penrod said the biggest striper he has caught in the Potomac was 12 pounds. He has seen bigger ones chase his lures through weedbeds.

"Stripers were once open water feeders here," Penrod said. "But now they feed in weedbeds. Sometimes when we are casting spinnerbaits for bass in weedbeds we see big stripers pushing the grass aside chasing our baits."

He has seen 20- and 30-pounders in weedbeds downriver. Favorite striper spots include the weedbeds in front of Mount Vernon, and Piscataway and Broad Creeks.

Mount Vernon reminded me of something I read about George Washington catching a 150-pound striper. If he told the truth about a cherry tree, why shouldn't we believe his fishing stories? His fishing kit was once on display at Mount Vernon, although from an angling standpoint it lacked the heft to wrestle 150-pound stripers. Plantation owners fished nets then, mostly to feed their workers.

As we passed the Blue Plains Sewage Treatment Plant, I commented on the odor, and recalled that many stripers were once caught over the Annapolis sewer pipe outlet near the mouth of the Severn River.

Penrod agreed: "One of our best striper spots is over the sewer outfall," he said, "They are stacked up there. You can catch all you want."

It was time to release the largemouth bass in the livewell. Penrod's anglers understand that they will not keep bass unless they catch a trophy.

"Think about it," Penrod said, "Our 15 guides make a total of 1,500 trips a year. With two anglers and a guide in each boat, and a five fish limit, that's 15 fish per trip, or 22,500 bass removed from this part of the Potomac each year. The bass won't stand that kind of pressure. If all of the guides here release their fish, we can maintain a quality fishery for tomorrow."

It would take a lot of tomorrows to fish every bit of this scenic river. The number of pilings, rip-rap seawalls, submerged trees, points, grass beds, and drop-offs that hold bass and stripers are mind-boggling, and each one must be fished differently. Although challenging to the angler, there is a world of fun in the trying.

Striper Cousins: Great Whites of Oahe

"Hot Dog!," said Steve Nelson as he, Carole, and I all battled white bass at the same time, "it's a triple-bagger!"

Steve had waded out on a sandbar below the dam at Lake Oahe near Pierre, South Dakota. He stood backlighted by the sun as he gently lip-lifted a three pound white. My wife, Carole, and I still had our hands full with two whites that ripped off more of our four-pound test line every time we got them near shore.

"Look at this one," Steve said, "Isn't that a beauty? I call them Great Whites."

Steve Nelson admires a Lake Oahe white bass.

It was a pretty fish to Marylanders who had not fished stripers since our moratorium. The shiny silver fish resembled two fish we have at home—white perch and striped bass. Steve's white bass reminded me of a three-pound white perch wearing striper stripes.

I had wanted to catch white bass (*Morone chrysops*) for some time. My all-time favorite game fish in Chesapeake Bay waters is the striped bass (*Morone saxatilis*), and its cousin, the white perch (*Morone americana*), is a close second. A fourth Morone cousin, the yellow bass (*Morone mississippiensis*) is a species I will try for another day. (Just checking the spelling of its last name is tiring enough).

We had come a long way from Maryland to find out if the white was as scrappy (and tasty) as its Chesapeake Bay cousins. Steve Nelson of Pierre volunteered to assist us in our search for this member of the Morone family.

We had some Chesapeake Bay lures with us. They worked as well on white bass as on our home-town stripers and white perch. Transferring lure technology over 2,000 miles to different waters and different fish is much the same as NASA's "Technology Transfer" to the private sector. I was about to transfer some Chesapeake technology to Oahe.

Shad darts and other Chesapeake lures were effective for Oahe whites.

Carole and I finally wrestled our whites to the beach. I climbed the bank to put our catch in the cooler. Steve and Carole continued casting into the "tide rip" that was formed by rapidly flowing water from the giant dam a mile away.

There was a lot of action. One white after another hit the Chesapeake lures I experimented with—until the turbines shut down. The water flow slowed. The comparison here between Oahe's water flow and our Chesapeake Bay tidal flow is curious—and similar.

In the Chesapeake, fish usually bite better on a moving tide—sometimes the flood and sometimes the ebb—but on slack tide, action stops. The fish either move or stop biting. The same thing happened at Lake Oahe when the water flow stopped—the fish either moved or stopped biting.

Popular local lures for Lake Oahe whites included Steve's favorites, small jigs with chenille and feather bodies, and grub or twister tails in white or chartreuse.

One favorite Chesapeake striper lure is a white 1/0 bucktail jig with real bucktail. Imitation hair does not attract strikes.

I tie white bucktail hair on my home made jigs with red thread, and paint large red eyes on the white jig head. Small spoons like tiny Tony Acettas and Drones are also good Chesapeake striper lures.

Chesapeake Bay white perch fall for our home-made spinner and grub lure with a $1/8$-ounce jig head, a white twister tail, and a French spinner blade. We have had days in shallow Chesapeake creeks where every cast of a spinner and grub lure resulted in a white perch. If you rate fishing success by numbers of fish caught per hour, Chesapeake white perching is the most productive fishing of all.

I rooted through my tackle box, hoping to find a Chesapeake striper or white perch lure the Lake Oahe whites *would not* take. I couldn't. Some lures, like small spoons, were not as productive, but whites still hit them. One of our best lures was my homemade 1/0 white bucktail jig, perhaps because I "worked" the jig at Oahe the same way I did in Chesapeake waters.

When we found small stripers in shallow Chesapeake Bay waters we cast small bucktail jigs to the fish. Occasionally stripers got lockjaw, and would not hit a jig retrieved steadily with no "jigging" action imparted by the rod tip. A slight "drop-back" action would sometimes attract strikes. As we retrieved the lure steadily, we would drop the rod tip back a foot or so toward the bait, then slowly sweep the tip back toward us, alternately slowing the jig then speeding it up. The stripers may have thought the meal was getting away from them, but the change in the speed or action of the lure sometimes resulted in a strike. Chesapeake Bay shallow water trollers use the jigging technique, too. Would it work at Oahe? It was worth a try.

Steve thought the white bass were still lurking just beyond the drop-off near the bar, though they had stopped biting when the current slowed. We tried everything in the tackle box with no luck.

Steve thought it might be a good time to head back to Pierre for lunch. I kept casting. I was stubborn. If the fish hadn't moved, there was a way to entice them.

As before, I cast the white 1/0 bucktail jig as far as possible and watched my line as the lure sank. I kept the line taut in case something grabbed it on the way down. When the line went slack, the lure was on the bottom. It was time for that slow retrieve that Chesapeake Bay striped bass like.

Out of habit gained from many years of striper fishing, I started to twitch the rod tip, and used the striper drop-back I just described. Something with broad shoulders and a mean disposition grabbed the jig and made off across Lake Oahe with several hundred feet of my four pound test line.

The "Chesapeake Twitch" turned the trick! It was a white bass turn-on. The Great Whites liked the same lure action as their East Coast cousins.

"If I caught a white perch this size at home," I told Steve as I held up a fat two-pound white bass, "I'd have it mounted." He deflated my ego: "That's a small white—though they're all Great," he added quickly.

"The fishing guides here only want walleye and salmon. They call the white bass a 'Chrome Carp' and won't even clean them," Steve said. "I think they are missing out on some good fishing."

"Some guides troll all day around one of the dam's concrete standpipes to catch one or two salmon a day. Many people like that kind of fishing. I like to walk the shoreline and cast for whites."

Steve told us that one group from Iowa has showed up every summer and stayed until they caught 400 whites. Then they went home and put on a giant fish fry.

"And in April, half of Minnesota comes over here walleye fishing, but they don't even fool with white bass," Steve said.

Back at Gene Cowan's Holiday Haus Motel in Pierre, we filleted our white bass, plus a few walleye and a saugeye (a sauger/walleye cross) that Carole caught. The fish and game cleaning shack in back of the motel was a necessity, owner Cowan said. Some "sports" had actually cleaned their gamebirds and fish in the rooms. One hunter cleaned his deer in the bathtub!

The restaurant chef cooked our filets for dinner that night. It was our 32nd wedding anniversary.

The white bass were cooked to perfection. Fellow outdoor writer Paul Jukes and his wife, Evangeline, heard it was our 32nd anniversary and sent over a piece of the salmon they caught that day. The salmon was excellent.

But, if we hadn't known which piece of fish on our plate was walleye, saugeye, or white bass, it would have been hard for us to tell the difference by taste.

I'm not a connoisseur, but I rate the flavor of the white bass right up there with our Chesapeake stripers and white perch. In fact, the white bass is the favored fish to cross with stripers, according to Maryland's DNR Hatchery Chief, Ben Florence: "The white bass x striped bass cross is hardier, fights better, tolerates warm water better, and it tastes the best of all the hybrids."

There were 26 varieties of mounted fish on the restaurant's walls, all caught in Lake Oahe. We had only skimmed the surface by concentrating on white bass. But that's what we came for, and that's what we got.

Steve Nelson agreed: "Great Whites, great fishing."

Striper Hybrids for the Pond
. . . July, 1983

"Jim," said Joe Boone to fellow DNR biologist, Jim Uphoff, "Every ONE of the fry must have survived."

We stood at the edge of a farm pond in Talbot County. Boone and Uphoff had just pulled their seine through the pond where they had stocked 15,000 tiny white perch x striped bass hybrids the previous spring. The net was chock full of struggling 2-inch hybrid stripers, and the biologists couldn't get over it. Usually, there is considerable natural die-off or cannibalism in grow-out ponds during the summer.

I asked Boone what the growth rate of the white perch/striped bass cross might be. He said it was a comparatively new breed, and they didn't have enough data to make comparisons yet. White bass x striped bass hybrids had been around longer.

Hybrids were once seen as a possible solution to the problem of striper migration. It was hoped that a hybrid fish could be developed that would stay in one river like a white perch, but grow and fight like a striper.

Smaller white bass x striper hybrids have been rumored in Bay tributaries, indicating the possibility of a successful spawn. Some biologists think striper hybrids are sterile, and do not reproduce.

That day, Boone gave me about 100 fingerlings for my new pond at home. Bluegill fingerlings were already stocked there.

I was curious about the new hybrid, and later asked Ben Florence what their potential might be. He said of the two hybrid crosses, one was dumber: you had to practically teach it to feed, and it would likely be too dumb to strike artificial lures. The other hybrid grew faster, fed well, and hit artificials like pure stripers. It tasted better, too. Guess which fish we have in our pond?

The frog population in our pond exploded. They croaked loud enough to rattle our windows at night. The hybrids didn't seem to like frog meat. I tossed in three adult largemouth bass. The few frogs we have left are afraid to go swimming now. If they sit on the bank, the Great Blue Heron has them for breakfast. If they jump in, it's largemouth dinnertime. Call it ecological balance.

When our pond hybrid stripers grew to eating size in 1984, we cooked two of them. They tasted like mud, a common problem with pond-raised fish. Not wanting to get into the science of aquaculture, we didn't eat any more of them. Later, Bill Perry told me the bad taste was in the skin. I should have skinned them before eating them.

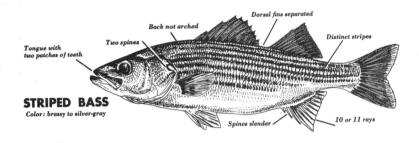

STRIPED BASS
Color: brassy to silver-gray

Tongue with two patches of teeth
Two spines
Back not arched
Dorsal fins separated
Distinct stripes
Spines slender
10 or 11 rays

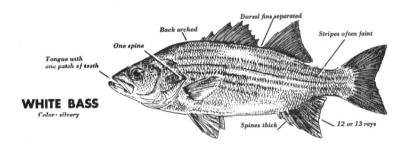

WHITE BASS
Color: silvery

Tongue with one patch of teeth
One spine
Back arched
Dorsal fins separated
Stripes often faint
Spines thick
12 or 13 rays

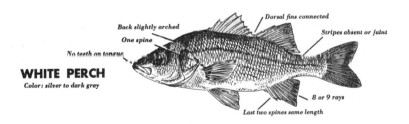

WHITE PERCH
Color: silver to dark gray

No teeth on tongue
One spine
Back slightly arched
Dorsal fins connected
Stripes absent or faint
8 or 9 rays
Last two spines same length

The white bass x striper cross has been successfully stocked in lakes throughout the south, and it is also a popular fish for pond aquaculture.

Scale sample analysis used to discriminate between hatchery and wild fish via computer is an accepted science. It has been used for years on salmon. Californians used it to tell hatchery stripers from wild ones. It is now being evaluated for enforcement reasons, being able to scientifically tell the difference between aquaculture stripers and wild ones.

It is hard for the lay person to tell the difference between pure stripers and hybrids. Ben Florence uses a quick reference: "Put the fish on the deck.

If it flares its gills, it's a hybrid. Flaring is a white bass/ white perch characteristic." That only works if the fish is still alive. With dead fish, scales will tell the tale.

Whenever open water aquaculture rears its ugly head, I think about the problems encountered in Canada. Dr. Robert Lippson told me about experiments with Atlantic salmon raised in net pens in the open waters of Maritime Canada. Although they had 30- to 40-foot tides in the test area, fecal material and excess food on the bottom was not scoured away. Pollution was a problem.

Chesapeake Bay tides in our creek average only a foot or two. Scouring action in the Chesapeake would be minimal. If the Canadians had pollution problems, even with their horrendous tides, what could happen here in Chesapeake Bay?

We saw another problem with open water net pen aquaculture near St. George, New Brunswick, Canada. Piracy. I got the definite impression the good 'ol Canadian boys would defend their net pens violently.

Perhaps striper aquaculture ponds on private property here in Maryland would be as zealously guarded.

"Those stupid hybrids are still in my pond," I told Ben Florence recently.

"They are too dumb to die," he said.

Match the Hatch: Try a Breadfly
. . . Autumn, 1984

The white perch x striped bass hybrids in our pond were notoriously lure shy in 1984. Largemouth bass and bluegills who lived there smacked lures and bait with abandon, but our hybrids ate nothing but the choicest parts of soft crab.

Practicing fly casting at the pond, I noticed some boils at a hair bug. I couldn't tell if they were bass or hybrids, because they didn't get themselves hooked and identified.

But, whenever we had some stale bread, I fed the bluegills with small chunks of it tossed on the pond surface. After a while, the hybrid stripers began to feed on the bread. It was fun to see them come up and roll as they scarfed bits of bread, just like rockfish do when they are breaking on the surface, chasing baitfish.

I remembered that Lefty Kreh chummed up bluefish with ground fish, then caught them on a fly rod. Lefty actually tied up a fly that looked like a piece of ground fishmeat chum. That may sound a little disgusting to a fly fishing purist, but it is very effective for anyone who wants to catch a big nasty fish on light tackle.

I called Wayne Grauer of Maryland Fly Anglers, who gives fly fishing seminars for Cortland Line Company.

"How can I tie a fly that looks like a piece of bread?" I asked Grauer. There was a long silence. You could almost hear him trying to figure if my rod wrappings had come loose.

"Why?" he finally asked.

I told him my pond hybrids would hit chunks of bread, but ignore any sort of fly cast amid the bread chunks. I wanted to fool the little rascals.

"Tie it with the hollow hair from a deer's body," Grauer said, humoring me. "It will stand straight out from the hook when you tighten the thread. That's the way they make hair bugs."

"The hair near the base of a deer tail is hollow," I said, "That's why some bucktail jig tiers won't use it."

"Try it," Grauer said.

The only small hook I could find was a black #1 hook with a bait holder crimp. I chucked it up in my workbench vise. I keep a couple of deer tails in the freezer for emergencies like this. They haven't been dried or cleaned, and still have meat on them. Keeping them in the freezer subdues most of the odor.

By golly, the hair near the base of the tail stood up vertically when the thread was pulled tight. It resembled a messy white hair bug. The hair went in every direction like a hippie's hairdo.

I jammed a slice of bread in my pocket and headed for the pond. A few pieces of bread had the hybrids rolling on the surface. I dunked the fly on the water. Not a professional presentation, but I was there to catch a fish. Most of my leader was still inside the rod guides, not recommended if big fish are in the area.

The breadfly, about the size of the end of your thumb, sat on the surface looking like a frazzled lump of white deer hair, which, actually, it was.

The hybrids scarfed up every piece of bread I tossed out. Didn't touch the breadfly. I tossed out more bread, "chumming" like they do for bluefish. The hybrids rolled on the surface, slurping bread like it was their last supper. Before the last piece was gone, a hybrid hit my breadfly. Success!

Now, I could hold up my head among the snootiest of fly anglers. I, personally, had tied a fly that matched the hatch!

The fish gave a pretty good fight. I knew nothing about fighting a nice fish on fly gear. He took quite a bit of line off the fly reel, heading for the far end of the 100-foot pond. He zoomed back, and I reeled like mad to try and regain all the limp line on the water. I thought he had tossed the hook.

Nope, there he was! The line came up tight. Actually, much of the fight was with most of the 9-foot leader in the rod guides, he was so close. I'm not sure that is an accepted practice among the brotherhood of fly anglers.

I led the hybrid to the bank, and lipped him as I yelled for Carole, in the house, to bring the camera.

No one would believe I'd caught a fish on a breadfly unless I could show photographs. I slipped the fish back into its pond home.

Ben Florence was right about the white perch x striped bass hybrids. They *are* stupid.

The author, the breadfly, and the hybrid.

14

STRIPED BASS WHITE PAPER COMMITTEE

Maryland Governor Harry Hughes had appointed members of rockfish "user groups" to a Striped Bass White Paper Committee (WPC) charged with deciding: "When the striped bass population has recovered to the point where fishing can be resumed, how different types of fisheries should be opened up in Maryland in a way that ensures the continuing health of the striped bass population?"

Before the first meeting of the White Paper Committee, the DNR's Dr. Paul Massicot defined (very well, I thought) problems to be worked out by the committee. He divided those problems into three broad areas. Three persons from each "user group" were to be selected to serve on subcommittees that would look at those problems.

When the WPC first met on September 1, 1987, the only non-committee members present were myself and my wife, Carole; plus Jim and Henrietta Price.

At that meeting, a commercial fisherman tossed a monkey wrench into Massicot's plans by suggesting, forcefully, that "it would take too much time to explain how his gear works" to recreational fishermen, and that he wanted to get together with his people [commercials] and they would decide what they wanted. The charterboat folks said they already knew what they wanted. Our recreational representatives were quiet. A fisheries scientist present brought them all up short by reminding them that no one had yet mentioned that the resource should come first.

I felt that Massicot soft-pedaled the rest of that meeting and did not regain the chairmanship role that evening.

A Red-Hot White Paper Discussion
... November, 1987

Eastern Shore MSSA members who attended a public meeting with the Sports Fisheries Advisory Commission (SFAC) at the Talbot County Free

Library in Easton were treated to a doozie!! They had a chance to air their gripes and ask questions of top Maryland DNR management including Secretary Dr. Torrey C. Brown and Fisheries Division Director Pete Jensen, about everything from new yellow perch regulations to rockfish to why there should be commercial fishing.

There were 32 people present, due mostly to advance publicity in *The Fisherman* magazine and in Bill Perry's *Star-Democrat* outdoors column.

John Kaestner questioned why there should be a commercial fishery on stripers at all. Jensen skillfully skirted the subject a bit, but the bottom line was, "It's the law."

Another question, "What God-given right does a commercial fisherman have to take an unlimited amount of rockfish just because of the type of license [recreational or commercial] he buys," was answered much the same way, but the ensuing discussion with a part-time net fisherman present was somewhat heated.

The saddest item discussed at the Easton meeting, from its impact on the future of the striped bass resource, was the suggestion that the Governor's Striped Bass White Paper Committee was being dominated by commercial fishing interests.

SFAC and WPC member, Kim Kaestner, was asked if commercial domination of succeeding White Paper meetings had diminished. "No," she said, "it's gotten worse." Kim also said something was unbalanced on the committee.

Unbalanced was hardly the word to describe it. There were four groups representing commercial fishing on the WPC. I counted 20 commercials and their supporters, about six neutrals, and three recreational representatives.

To me, that meant that 500,000 recreational anglers had *three* White Paper representatives, and less than 400 commercials had at least 20 representing them!

When the Easton meeting of the SFAC began heating up, Secretary Brown skillfully ended the discussion about commercial domination of the WPC by saying, "It does not always follow that whoever talks the loudest, wins."

Dr. Brown must have forgotten that a few loud-talking folks were able to convince the Maryland Legislature a striper moratorium was not needed in 1983, although the fishery was crashing.

Maryland White Paper Recommendations
... January, 1990

Considering that the balance of power tilted strongly toward commercial fishing on the Governor's Striped Bass White Paper Committee (WPC), their final proposal was surprising to many recreational anglers. It allocated the striper take between recreationals and commercials at 42½ percent each, and 15 percent to the charterboat fleet.

The White Paper Committee's proposal, listed below, was approved by the ASMFC on May 15, 1990. The Maryland DNR can close any fishery when its quota has been filled. The overall quota of 750,000 pounds in 1990's "transitional fishery" (estimated 18 percent mortality rate) would be divided as follows:

- Charterboats: 15 percent, or 112,500 pounds.
- Recreational fishery: 42½ percent or 318,750 pounds.
- Commercial fishery: 42½ percent or 318,750 pounds.

A "more robust recovered fishery" (30 percent mortality rate allowed) would be proposed to the ASMFC when "the juvenile index reaches a three-year-average of 8.0 and at least 10 percent of spawning stock is equal to or greater than Age VIII."

Maryland seasons approved as of May 15, 1990:

- Charter and Recreational: October 5 to November 9, 1990, plus a "trophy fish" season in May, 1991.
- Commercial: Drift gill nets, January 2–31, 1991.

Size limits proposed: an 18 inch minimum for the Chesapeake Bay, with a maximum size limit of 36 inches, except during the May trophy season when the minimum size will be 45 inches with no maximum.

Creel limits proposed:

- Recreational: Two stripers per day per person.
- Charter anglers: Five stripers per day per person.

NOTE: These are highlights of the approved regulations. The entire set of regulations is much longer, and subject to change. Check striper regulations before you go fishing.

"The Sports Fisheries Advisory Commission (SFAC) opposed a separate creel limit [two recreational and five charterboat]," said WPC and SFAC member, Kim Kaestner, "The Commission also opposed striped bass tournaments and the May trophy fishery."

"First, we didn't think a five-fish creel is in keeping with good conservation; and secondly, it's bad PR to have a [May] trophy fishery on a spawning fish," Kaestner said.

A Trophy Striper Season?

There are many good reasons not to pursue and kill big spawning stripers. First: Most stripers over 45 inches are cows. Male stripers rarely grow that big. For each 10 pounds of body weight a big cow striper can cast 1 million eggs; therefore, a 50-pound striper can potentially spawn 5 million eggs a year. Killing a 50-pound striper will take 5 million eggs out of production every year afterward. A "directed" trophy striper season in May will guarantee that many big spawning cow stripers will be dragged behind trolling boats for long distances, and badly stressed. These stripers are our brood fish, the future of striper fishing. Enough cows will be caught and released in a May bluefishery, anyway. Why have directed trophy fishery that will kill many of the last of these big cows?

Second: Big stripers are near the top of the food chain. A rockfish biologist told me big fish concentrate poisons they get from smaller fish they eat. In the halcyon days of rockfishing around the Bay Bridges, that's all we caught—big fish from 10 to 30 pounds. So, I guess I've eaten my share of toxic chemmies. But, we didn't know that then. We do now.

Third: What else can you do with a 50-pound striper if you don't eat it? Drag it around in the back of your pickup until it rots so you can show it to the neighbors? No?

Mount it for the wall? Not really. Skin mount fish crack and look nasty with age. Plastic mold copies of any size or specie of fish, in almost any position, can be ordered through your local taxidermist. Mold copies are already in stock, so you don't have to kill your big fish. These fiberglass copies look better and last longer.

Then what can you do? My suggestion is to release the big cow as soon as possible. Take photographs of you releasing the fish and have a poster-sized print made for your wall. Or, video tape the battle and the release, then invite the neighbors over to watch your catch on TV. Or both. Catch, Photograph, and Release (called "CPR" by one camera company). You'll feel better, and you'll help restore the troubled striper.

White Paper Rec Reps Talk Back
... Summer, 1990

There were three recreational fishing representatives on the Striped Bass White Paper Committee (WPC):

Yvonne Giguere and George Hemelt from the MSSA; and Kimberly Keene Kaestner as liaison from Maryland's Sport Fisheries Advisory

Commission (SFAC). A third MSSA representative belonged to both the sport and commercial advisory commissions, so I don't feel that person represented me as a sport angler.

Only three people on the WPC represented Maryland's 500,000 sport anglers, and at least 20 people on the WPC backed less than 500 commercials. Knowing that, the great surprise to me was that rec anglers were allocated any rockfish at all.

That allocation, said committee member, Kim Kaestner, was "whacked up" at the group's Christmas party meeting on the Governor's yacht: "It was late, and everybody was tired. Pete [Jensen of the DNR] asked George [Hemelt] how he would apportion the fish. George said 98 percent recreational, two percent commercial. They laughed at him. I recall Pete said, 'Suppose we split it down the middle [commercial—recreational], and each group gives up $7\frac{1}{2}$ percent to the charterboats.' If you ask Pete now, he'd say it [allocation] was based on history. Pete pretty much ran the show [the White Paper Committee]. Everything in these regs was initially voiced by the DNR. The DNR could have written them. The final say was the DNR's anyway. Maybe that's not wrong. Maybe they shouldn't establish a lay group and ask them to set regulations."

Yvonne Giguere is an MSSA Board member. She is also President of the Conservation Federation of Maryland (a National Wildlife Federation affiliate). As an MSSA Board member, she backs that organization's move to make stripers gamefish. "The White Paper Committee was wrong, unfair," Giguere said, "It was obviously set up by people who thought they were considering the bulk of the voters. And, my feeling was that Pete's [Jensen] mind was made up and that it didn't matter who was trying to make changes. . . . There was never a vote taken."

"The controversy over the White Paper opened some eyes in Maryland, though," Giguere said, "It let the watermen know that we [recreational anglers] can get organized." On allocation: "At the Christmas party Pete said something had to be done by early January. There was a big argument. Pete finally threw up his hands and said 'Let's split it down the middle.' I said, 'Let's *start* from there.'"

"We did win by getting 50 percent of the rockfish—they [the commercials] wanted 80 percent," said Giguere. "Commercials also wanted a 16 inch fish. We held out for an 18-inch minimum. If you disagreed, who could you complain to? There was no appeal."

George Hemelt net fished with an uncle as a kid. He is now 58, and an avowed sportfisherman: "I was out of my league on the White Paper," he said, "I'm a tool and die maker. But, we all felt throughout the proceedings that Pete [Jensen] was steering us. We always referred back to the DNR's expertise. Pete took everything we said and shuffled the cards and came back with whatever *he* wanted."

"*Maybe* it was all worthwhile, but I think we spent a lot of time getting nothing done," said Hemelt. "We continually asked, 'Who is going to be on the Striped Bass Advisory Committee?' But, it was never addressed."

Kim Kaestner checked the number of commercial netting licenses on May 21, 1990. She was told by DNR Licensing there were 365 gillnet licenses as of that date. (There is now a two-year waiting period for new commercial license applicants). DNR figures indicate 500,000 recreational Chesapeake Bay anglers. Kaestner said she still has not changed her mind about "the commercials being one percent of the user group who got nearly half the fish."

Pete Jensen Replies
. . . June, 1990

Maryland DNR Fisheries Division Director, W.P. "Pete" Jensen, defended the WPC. "We didn't steer at all other than trying to keep it within the reach of the law which meant we had to open it to all three groups [recreational, commercial, and charterboat]. And, there were biological limits as to how far we could go."

On allocation: "They [the WPC] didn't agree on allocation until the last meeting; then they were so tenuous about it. They finally said, 'O.K. for one year.'"

Jensen said the recreationals wanted 100 percent, the commercials wanted 100 percent, and the charterboats wanted 20 percent. "That's 220 percent, we told them," Jensen said, "That's not possible. We threw out some alternatives. The one that came down in the end was, split it 50-50. They couldn't agree on anything else. It wasn't our decision, it was their decision. Every meeting, we'd say 'Hey, if you don't agree on allocation, it's not going to work.' So then they agreed to split it 50-50 and agreed to take 7$\frac{1}{2}$ percent out of each allocation for the charterboats. Then we [DNR] applied that to the quota [750,000 pounds total]. We said, 'How do you want to structure the seasons and creel limits?' Out of that formula comes the seasons and bag limits. It protects the resource, stays within the quota. We know the basis for the numbers we use, how many participants. We estimate how many trips for recreational and commercial. So, if we start departing from that based on these equity arguments—and I understand the equity arguments—we take a step backwards from a structure system. We get right back to the dogfight we've had for years."

"A lot of times they [rec reps] didn't say anything," Jensen continued. "We would ask them what they had to say about this, and they'd just sit back and nobody would say anything.... They did have their differences, kibitzing, in and out, about me. Same thing with the commercial people; they had their differences depending on what part of the Bay they were from. You didn't really have three groups negotiating; you had 15 or 20 negotiating. It was an interesting process. I don't necessarily accept any criticism that I steered that group. You know the strong personalities involved. I couldn't steer them if I wanted to."

Ben Florence told me he had attended several meetings of the WPC, I asked Ben about fair representation: "They [rec reps] didn't say anything," Ben said, "Every time I went, they just sat there."

I posed the same question to Rich Novotny, Executive Director of the MSSA: "I started attending [WPC] meetings, and they [rec reps on the WPC] were pretty quiet. If I saw something wrong, I held up my hand [Novotny was not a WPC member] and said what I thought. I think I came pretty close to getting tossed out."

Jensen about the WPC being unbalanced toward commercials: "I don't see the unbalancing Novotny is talking about. The WPC was set up through the legislature, but for this one [the DNR's new Striped Bass Advisory Board] we set the numbers and appointed them."

Maryland's New Striped Bass Advisory Board
... June, 1990

"We tried to pick people who were responsible and who represented the different views we knew that existed out there," Pete Jensen said about the new Striped Bass Advisory Board. "Also, we didn't want a group as big as the White Paper Committee."

Jensen continued: "We picked Charlie Ebersberger (Angler's Sporting Goods, fishing tackle), Robert Eurice (Tidal Fisheries Advisory Commission, commercial fishing), Jim Gilford (Chairman, Sports Fisheries Advisory Commission), William Goldsborough (Chesapeake Bay Foundation), Buddy Harrison (charterboat fleet and hotel owner), Bill Huppert (MSSA, sportfisherman), Fred Meers (MSSA President and tackle manufacturer), Ed O'Brien (charterboat captain and Sports Fisheries Advisory Commission), Larry Simns (Tidal Fisheries Advisory

Commission and Maryland Watermen's Association), and Bill Woodfield (Tidal Fisheries Advisory Commission and seafood dealer)." Jensen said more may be added later if the DNR decides that other user groups need to be heard from.

15

POLLUTION

Pollution Versus Stripers
... May, 1989

By the year 2025, U.S. coastal fish stocks will support more than 211 million angler-days of fishing, an increase of 40 percent over 1985, according to the Sport Fishing Institute. Huge northeast populations will put ever-increasing pressure on coastal fish. Even worse, it is this very density of people that will wreak the most havoc on nature's attempts to replenish fish stocks.

Ironically, the creature comforts we demand create the industry which in turn creates more pollution of all types. Ever denser populations also put more pressure on antiquated sewer systems. Pesticide and nutrient runoff from well-manicured lawns and farms will eventually wind up in our rivers and bays.

Automobiles cause problems, too—lead and oil run off into waterways because the paving our vehicles need covers much of the soil that would have absorbed the pollutants.

If one considers the fish most likely to be affected by pollution: "It is safe to say that there is decreased reproductive success in estuarine spawners all along the coast," said Dr. Robert Lippson, Assistant Director of the Northeast Region of the National Marine Fisheries Service (NMFS). This includes anadromous fish like striped bass, herring, and shad, which spawn in fresh water but spend their adult lives in the ocean. Semi-anadromous fish, those who spawn in fresh water but live just downstream in brackish water like white and yellow perch are in trouble, too. Open-water spawners that swim into estuaries to feed include bluefish and weakfish. Their stocks are healthy. Ocean spawners that stay in the ocean have good reproductive success, but are more subject to overfishing.

We must look, then, to the estuaries for a key to the decline in reproductive success of anadromous fish like the striper. Aside from

The battle to save anadromous fish will be won or lost in the estuaries, say some experts.

overfishing, why are coastal stripers numbers down? What is killing them? A five year study by the U. S. Fish and Wildlife Service (USFWS) is yielding some clues:

"We are finding some real horror stories in Eastern Shore rivers [in Maryland]," said Robert Stevens, Chief of the Office of Research Support of the FWS. "The pH of the Choptank and Nanticoke Rivers dropped below 6.2 after heavy (acid) rains, and the low pH has killed striped bass larvae after the spawn for three years now [1986, 1987, 1988]. In the Potomac River heavy metals kill striper larvae even when we don't have acid rain pulses. Problems stem from automobiles, illegal releases of chemicals, and agricultural runoff."

Cold weather and acid pulses after heavy rain normally occur in the spring when these fish are spawning. Suppose we had a dry spring? Not good either, Stevens said. Some rain is needed to grow the little critters that striper larvae feed on. A no-win situation in some rivers—but not in Virginia where there has been record striped bass reproduction. Studies are underway to compare differences in water quality in Maryland and Virginia spawning rivers. The bottom line?

"Something is killing the larvae," Stevens said. "The more we fail to get a good juvenile index, the more we feel that contaminants are the main factor."

Acid rain is not the only contaminant to fall from the sky, according to a recent Environmental Defense Fund report. Up to 25 percent of the nitrogen pollution in the Cheseapake Bay came from airborne sources, according to the report. Nitrogen and phosphorus are nutrients that cause an algae bloom. When algae die and decompose they consume the same dissolved oxygen that supports other marine life. When dissolved oxygen levels are low, strange things happen. Crabs are seen trying to crawl up on crab pot buoys. Dead fish are floating everywhere.

Dead fish like this black drum are the most visible sign of an estuary in trouble.

Point source pollution is relatively easy to find. Industrial discharges and sewage treatment plants are examples, though they are not always easy to clean up. Stopping an industrial polluter puts people out of work, so many industrial plants have permits to discharge. Basically, the same problem exists with sewage treatment plants that are rapidly outgrown as we continue building.

Non-point pollution includes not only airborne, but pesticides and herbicides our farmers need to compete in today's marketplace. One retired farmer told me he used chemicals because "there is no way that two men can farm 1,000 acres and make a profit without chemicals." Another farmer said that to "chemical farm" he didn't even need soil: "Give me the right chemicals," he said, "and I can grow soy beans in your hat!" Does that mean there are more chemicals poured on farmland than are absolutely needed?

At the price of chemicals today, not likely. But, consider this—maybe "enough" is "too much."

Another possible source of waterway pollution will have to be dealt with soon—the application of sewage plant sludge on farmland. On one hand, it does get rid of the awesome pile of sludge around sewage facilities. On the other hand, there are doubts about whether heavy metals or some of the 2,000 new chemical compounds that come out every week are present in the sludge, and whether the sludge is even examined for these. Once sludge is worked into the soil, will toxic chemicals in it leach down to the water table to poison us later, or run off farmland into waterways to kill fish larvae now? Or both?

If one looks at the first industrial cities in the northeast, it is easy to figure which ones have polluted their waterways for the longest amount of time: Providence, Rhode Island; Boston, Massachusetts; New York, New York; Philadelphia, Pennsylvania; Baltimore, Maryland; and Washington, D.C. From north to south, let us talk to some folks along the coast about pollution and fisheries.

Mark Galasso worked on a NMFS research ship taking sediment samples along the Atlantic coast. "Narragansett Bay had the worst sediment we saw from Nova Scotia to the Dry Tortugas," Mark said, "It was the consistency of mayonnaise and smelled so bad we were afraid to touch it. We wore rubber gloves." He said that even Raritan Bay sediment was not as bad as that from Narragansett.

"The Narragansett Bay area was the heart of the American Industrial Revolution," said Chris Little, President of Rhode Island's SAVE THE BAY. "There are more than 200 years worth of contaminants in river bottom sediments," he said, "and in heavy storms they come into the Bay." In adjacent Mt. Hope Bay defective septic systems and industrial contaminants have caused problems. Little anticipates new sewage systems will allow some parts of Mt. Hope Bay to be open to swimming and shellfish harvesting soon. Little complained that "it is hard to get the recreational fishing industry interested in habitat."

Barry Gibson, Editor of *Salt Water Sportsman* magazine based in Boston, remembered that Boston Harbor had the "best winter flounder fishing in the world until four or five years ago. Pollution finally got to it," Gibson said. He cited cancerous lesions on fish, and added that Salem Harbor is just as bad.

"New York is cleaning up its act," said Dr. John Waltman of the Hudson River Foundation. "PCB levels are dropping slowly, and new sewerage treatment plants are helping, but bottom sediment still has to be cleaned up."

"PCB pollution in the Hudson has helped the striped bass recover," said Dr. Waltman, "the fact that they are inedible doesn't seem to hurt the fish themselves. Hudson River bass have been increasing dramatically."

One theory blames the failure of striped bass spawning in the Chesapeake Bay on its lack of buffering capacity in an acid rain, and credits the successful spawns in the Hudson River to large deposits of limestone which buffer acid rains there.

Dr. Waltman was positive about other species in the Hudson: "Our shad run this year was tremendous. Last year the blue crab run was amazing, but there was cadmium and other heavy metals in certain body parts and in their fat. There is also a large population of Atlantic and shortnose sturgeon in the Hudson."

Since Pennsylvania and Delaware have worked to clean up the Delaware River, the pollution block that once stopped anadromous fish at Philadelphia is pretty much gone. Charlie Lesser, Manager of Fisheries for Delaware's Department of Natural Resources and Environmental Control (DNREC) said, "Oxygen levels in the Delaware River are better now, and fish are getting through to spawn. Shad, historically a big fishery, are recovering. Striped bass are spawning in the river again. Walleye, striper hybrids, and tiger muskies are coming down the Delaware River from releases in Pennsylvania, which was unexpected."

"By poundage, over 90 percent of Delaware's fishery is recreational," said Lesser. Lesser feels that one day migratory species of fish like the striped bass will be managed on a national level like waterfowl: "The feds will set maximum limits, and the states will be able to set their fishing regulations within that framework."

Dr. Edward Christoffers is the NOAA/Chesapeake Bay Science Coordinator appointed as liaison between Maryland, Virginia, Pennsylvania, the District of Columbia, EPA, NMFS, FWS, and the Soil Conservation Service. His emphasis is on marine resources and habitat. He feels good about the progress being made in cleaning up the Chesapeake Bay:

"Our progress is slower than many would like," Dr. Christoffers said, "but it is faster than many anticipated." He cited the 1987 Chesapeake Bay Agreement that was signed by MD, VA, PA, DC, EPA, and the Chesapeake Bay Commission, and their goals and commitments.

"Our main goal is to attain water quality conditions necessary to support the living resources of the Bay," Dr. Christoffers said. Toxics entering the Bay are now being inventoried, and will soon be controlled. An immediate goal is a 40 percent reduction in nitrogen and phosphorus.

The Chesapeake Bay Commission adopted a fish passage strategy in December, 1988 where fishways will be installed at dams in Maryland and Virginia rivers, allowing spawning fish access to many additional miles of river habitat. Over 700 spawning river miles will be gained in the Susquehanna, Potomac, and Patapsco in Maryland, and the James and Rappahannock in Virginia.

Maryland passed "Critical Areas" legislation that may become the model for other coastal states. All the land that lies within 1,000 feet of the Chesapeake Bay or its tributaries will be regulated as to buffer strips of vegetation and other natural filters, plus a 20-acre minimum lot size in new subdivisions near the water.

In this seemingly endless inventory of estuarine pollution problems, is there any good news? You bet.

"It's not all doom and gloom," said Barry Gibson, "The Kennebec River [in Maine] is a good news story," he said. "Once this was one of the worst. Factory pollution was unchecked. But, it is cleaning up now. Stripers, blues, and salmon are back."

The Hudson is cleaning up, and the Delaware, too. That's good news. Even Baltimore Harbor, where crabs are caught now.

The Potomac River at Washington, D.C. is another cleanup success story. Largemouth and striped bass are now caught within sight of the Washington Monument, right downtown!

The bottom line? Barry Gibson: "We need tighter zoning laws to curtail development of all coastal areas. We run around and put out [environmental] brush fires, but are we putting them out faster than new ones are being lit?"

We hope so.

Acid Rain at Ganeys Wharf
... May, 1986

I knelt, in an almost prayerlike stance, to get a closer look at one of 35 quart-sized glass laboratory beakers that contained tiny 15-day-old striped bass larvae. The beakers were arranged in five tiers so that seven different mixtures of Choptank River water and the "ideal" Manning Hatchery water (pH 7.0) dripped down through the separate temporary glass homes of the stripers.

An incredible array of pipes and sheds lined the bank at Ganeys Wharf on the upper Choptank River that day. Several times each day University of Maryland and DNR technicians sampled the water and the larvae, a laboratory-controlled experiment that was intended to duplicate the massive die-offs of striped bass larvae after a "rain event"—one or more inches of rain in a 24-hour period.

A rain event, coupled with a die-off, would give fisheries scientists samples of water and larvae to analyze immediately after the event. This could have been one of the most significant experiments in the entire array of striper studies planned Baywide that spring spawning season.

The experiment was set up in a small shed, like those used in back yards for lawn mower storage. Pumps and piping were everywhere along the ground outside the shed, some connected to giant tanks of the ideal hatchery water, some pipes providing pickup and discharge for raw Choptank River water. A laboratory trailer and two rented camping trailers provided space to work, eat, and sleep—for sampling went on around the clock.

Adjusting my bifocals for a better look at the quarter-inch long semi-transparent, partly-formed animals in the beaker, I noted that the most prominent features of the tiny stripers were large eyes and a yellowish-brown substance visible in their stomachs. Brine shrimp. A good sign, I was told. They were feeding.

So this is the way they start their lives, I thought. These tiny creatures, if they survived the low pH of an acid rain, would grow into the same gallant striped bass that put up such courageous fights at the end of a fishing line. Stripers! Always eager to take a clam bait or peeler crab with a hook imbedded in it.

I remembered the heart-stopping action when a twenty-pounder feeding in three feet of water knocked my surface popping plug several feet into the air in the middle of a bathtub-sized swirl, and inhaled the lure as soon as it fell back to the water. I could not forget the powerful tug, unlike any other, when a 10- to 15-pound striper struck my bucktail or live eel near Chesapeake Bay Bridge pilings.

Dr. Eric May, the University of Maryland pathologist responsible for this experiment, jarred me out of my reverie.

"These guys are not doing too good," Dr. May said, as he held up a pipette containing Choptank River larvae in Choptank water. "These first two rows [of beakers] may be the only Choptank River larvae that see Choptank River water," Dr. May continued. Larvae for the experiment was hard to get.

The reason for the shortage of Choptank River larvae was thought to be the cold snap that hit just as Dr. Reggie Harrell of the University of Maryland's Horn Point Lab at Cambridge spawned several large cow stripers at Ganeys Wharf with only minimal survivability.

Dr. Eric May examines striped bass larvae that have been exposed to varying amounts of pure well water and Choptank River water. Following a rain, shore-based pollutants enter the river in runoff.

I had watched Dr. Harrell as he squeezed ripe eggs from a 60-pound cow striper into a stainless steel pan and fertilized them with the milt (sperm) from four different male fish of about five pounds each. Although a female striper will cast 1 million eggs for each 10 pounds of body weight, survivability of the Choptank eggs was less than one percent. By the time the cold weather abated, the Choptank River striper spawning season was nearly over.

SIX p.m. Time to sample water and larvae. Roman Jesien, a doctoral degree candidate, checked the Choptank water for pH, salinity, and temperature. Volunteer "lab assistants" Jack Wiley and Jimmy McCafferty measured and saved water samples, then took several larvae samples from each beaker to be kept in preservative for later examination by Dr. May.

"I'd rather be here trying to learn something than home watching television," McCafferty said as he placed larvae samples into vials of preservative. "Maybe I can help, so that one day we can catch another rockfish," he added.

Jimmy McCafferty at 24 looked much younger, but his level of maturity and responsibility was much beyond his tender years. He had fished this part of the Choptank with his stepfather, Bill Price, picking rockfish out of gill nets with frozen fingers in mid-winter. Since the Maryland moratorium on stripers, Jimmy had found a new career on a surveying crew.

Helping Jimmy sample the water and larvae was sportfisherman Jack Wiley, a retired farmer and a member of the Talbot County Chapter of the MSSA. Wiley had been active in conservation organizations in his previous home state of Delaware. When the call came from the MSSA asking for volunteer help at Ganeys Wharf, Wiley stepped forward. "It's a really interesting experiment," Wiley said, "And it feels good to be a part of something that might help the fish."

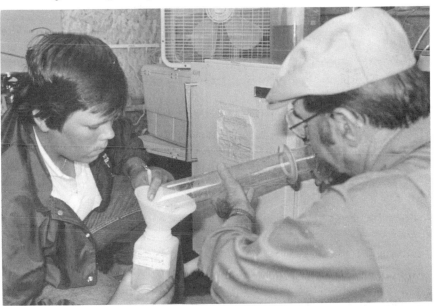

Jimmy McCafferty (left) and Jack Wiley collected and measured Choptank River water samples.

After the sampling, a diverse group met in the office trailer over coffee. A pathologist, a reporter, two sportfishermen, and a commercial fisherman. Ten short years ago, just getting sport and commercial fishermen in the same room would be quite a feat, much less getting them to pay rapt attention to a scientist discussing striped bass pathology! Things really changed when our favorite fish were in trouble.

"Right now we need a rain event," Dr. May said. Historically, die-offs occur after a rain event. "We should have been able to track a normal spawning event and be done by the end of April," he added.

Dr. May had collected data from almost 11,000 fish. He looked for small changes that occur in the fish, correlated with analyses of river water.

Water quality was checked for pH, temperature, heavy metals, salinity, and agricultural chemicals in the run-off after the rain. Dr. May added that 2,000 new chemicals appear on the market every year; many of them that can't be detected in laboratory analysis.

"The Chesapeake Bay is one of the cleanest bodies of water in the country," Dr. May said, "because it does not have large concentrations of heavy industry." That statement is sure to raise the hackles of those who look forward to a lifetime career of saving the Bay, but Dr. May based his statement on his experience in many other areas of the country that have much worse pollution problems. He gave Puget Sound with it's creosote industry and the PCB-laden Hudson River as examples.

NINE p.m. Time for another sampling. Volunteers with possibly opposing viewpoints tripped across the labyrinth of pipes between the trailer and the shed in the gathering darkness. They again sampled the health of a major spawning river that once helped produce enough striped bass to supply a 5-million pound annual commercial fishery, plus hundreds of charter boats that carried at least six anglers every day from May to December. Even with all that pressure, there were so many rockfish left over for sportfishermen that creel limits were rarely even discussed.

That evening at Ganeys Wharf there was indeed a strange symbiosis. Scientists, commercial and sportfishermen, and reporters who gathered that evening on the Choptank River shore may have had differing viewpoints— but they also had much in common. When stripers were plentiful most fishermen only wanted to know where, when, and how to fill the fishbox. There was no tomorrow, no limit to what the Bay could supply.

But, there at Ganeys Wharf fishermen volunteered, willing to help with repetitive tasks so that the scientists could devote more of their time to analysis.

Are rivers sick, or the Bay? Are the fish sick? Will scientists like Dr. May be able to analyze the problems in time?

I knelt for another peek at the beakers and the tiny striper larvae that might provide the key to a declining species. Watching the striper larvae swim in a tiny world that could turn lethal after an acid rain, I wished that all striper fishermen, everywhere, had the opportunity to see these tiny creatures, and speculate on their future.

16

STRIPED BASS AND LAW ENFORCEMENT

Consider the striped bass. No fish in the history of Maryland has generated as much raw emotion, greed, pleasure, printer's ink—and profit.

According to many knowledgeable anglers, white perch are better table fare, and bluefish give a better account of themselves on sportfishing tackle. Then why all the fuss?

To understand, one has only to hold a rockfish, freshly taken from Chesapeake Bay waters. It is a thing of beauty, with black spots that form longitudinal stripes down it's silver sides. From its slightly pointed snout to a gently rounded forked tail, it is esthetically pleasing to view.

A rockfish will strike all manner of lures from surface plugs to spoons and bucktails. It will bite on almost any bait, from clams to shrimp to eels and crab. It has provided a living for generations of commercial fishermen and charterboatmen, and thrilling sport for countless numbers of recreational anglers.

In the pursuit of striped bass, men have drowned, frozen, or keeled over with an overtaxed heart. Others have forsaken family, friends, sleep, jobs,—and sanity. Some poor unfortunates will never understand "Striper Fever"—but some of us do, don't we?

When we talk about enforcing striped bass regulations, there are two groups of people that officers must deal with. On one hand there are recreational anglers who break the law—for who knows what reasons—but not for monetary profit. The second group are commercially oriented—those who sell illegally taken striped bass for profit.

Let's take a look at striper poaching; both commercial and recreational.

$triped Ba$$

In our system of supply and demand, shortages of commodities like striped bass only drive up the price. When the price is high enough, even if the merchandise happens to be an endangered or threatened species, there are those who will risk fines and jail for the big money that can be made.

Most recreational fishermen have not had the opportunity to fish nets for stripers. It was a thrill for me to see big striped bass captured in nets, even if I couldn't comprehend how it felt to sell several thousand dollars worth of stripers for one day's work.

I have never sold a striper, but I have given away literally tons of them to friends and neighbors. It never crossed my mind to charge for something that was so much pleasure to give away. (Young girls get in trouble the same way, but our subject is stripers).

Skip Bason returns a 60-pound cow striper as Bill Price checks gill net.

No "ripe" cow fish were found the day I net fished with Skip Bason in the Choptank, gathering cow stripers for his hatchery work. All of the 40- to 60-pound stripers we caught were gently released. Our commercial fisherman host, Bill Price, asked, "Do you know what we just put back overboard?"

"Yes," I answered, "19 of the most beautiful striped bass I have ever seen."

"No," Bill replied somewhat sadly, "We just put back $5,000."

We had been fishing for less than 20 minutes. In my mind's eye, I saw the sport these grand fish would have provided, and some excellent eating.

Price saw the dollars—new shoes for the kids, groceries for the table, maybe a new pickup truck. Such differing perspectives have kept commercial and recreational fishermen at each others' throats for generations.

Although these oversized fish would have been illegal to sell in Maryland, another commercial fisherman told me—"If I get him across the state line, he's a legal fish."

One young commercial fisherman, still in his 20s, told me that he caught 10,000 pounds of rockfish in one week in the fall of 1984. The value of his week's work, depending on market prices, was somewhere between $5,000 and $50,000. One could understand his reluctance to give up rockfishing.

On January 16, 1985, federal and state wildlife agents arrested 13 Maryland commercial fishermen and seafood dealers for allegedly selling 6,700 pounds of illegal oversize rockfish caught in the Chesapeake Bay or Potomac River. Strangely, in some areas around the Bay, poachers are still not looked on as thieves stealing from a resource belonging to all of us equally. They are revered as folk heroes!

In some local courts, alleged poachers were given a slap on the wrist because "They are just good 'ol boys tryin' to make a living."

In Anne Arundel County, a DNR officer invested two weeks of night duty to apprehend an alleged violator who was charged with gill netting illegally. The judge handed down a fine of $20. As a result of questioning by reporters, the DNR additionally charged this alleged violator with fishing a commercial net without a license.

One Baltimore County judge was tougher. He levied a $500 fine for an illegal gill netting offense.

Fines for those who don't make a living on the water have been tougher than that. Several years ago the court confiscated the boat and motor of an individual who was alleged to have robbed a commercial crabber's pots along the Gibson Island shore.

Sportfishermen hoped the federal judge in the fish market striper sting case would hand out sentences that reflected the seriousness of the crime— jail instead of fines.

A cow striped bass will cast about one million eggs for each 10 pounds of body weight, so consider how many eggs were lost from those 6,700 pounds of oversize fish. Potentially—nearly one billion eggs! What devastating effect did that have on the future of the striped bass fishery?

Minimal fines are also a problem in the Exclusive Economic Zone, called the "EEZ," (from 3 to 200 miles offshore) overseen by the National Marine Fisheries Service (NMFS). Dr. Robert Lippson, Assistant Director of NMFS' Northeastern Region said, "Fines are looked upon by some 'pirates' as a business expense—a license to fish." Lippson added, "When these pirates weigh a $40,000 load of scallops against a $500 fine. . . ."

The problem of illegal striped bass poaching is national. It extends from the East Coast through many southern lakes stocked with stripers, to California—where a striped bass black market was cracked in 1984. California sportsmen formed the United Anglers of California for the express purpose of writing to judges and packing courtrooms so the judges would hand out jail sentences instead of fines. The poachers made $50,000 tax free for a summer's work. Is it any wonder that stripers are in trouble in California too?

Recreational fishermen were not immune to greed, either. In the fall of 1984 many Maryland "sportfishermen" bought the $50 hook and line commercial license so they could keep unlimited amounts of rockfish instead of the sport creel limit of five fish per day.

Charterboat Captain Gil Pumphrey of Cape St. Claire was hopping mad when I saw him in March, 1984: "Eighty percent of the charterboat captains bought the hook and line commercial license last fall," Pumphrey said. "They were taking out parties and catching as many rockfish as they could. The parties kept their five fish per man, and the captain sold the rest."

Although this was perfectly legal, Pumphrey's face reddened even more when he told me that one of the charterboat captains who did this was also an outdoor writer who wrote about conserving rockfish.

Everyone on the fishing scene had a solution, but Mike Pivec, then President of the MSSA, felt his was the best one. He said he would introduce a bill in the Maryland Legislature to make the striped bass a game fish. This would take the striped bass out of the commercial marketplace.

Gamefish status for stripers in the Chesapeake Bay could have the effect of replacing a very small commercial fishing fleet with a very large charterboat fleet. Pivec was realistic about his bill's chances.

"It might take three years to get it," Pivec said, "but we will have a full legislative program—letters, lobbying, everything. Once the DNR sees how many people are buying the Chesapeake Bay Sport Fishing License, they will support us."

Pivec's campaign was to be patterned after that of the successful Gulf Coast Conservation Association (GCCA), which was able to make redfish and spotted seatrout game fish in Texas.

Dick Schaefer of NMFS didn't want to comment on the possibility that some Atlantic coastal states would be closed to striped bass fishing under the federal Studds amendment, as the feds were in the process of evaluating coastal states compliance to the 55% reduction in striper mortality. Some, like Maryland, obviously complied. Others did not.

Schaefer did say, "The days of an unrestricted commercial fishery are about over. Commercial gear has become too efficient."

"Sportfishermen will have to bite the bullet, too," Schaefer said. "Reasonable limits will have to be set—three porgies, two tautog, four flounder—whatever. We [he fishes with hook and line too] should only be able to take as many fish as we need—no more." Most sportfishermen would agree.

Did Schaefer think Maryland would pass a striped bass game fish bill? "With the moratorium in place," Schaefer said, "commercial fishermen have found other things to do. And when the politicians see how many people are buying the Chesapeake Bay Sport Fishing License they will respond to those numbers."

Choptank Striper Patrol
. . . August, 1986

Corporal Burton Wheedleton of the Maryland DNR Police had received reports that fishermen on the Emerson Harrington bridge at Cambridge were catching and keeping rockfish that were protected under the moratorium.

"Officer Charles Creason and I were in plain clothes fishing from an unmarked boat under the Choptank River bridge," Corporal Wheedleton said. "There were several anglers fishing from the bridge above us."

"It was about 9:30 p.m. We could see the fish the anglers were catching because the fish practically went past our noses when they were reeled up, and bridge lights were reflected in the water," Wheedleton continued.

"First a small perch went up. Then another one. Neither one was thrown back." No problem. There was no minimum size on white perch.

"Then a small rockfish went up, about 11 or 12 inches long. There was a long wait, and we heard a splash on the other side of the bridge. I saw a rockfish floating on the surface, stunned by the fall. We untied and went over to it but it revived and swam away."

"We tied to the piling again. Several more perch went up and nothing came back. An oyster toad went up and came back down. Then a larger fish went up—a rockfish, about two pounds—but it didn't come back. We waited quite a while to see if it would be returned. It wasn't. Then, another rockfish went up and didn't come back."

It was decision time. If the officers ran their boat several miles back to the ramp at Trappe Creek and returned with their car, too much time would be lost.

Only one choice. Climb the bridge. They untied their boat and motored to the bridge's turntable center span as quietly as possible, using the rumbling of passing cars above to mask their noise.

Wheedleton looked up at the center span. Maybe 30 feet or more above the water. Wheedleton didn't mind heights when he was younger, but at 42 years of age he had some second thoughts about climbing. Wheedleton stands a lean, rugged 6'2" tall. His shock of reddish hair combined with the intense look on his face would prevent most folks from kidding him about a fear of heights.

The officers knew they should have carried fishing rods with them so they would look less conspicuous, but a climb up the center span of the bridge precluded carrying too much. They decided to take only the essentials with them—a pistol and a flashlight.

Someone had nailed 2x4s to the wooden bulkhead that surrounds the center span turntable, which provided a handy but wobbly access to the top of the bulkhead. Then, they walked across the grease-coated center span turntable to a rusty ladder that led up to road level.

When they started to climb the ladder they discovered the rungs were loose and nearly rusted through. Wheedleton looked down. The cross braces inside the bulkhead 20 or 30 feet below were awash.

The officers had been staring at the underside of the badly deteriorated bridge for several hours from their boat. One look was enough to give anyone the willies about riding across it in a car. Soon after the adjacent new Fred Malkus Bridge was funded, the state's interest in maintenance on an old center span that was about to be dismantled was less than enthusiastic. Climbing this decrepit bridge in the middle of the night was plainly the sort of thing medals are given for.

The officers breathed a sigh of relief when they reached the roadway. They surveyed the alleged poachers. Plain clothes or not, two clean-cut gents with big bulges under their jackets, but minus fishing rods, striding purposefully toward two jumpy rockfish poachers in the middle of the night on a deserted bridge moved the alleged perpetrators to act quickly. One of the anglers said something to the other, then picked up a bucket and tossed the contents overboard. The two officers on the bridge stared down at the alleged evidence slowly sinking below.

Oops.

"You threw fish over?" Wheedleton questioned one of the anglers.

"Yes I did," the angler replied, "but they were funny looking. I wasn't sure what they were so I threw them back."

That late night stake-out and hair-raising bridge climb didn't net those alleged violators. At other times, alleged poachers got away when the officers couldn't get a boat quickly enough to chase them, or the poachers kept their illegal catch tied overboard on a string that could be quickly cut when the officers approached.

Spending long hours trying to catch violators and then not having enough evidence to make a case was demoralizing, but Wheedleton painted rosier pictures of other arrests:

• He was randomly checking boats at landings when he found a rockfish in the bottom of a bucket of perch. Fine: $350.

• Wheedleton walked over to a group of people holding fishing rods on a parking lot near the old Choptank Bridge. He checked their Chesapeake Bay Sportfishing licenses. O.K. Catch anything? Right there in the bucket. All white perch. But what about this rockfish tail sticking out from under a jacket in the trunk? Rockfish? What rockfish? Oh, *that* rockfish! Well, one of our group made several trips to the car but we didn't know what he was doing. Which member of your group? Well, we don't know. Well, then, how about a ticket for illegal possession of striped bass for the owner of the car since no one will admit who caught it?

Fine: $100 plus costs.

Preventative law enforcement is as good as making arrests, said DNR Officer, Corporal Nickolas F. Nazare, Jr. He and his partner, DNR Officer 1st Class C. Gary Bridges stopped John Fairbank and I to check for rockfish. Nazare said that the high profile of uniformed officers in a marked police boat is a good deterrent. Nazare wished, however, that covert operations could be stepped up. Gas and oil are in the budget, he said, but covert boats were hard to come by. He felt that confiscated boats and vehicles "with a few dents" might be used in undercover operations before being auctioned.

Undercover officers can be more effective in certain situations, and might be safer, too, Nazare said, adding that it was dangerous to go on the bridge in uniform: "Burt [Wheedleton] had a bottle thrown at him from a passing car."

It is hard to miss the distinctive appearance of the Boston Whaler police boats with a flasher light mounted above the console. And the Whalers have a distinctive wake, Nazare said. Seasoned watermen can tell the wake of a police Whaler from a long way off.

Netters were going out of their way to avoid areas where they might catch rockfish, Nazare said. Even though they used smaller mesh net for

Officer First Class C. Gary Bridges and Corporal Nickolas F. Nazare, Jr. of the Maryland DNR Police discuss a Choptank River white perch with John Fairbank.

perch it could be possible to catch a rock by the lip in the small mesh and they didn't even want to be seen near a striper.

One rainy night, Cpl. Wheedleton and two other officers crossed the Choptank River bridge in an unmarked car. They saw a man pull up a rockfish, but he didn't toss it back overboard. The officers went on to Easton, picked up a marked police car and returned to the bridge. Wheedleton let the other officers out on the bridge and drove to the Cambridge side so he wouldn't block bridge traffic. The officers kept in contact on hand-held radios.

"They called me on the radio. The man had an eight-pound rockfish in a duffle bag hung over the side of the bridge," Wheedleton said.

How did they know who owned the duffle bag? To keep his wallet dry in the rain, the alleged poacher placed it in his duffle bag with the rockfish.

Fine: $300.

Big Fines: A Deterrent?

MSSA Legislative Chairman, Dale Dirks, was proud of the first bill the MSSA ever got through the Maryland Legislature. Called the "Rockfish Preservation Act," it was passed in the 1990 session. It provides for fines

DNR Police Corporal Burton Wheedleton with frozen-evidence stripers.

up to $1,500 for each illegal striped bass, first offense; and $2,500 per striper, second offense—plus confiscation of all property used to take illegal rockfish.

It sounds great, but will it preserve any rockfish? Will judges hit offenders with top fines? Or will equipment be returned and fines reduced as is usually the case?

While the MSSA can take credit for backing such a bill, part two is monitoring how effective a deterrent it is. With 6,000 members, the MSSA should be able to keep in touch with judges who let offenders off with minimal fines.

Pursuing Stripers: Legal or Not?

"We are not reopening the fishery," said DNR Assistant Secretary James Peck, "We will still have an 11-month moratorium."

Before any fishery on stripers could be opened in Maryland the striper must be downgraded under the Endangered and Threatened Species Act (the Act), from a Threatened Species to the lowest level of protection—a "Species in need of Conservation."

The official status of striped bass in Maryland—Threatened Species—coupled with the public perception that the stripers are out of trouble, has given the DNR a lot of heartburn.

First, it is illegal under the Act to pursue a threatened species, like stripers. If you catch one and release it, fine. If you catch a second one in the same place, you are in violation, according to DNR officials. You should have moved after catching the first striper. If not, you are pursuing. You are participating in a "directed fishery" for striped bass.

Second, consider the angler who has not been able to fish for stripers since January, 1985. It is late autumn, 1989. He is surrounded by acres of breaking rockfish, tearing up the water in all directions as far as he can see. Gulls are swooping and diving all around his boat, picking up baitfish sideswiped and stunned by stripers. The few summer bluefish have left, and the ratio is one blue for every 10 stripers. He remembers that DNR officials and Governor Schaefer were quoted in the papers saying, "the fishery is restored." What would you do?

Third, many charterboat and private anglers who were trolling for the bluefish that didn't show up in the spring months of 1989 and 1990 caught (and released) tons of stripers, many without catching a single bluefish. Dead rockfish floated up on beaches, and people were upset about that. The MSSA's 1990 Bluefish Tournament, with 1,600-plus boats trolling the Bay, caught just over 90 bluefish—total.

Fourth, charterboat captains were in a bind. Trout hadn't showed up yet. Bluefish swam up the ocean coast without making their traditional spring appearance in the Chesapeake Bay. Black drum showed for two days and disappeared. There was nothing to fish for except rockfish. Many captains went catch-and-release striper fishing, some even using bucktails. Some used big spoons so they could say they were bluefishing, but caught rock anyway. Others cancelled parties rather than pursue stripers. Some charterboat anglers, after catching and releasing 30 to 50 stripers, refused to pay their captains because they had no fish to take home!

"It's one of the things that comes with an abundance of fish," said Maryland DNR Fisheries Chief, Pete Jensen. "The more you increase the stock, the bigger the problem is going to be. I'm not concerned about background F [mortality from catch and release, discarded commercial bycatch, and illegal fishing]. It's not a directed fishery, because there are too many fish. You can be too successful at this game [restoring fish populations]. It's an extremely difficult situation."

Is pursuing legal? Officially, no. Is it happening? Yes. Can it be enforced? No, there are not enough officers in the *world* to stop the illegal pursuit of rockfish in the Chesapeake Bay.

One can judge public perceptions by the remarks I hear all the time:

"Those stripes? They fry right off."

"My neighbor is frying the two rockfish he just caught off the jetty. I can smell them from here. Yuuuum!"

"I caught a couple of rock off my dock," said one woman, "I got them into the frying pan before anyone saw me."

"THAT GUY? (alleged poacher) He never even *fished* for rockfish until it was *illegal*"

One waterman regales me with stories about an alleged illegal hook-and-line commercial fishery that has never stopped since the 1985 moratorium was declared! The alleged poacher fishes several times a week, and has to have a market for *that* many fish. Locals all know about it, including several DNR officers who haven't been able to catch the alleged offender—although they have come a lot closer than they know. The stories about his nearly getting caught would fill a book.

Pete Jensen's "background F" may be a lot more significant that he thinks. It is easy for fisheries managers to sit in an office and scan numbers on a computer printout. If the DNR Secretary directed his fishery managers to spend at least one day a month in the field with their biologists and police officers, and another day a month afield talking to real fishermen (not political appointees on advisory commissions), you'd see striped bass management step out from behind desks and charts into the real world.

Poachers: No Place to Hide

"Things were pretty quiet this year," said DNR Police pilot, Sergeant Scott Zimmerman, "We made a number of night flights over the Nanticoke and Choptank Rivers, and over Fishing Bay. That's where the fish were." The DNR pilots get their flight requests from field officers. They had no requests from the upper Bay in 1990.

The DNR officers were checking striped bass spawning areas on spring nights, looking for illegal fishing activity. If anything unusual had been spotted, the pilot could turn on a powerful spotlight suspended under the aircraft, aptly called a "Night Sun."

Sgt. Zimmerman's night flights were in the DNR's Bell Ranger helicopter. He wore the night vision goggles that proved so effective in the Vietnam War.

DNR Police Pilot Sergeant Scott Zimmerman adjusts his night-vision goggles at dusk. "Night Sun" is visible in lower left.

More than one deer jacklighter can thank the DNR Police for using night vision goggles. The goggles amplify low levels of moon or starlight so a jacklighter's tiny flashlight or vehicle headlights look like beacons to the goggle-wearing airborne pilot, who then directs officers on the ground to the jacklighter.

Hanging on Sgt. Zimmerman's office wall is a commendation plaque signed by Governor Schaefer. It was awarded for his participation in a big drug bust, where property was confiscated. What does that have to do with striped bass? Well, when the confiscated drug bust property is finally sold, the DNR Police will get a portion of the proceeds for needed equipment. They have their eyes on something better than night vision goggles for their night flights. It is called "Forward Looking Infra-Red," or FLIR. Maryland State Police have four of the $100,000 units. Soon the DNR Police will have one.

FLIR does not amplify starlight or other visible light. It operates in the infrared range. It records heat. Body heat. Car engine heat. Boat engine heat. It can pick out a person hiding under foliage, the hottest engine in a parking lot, hot tire tracks, boat engines, even a boat's wake. Plus scuba divers or fish near the surface. It will sense a 2/10 of a degree difference in temperature. From 10,000 feet in the air. In the darkest night. Get the picture?

Poachers have no chance against a FLIR. There is no place to hide. If anything will take the fun out of striper poaching, it is FLIR.

17

REOPENING

"Asking politicians and bureaucrats to clean up the rockfish mess is like asking the pigeons to clean up the statue."

— A rockfish biologist

A Very Controversial Reopening

The ASMFC voted 10 to 2 in October, 1989 to allow 20 percent of the historical striper harvest at a meeting in remote Dixville Notch, New Hampshire.

Tom Fote, president of the 30,000-member Jersey Coast Anglers Association (JCAA) rebelled. "They hold the meeting so far up in the woods nobody can get there," said Fote, "Then they take an important vote like that. One commissioner told me 'We are the Commissioners. We know what people want.'"

Newspapers, fishing magazines, and angler's organizations were quick to jump into the controversy that arose after the DNR's August, 1989 announcement that Maryland would reopen its striper fishery.

So much negative response was generated that hearings were held in the Maryland Senate and U.S. Congress about the YOY "anomaly" and the "headlong rush to reopen."

On the state level, DNR officials were questioned at length by members of the Maryland Senate Economic and Environmental Affairs Committee on October 24, 1989. Maryland Senator Gerald W. Winegrad asked DNR officials in that hearing, "What is the compelling state interest in reopening a fishery under moratorium, taking state resources in law enforcement away from other areas? Why not wait another year? Maryland's reopening a fishery signals to Atlantic coastal states 'Go at the fish'."

"What I am suggesting," said Senator Winegrad, "Is that we should wait a year out of an abundance of prudence."

233

News Release dated October 18, 1989

CHESAPEAKE BAY ACID RAIN FOUNDATION, INC.
P.O. Box 1538
Easton, Maryland 21601

Maryland 1989 Striped Bass Juvenile Survey Results

Area	Site	Round 1	Round 2	Round 3	Total
Choptank R.	Tuckahoe	31	48	4	83
	Warwick	63	185	287	535
	Hambrooks Bar	265	1,162	60	*1,487
	Castle Haven	227	16	0	243
Upper Bay	Worton Creek	0	3	4	7
	Howell Point	37	76	24	137
	Ordinary Point	71	60	85	216
	Parlor Point	17	4	0	21
	Welch Point	39	73	132	244
	Hyland Point	22	61	100	183
	Elk Neck Park	0	4	4	8
Nanticoke R.	Sharptown	7	11	2	20
	Lewis Landing	2	2	3	7
	Chapter Point	11	20	4	35
	Tyaskin	3	3	1	7
Potomac R.	Fenwick	1	9	2	12
	Indianhead	2	7	4	13
	Liverpool Point	11	0	3	14
	Blossom Point	15	18	17	50
	Morgantown	0	2	1	3
	Rock Point	1	1	0	2
	St. Georges Isl.	0	0	0	0
				Total	3,327

3,327 Striped Bass divided by 132 hauls = 25.2 Striped Bass Per Haul

* According to the fisheries biologists and scientists that I have consulted, the Hambrooks Bar results are an obvious anomaly and should not be counted as part of the survey. The 1989 Striped Bass Juvenile Index of 25.2 would be reduced to 14.6 if you exclude the Hambrooks Bar Site. The Atlantic States Marine Fisheries Commission voted to open up the Striped Bass fishery during their meeting October 2–5. The State of Maryland did not act properly by withholding this information from the ASMFC prior to the scheduled meeting when they knew the vote to open the fishery would be taken.

DNR Assistant Secretary, James W. Peck, answered that other states would be fishing, and it would be unfair for Maryland's fishermen to sacrifice while other states fish.

Senator Arthur Dorman, looking at Jim Price's press release showing the large YOY catch at Hambrooks Bar, said, "The index is skewed by a high catch at one Choptank River site."

Peck: "The sites are chosen in advance and are always the same to keep the scientific validity of the [YOY] index."

Captain Jim Price testified, "There is no compelling reason to re-open. We on the east coast are not starving. We have no need for this fish. Few commercials will benefit [his family fished commercially for five generations]."

Price also read a statement in the Senate hearing by retired DNR biologist, Joe Boone, who designed the YOY index: "The 1989 juveniles do not compose a dominant year class because they are not evenly distributed throughout the Bay."

Price added: "The State of Maryland did not act properly by with-holding this information [Hambrooks high index] from the ASMFC prior to the scheduled meeting when they knew the vote to reopen the fishery would be taken. The 1989's will not be able to spawn for another seven years. And the fishery should not be reopened until 1992 when the 1989's will be 18 inches."

Captain Bill Price (Jim's brother, who is a commercial Choptank River net fisherman), testified that the Choptank commercials he talked to "would rather wait two years before reopening the fishery, and they were not sure about the data from the Hambrooks site."

William Goldsborough of the Chesapeake Bay Foundation testified that the ASMFC's 1985 target of a three year average of 8 had been met, indicating that the status of the stock is such that it can bear a limited fishery.

After all of the striped bass testimony, striper interests filed out of the hearing room. The next hearing, on critical areas, was about to start.

I did a quick turnabout when Critical Areas Commissioner, John C. North II, prefaced his testimony about critical areas by a reference to striped bass: "I've been around rockfish all my life, but this is a change of position: The conservationists want to reopen—and the fishermen want to keep it closed!"

Tempers Flare on the Eastern Shore
... March 21, 1990

Bill Perry, an Atlantic Coast Conservation Association (ACCA), Capital Area Chapter Director, organized a membership drive meeting at the Tidewater Inn in Easton. Speakers and their assigned subjects were: Ken Penrod, Bass fishing; C. Boyd Pfeiffer, Fly fishing; Joe Reynolds of Field & Stream, Eastern Shore small boat fishing; Clay Gooch III, International fishing; Captain Chris Rosendale, Weakfishing tactics; Captain Levin F. "Bud" Harrison IV, Bluefish and black drum methods; and this writer, Center console boat fishing. There were 93 people present, a good turnout for the Eastern Shore.

As I remember that night, the first speaker was Penrod, who made an impassioned plea for a continued striper moratorium. After that, the meeting turned into a heated striper discussion. Pfeiffer gave his reasons for not striper fishing yet.

The charter captains were getting hot. They had been asked to talk about fishing, and they didn't think they were going to hear anything about stripers that night.

Next up was Joe Reynolds, who said he didn't give a hang about recreational fishermen, commercial fishermen, or charterboat captains —he cared about the fish. Reynolds asked for a show of hands, "How many support a continued moratorium?" Almost everyone held up their hand.

"How many want to see it reopened?" Reynolds asked. Six people: three charter captains, one charter captain's wife, and two men in the front row I didn't recognize, held up their hands.

When "Bud" (Buddy Harrison's son) Harrison got up to talk, he was mad. He turned to Reynolds: "Where were you when we were trying to get the rockfish stamp passed? [Harrison's $25 Rockfish Stamp bill was to provide funds to buy out commercial rockfish netters]. I didn't see you down there [at the Legislature] testifying." [Maybe Bud didn't know that Reynolds single-handedly closed Maryland's crashing shad fishery using the Endangered and Threatened Species Act].

Then, Bud gave an excellent talk on drum and bluefishing. Chris Rosendale, the other charter captain on stage, said a few words about rockfish and gave his talk about Bay trout fishing. Tempers were still hot.

Reynolds got up again. "My point is that there are reasonable people on both sides of the moratorium issue," he said, "and since that is the case, why not err on the side of the fish?"

Before things could disintegrate further, moderator Bill Perry brought the meeting to a close. "Thanks for coming out tonight," he said, breathing a sigh of relief.

What Did Maryland's Anglers Think?

Callers to Allan Ellis' "Maryland Sportsman" radio show on WCBM-AM 680 (103 callers in one hour) voted 94 to nine to continue the striper moratorium. "Included were a seafood restaurant, MSSA members, and many women anglers," Ellis said.

"MSSA Northwest Chapter President, Bert Gelvar, called in for his entire chapter," said Ellis, "He gave us 160 votes to continue the moratorium, but we couldn't count them—only his vote."

The Talbot County Chapter of the MSSA voted unanimously to continue the moratorium, along with several other MSSA chapters. The ACCA of Virginia (with 300 members in Maryland) voted to support a continued moratorium.

Meanwhile, the DNR stepped up its publicity to support the YOY data and reopen the striper fishery. Letters to the Editor and Guest Commentaries appeared in local papers all over Maryland from DNR officials, justifying their position.

Outdoor writers were still skeptical. Angus Phillips of the *Washington Post* interviewed people on both sides of the argument from Maryland to New England. Phillips quoted Joe Boone, Jim Price, Bob Pond, and Dick Russell, all of whom questioned reopening the striper fishery based on the Hambrooks Bar data. He quoted the DNR's Pete Jensen, who said "Next year's extremely conservative regulations—a one month season for both sport and commercial fishing—won't slow the recovery of rockfish from record low populations in the early 1980s." Phillips was puzzled by this "seemingly backward situation," where fisheries managers say, "Go get 'em," but fishermen urged restraint.

Even all of the feds were not convinced by the Maryland DNR that the moratorium should be lifted, including Dr. Robert Lippson, Assistant Director for the Northeast Region of the National Marine Fisheries Service (NMFS). Dr. Lippson is also Chesapeake Coordinator for NOAA, and has recently been assigned as liaison to Chesapeake area sportfishing groups [he supports commercial fishing, too]. Dr. Lippson: "I think they are skating on thin ice. They should keep the moratorium another two or three years. This puts too much pressure on the decision makers. My sense was that fishermen were ready not to fish for another five years, anyway."

I asked another NOAA official why NMFS would support lifting the moratorium before Congress, while at the same time they were moving to close the striper fishery in federal Atlantic coast waters. He turned to me, smiled, and summed it up in one word: "Politics."

The North Carolina Cows
... Winter, 1989/90

When the Mid-Atlantic Fishery Management Council met in Ocean City, Maryland in December, 1989, a motion was made to send a letter to the ASMFC requesting the striped bass fishery not be reopened in 1990. The motion was defeated 8 to 7 by a voice vote. Unfortunately, those council votes were not recorded, because accountability is the cornerstone of honesty. Well-paid council members are selected by a complicated process that begins with an appointment by state governors. Would state representatives be reappointed if they voted counter to the party line? Sure. You betcha.

John Bryson, the council's executive director, was hopping mad about the vote. He was concerned about North Carolina's imminent 96,000 pound commercial ocean striper fishery. The big 20- to 40-pound cows that winter off North Carolina would soon move into the Chesapeake Bay and other spawning areas.

"We thought it was important to let those big cow rock come back to spawn one more time," Bryson said. "Millions of eggs will be lost."

A warm winter moved most of the big fish northward early, and North Carolina's strict monitoring system discouraged many commercial draggers from participating. About 1,000 pounds of stripers were reported caught, mostly by beach haul seiners.

It still doesn't seem to me that those eight council members can take any pride in their vote.

Congress Hears About Hambrooks
... January 31, 1990

"It is my personal hope that the Atlantic States Marine Fisheries Commission will reconsider its decision and decide to wait at least one more year."
— U.S. Congressman Gerry Studds (MA), to Dick Russell.

Public sentiment against reopening the striper fishery based on a questionable 1989 Maryland Young-of-the-Year (YOY) index prompted U.S. Congressman Gerry Studds to hold a hearing of the Subcommittee on Fisheries and Wildlife Conservation and the Environment which he chairs. He wanted to hear more about the Atlantic States Marine Fisheries Commission's (ASMFC) decision to reopen the fishery, and the information on which that decision was made.

Recreational anglers hoped the hearing was a good chance for Congress to hear from conservation-minded sport anglers, and that their concerns might influence Congress to request the ASMFC to reconsider reopening. The ASMFC is an organization of states, and the Congress usually prefers not to interfere in states' rights.

Meanwhile, state and federal fisheries managers drew their wagons into a circle, and held meetings so they would all speak with one voice. Outside the bureaucrats' circle of wagons rode hostile Indians from the outdoor press, and representatives of associations representing tens of thousands of recreational anglers who wanted to see the fishery remain closed until there was no risk of losing their precious stripers again.

Only two of the "Indians" from outside the bureaucratic wagon circle were chosen to speak: Robert E. Lick of the New Jersey Marine Fisheries Council and James E. Price of the Chesapeake Bay Acid Rain Foundation, Inc.

Questions from Congressmen on the committee reflected their constituencies. Congressman Studds stated the concern of some people that "the survey of juvenile bass on which the Commission [ASMFC] decision rests did not provide a sound scientific basis for relaxing striper guidelines." Studds was also concerned about enforcement. He reiterated the Congress' policy of leaving management decisions to the states.

Congresswoman Claudine Schneider (RI) stated her concern that the reopening was premature and five years of sacrifice would be squandered. Her constituents told her they didn't trust the YOY survey and they begged to continue to make sacrifices to assure the stocks are truly healthy.

New Jersey Congressmen Frank Pallone, Jr., William J. Hughes, and Jim Saxton wanted a delay in ASMFC Amendment #4 for at least a year. Pallone announced he had filed H.R. 3903 that would designate Atlantic coast striped bass as gamefish. Saxton was surprised to learn it was the fishermen who opposed the relaxation of conservation measures. He said the fishermen realized they were headed for a problem.

Congressman George J. Hochbrueckner (NY) pled for relief for his commercial fishermen. He emphasized that most of the fish in his area are not from the Chesapeake, but from the Hudson.

Phil Coates, Chairman of the ASMFC's Striped Bass Board supported his commission's Amendment #4 decision to reopen the fishery. He stated confidence in the YOY index.

Jim Price of the Chesapeake Bay Acid Rain Foundation, who disagreed with the reopening, said the striper was still considered a threatened species in Maryland until such time as evidence warrants a change in that listing.

Price said YOY data clearly showed the 1989's were not a Bay-wide dominant year class. He suggested if data from two auxiliary Choptank sites were used in place of the high number from the Hambrooks site, the annual index would have been 15.0 instead of the reported 25.2. Good news but not enough to meet the mathematical trigger for reopening the fishery.

"Following six years of the lowest reproduction ever recorded," Price said, "it is difficult to believe that a species which had reached the point of total collapse in 1984, could be restored to a level that would even allow a limited fishery at the present time."

John Turner of the USFWS and John Douglas of the NMFS expressed confidence in the Maryland figures and the ASMFC's decision to open.

Robert E. Lick of the New Jersey Marine Fisheries Council said his long-time support of the ASMFC ended when they agreed in October, 1989 to permit the increased harvest of striped bass.

"I hope this Committee can determine why the ASMFC is so hell-bent on easing the restrictions on fishing for striped bass and ignoring the tremendous outcry of protest from most user groups throughout the striped bass range," Lick said. "On Long Island, New York fisheries managers heard testimony in excess of ten to one in favor of maintaining the restrictions for the taking of striped bass." Lick criticized New York's ASMFC representative for ignoring this overwhelming opposition and voting to reopen the fishery at their [ASMFC] meeting in New Hampshire in October. Lick also said ASMFC meetings should be made more public, and not held in remote locations.

The Maryland DNR's position, supported by USFWS and NMFS, and stated by DNR Assistant Secretary, James Peck, was that the YOY survey's science was good, and that the data was not "inconsistent." Under questioning, Peck said, "We invited lay people such as Mr. Price and others [including Bob Pond and this writer] to go out on these surveys—and they don't realize how the general index works and its history in the past, and the great variability and strong influence by one particular site than others."

Price had attended for 12 years. This writer attended surveys in the Choptank for six years, during which time I never saw Peck on the survey. My money says he'll take my place in the DNR boat in 1990.

Congressman Jim Saxton (NJ) asked Peck if Hambrooks was a new site.

"Yes, it was a new site," Peck answered.

"And sixty-three percent of this number came from one site?" Saxton asked.

"Yes," Peck answered.

Saxton asked if that was unusual. Peck answered it was not unusual at all.

Saxton later asked: "So, we are now contemplating permitting commercial fishing based on the sampling of one site, and a number which never occurred before in the history of this sampling process; is that correct?"

Peck answered commercial fishing was also based on other biological samplings that showed increased spawning, a five time increase in spawning females and juveniles, and the index confirmed those trends.

Turner of the USFWS stated the predicts for 1990 were for an even larger YOY stock, and he called Dr. Paul Rago for backup. Dr. Rago stated a "projection of the median value of 18.2, with a range between 5.7 and 55.5."

"That's a pretty safe bet," Studds said.

[Laughter.]

And so it went. For the interested striper angler who doesn't mind plowing through a lot of testimony to make up his own mind, the entire proceedings may be purchased for $4.25 from: Congressional Sales Office, Main Government Printing Office, Washington, D.C. 20402-9315. Order Serial #101-68 dated January 31, 1990, Stock No. 552-070-079-93-9.

Was the hearing a whitewash? Well, everyone got to speak his piece, though the tightly circled bureaucrats outnumbered the Indians. No decisions were made, but none were really expected. All in all, a colossal show, at great expense, with no end product. If you ever worked for the guvmint, you'll understand.

18

CATCH AND RELEASE

Catching and releasing sport fish has been in the public eye lately. The conservation ethic of releasing fish that began with fresh water trout and largemouth bass has spread to Chesapeake Bay waters.

Since the striped bass crash, concerned anglers have cheerfully returned the troubled stripers to the water. Many anglers have begun to release bluefish that will not be used for food.

Releasing fish does require some planning before the trip. Trollers who drag a rockfish a mile on heavy tackle before boating it are unduly stressing the fish. Medium tackle fished from a stopped boat allows fish to be brought to boatside relatively quickly. Others say ultralight tackle lets a fish fight too long, thereby causing stress.

Fishing with bait increases chances that a fish will swallow the hook, and later die. Small hooks and small bait like grass shrimp, said Captain Bobby Marshall at a Talbot MSSA meeting, kill a lot of stripers.

Barbless hooks have seen increasing use in recent years. I have replaced the two treble hooks on most of my surface popping plugs with a single barbless hook. Hook barbs can be filed off or bent flat with a pair of fishing pliers. This allows for the quick release of unwanted blues or illegal rock.

Biologists recommend leaving the fish in the water if possible, because handling a fish removes its protective coating of mucous. If the fish must be handled, wet gloves or a rag are easier on the fish.

In handling fish, don't hold it by sticking your hands into the gills. Biologists say that is like jamming your hands into someone's lungs, and can kill the fish.

The combination of a single barbless hook and a long-handled hookout (made like an old-fashioned button-hook) make releasing fish easier.

The barb on this lure's single hook has been filed off. A frazzled dressing of bucktail hair helps stabilize the plug as it moves through the water.

Slide the bend of the hookout down the leader until it engages the bend of the fish hook. Keep tension on the hook and raise the hand holding the hookout higher than the hand stretching the leader. Next, slide the fish off the barbless fish hook into the water.

If the fish is exhausted, hold it upright in the water, working it back and forth to force water through its gills until it swims away under its own power.

Hook-and-Release Mortality, Choptank
...August, 1988

"He out-catches me four to one on hook and line," said commercial fisherman Bill Price, nodding his head toward his brother, Charterboat Captain Jim Price who was busy reeling in a rockfish, "But, I'm better with nets," Bill added, a twinkle in his eye.

It was a hot, steamy day on the Choptank River. The order of business was to catch 80 stripers for a hook-and-release stress study conducted by DNR pathologist Dr. Eric May of the Oxford Lab.

The study was prompted by large numbers of stripers found floating below the Conowingo Dam, fish some thought had been overstressed by being repeatedly caught and thrown back—some from the high catwalk on the dam. Dr. May and his group investigated the Conowingo fish, and found that over 90 percent of the dead fish had hook damage around the mouth. Not necessarily conclusive because they also found dead catfish, carp, and largemouth bass.

On the Choptank, we fished from Captain Jim Price's 20-foot Mako. Looking around at the advertising t-shirts and baseball caps everyone seems to wear these days, one could see we had a diverse group, indeed. Jim wore a "Maryland Charterboat Association" shirt; his brother, Bill, wore a "Maryland Watermen's Association" cap; and I wore a "Maryland Saltwater Sportsfishermen's Association" shirt. In the days before the rockfish moratorium, the likelihood of seeing all three of those groups represented in one boat—much less speaking to one another—would have been pretty slim.

The fourth member of our group was Tara Cannava, a biologist working for the summer for the University of Maryland. She once worked with her brothers in Alaska, commercial fishing. She had the time of her life as rockfish came aboard: "This is fun. I can't believe I'm getting paid for this!"

Jim and Bill Price had fished the day before, taking 19 stripers on peeler crab, and by trolling. "It was a tough pick," said Jim, "the fish were hard to find." For those who are not familiar with the Prices rockfish expertise, both brothers commercially fished the Choptank, and their father too, for many years—Bill and his father with nets, and Jim with hook-and-line. They know every nook and cranny where rockfish hang out, and how to catch them. If they say it's a tough pick, believe them. It is.

On that first day, the fish we caught were badly stressed, according to experiment director, Dr. May. The fish were handled the way an average angler would in catching them, then the stripers were placed in net pens in

Jim and Bill Price show Tara Cannava a brace of Choptank stripers.

the Tred Avon River at the Oxford Lab for 72 hours. Fish caught the next day were placed in different pens.

On the day I fished with the Prices, the DNR had a 25-foot open "chase boat" standing by, equipped with a 500-gallon holding tank. As the Prices caught fish, the chase boat came alongside and the fish were transferred to the big holding tank. To relieve the fish of as much stress as possible during transport, oxygen was added to the water in the holding tank, plus salt and a tranquilizer.

DNR biologists Jim Van Tassel and Rudy Lukacovic manned the chase boat, along with their helper, college biology student Sandy Wagner.

"These fish are hard to catch," Jim Price said as he steered his Mako over a favorite bottom lump watching his depth finder, "there are not that many here." Jim picked up his lines to try another spot.

"The fish will stay in shallower, hotter water this time of year than Eric [Dr. May] thinks," Jim said. The sun beat down on us unmercifully. Air temperature was 95 degrees with humidity to match. Water temperature was in the high 80s. "We've caught them this time of year in water so shallow we were hitting bottom with the prop," Jim added.

"The heat and humidity around here kills me," Tara said, "I miss the mountains." Tara was raised in Anchorage, Alaska, where she said the humidity is "zero" and summer temperatures may average in the 60s or 70s.

"My golly, I've got a big one on," Bill joked as he strained at his boat rod, "I'll bet he measures six inches—between the eyes."

When there were 20 stripers in the chase boat's holding tank, I joined Van Tassel, Lukacovic, and Wagner for the ride back to the net pens at Oxford. The Prices continued to fish, finally catching that day's goal of 60 stripers by 3:30 p.m.

As Van Tassel and Lukacovic gently placed the stripers in their proper pens, Dr. May explained that none of the fish from the preceding day had died. "They've got it made," Dr. May said, "Look at all that natural feed inside the nets."

Dr. May said that striped bass are less stressed in more saline water because stripers are basically animals from a saltwater environment. Anglers who fish for striped bass in freshwater lakes would agree. It is nearly impossible to successfully release badly stressed hook-and-line stripers caught in fresh water when the water and weather are hot. Anglers in southern lakes keep their stripers.

The Choptank River stripers the Prices caught were released from the net pens starting at 72 hours after their capture. "We had 79 fish, total, and seven died," Dr. May said after the test, "Six of the seven we lost we

Dr. Eric May found no dead stripers floating in his net pens, indicating good survival of lower Choptank hook-and-line caught stripers.

attributed to anesthetic death. The other one died from delayed mortality due to transport and confinement."

The bottom line is that no fish died that could be attributed to being caught on hook and line by the Prices. But, please note that the Prices are expert fish handlers. Stripers will not survive the rough treatment you sometimes see out in Chesapeake Bay waters when fishermen angrily throw the fish at the water because they cannot keep them. Handle rockfish gently and as little as possible.

What next? Dr. May repeated the hook and release experiment in the upper Bay where water salinity is considerably less than it is in the Choptank River near Oxford. Results were interesting.

Hook-and-Line Survey, Susquehanna
. . . August, 1989

At 73-years young, Captain Earl Ashenfelter has fished the Susquehanna River between Port Deposit and Conowingo Dam for 57 years. He knows every rock in that part of the river personally, and what volume of water has to be released from the dam's turbines before he can get over those rocks to his favorite "holes" below the dam.

Not only does Captain Earl know every rock, but he has a name for each one, not all of them printable. Bang around these rocks for 57 years with your outboard motor (rowing in the early days) and you'd have some fancy names for them too.

"Here's as far as Captain John Smith got in 1607," said Captain Earl, pointing to appropriately-named Smith Falls near Port Deposit.

Conowingo Dam had just opened "five and three" turbines, and the water level in the Sussky was rising fast. Captain Earl steered a course between huge boulders. I wouldn't recommend anyone trying this with less than 50 years experience on the river. Even then, his motor banged over a few big ones, with some appropriate remarks from the captain. Knowledgeable Sussky anglers like Ashenfelter affix the tines from a pitchfork in front of the prop on their outboard motor lower units, and leave the motor in the "tilt" position so it will kick up over rocks without damaging the prop.

We were rockfishing this morning for the Maryland DNR. Captain Earl is one of the Bay charter captains who is paid to fish under the Watermen's Compensation Program that was instituted when the striper fishery closed. The DNR needs data about the status of the fishery. Charter captains fish a certain number of days to gather data called catch-per-unit-of-effort (CPUE), and the general health of stripers.

A DNR biologist with a scientific collection permit is always present on these trips. That day, the biologist was Dale Weinrich, who also works with herring and shad when they are running. Dale kept 10 rockfish over 18

DNR biologist Dale Weinrich weighs a Susquehanna striper.

inches long, sexed them, checked stomach contents, weighed and measured the fish, and took a scale sample from each one.

DNR Stock Assessment Coordinator, Steve Early had two objectives in the Bay-wide hook and line study that included our Susquehanna trip. First: "To evaluate the availability of 18-inch and larger striped bass to a hook and line fishery in Maryland's part of the Chesapeake Bay." With that data the DNR could apply the success rates to the number of anglers and determine how quickly they could catch up their quota (when the striper fishery is reopened). Creel limits would be included in a formula that includes CPUE and the number of fish available, and a season length could be determined.

"The second objective of the survey is to evaluate the composition of the stock Baywide," Early said. "What fish are where, and when, and their sex distribution. Also, if we divide their length by their girth, we can determine their physical condition. We already see that most of the Susquehanna River fish are over 18 inches."

Hook-and-line sampling is also taking place near Kent Island and the Bay Bridges, the Patuxent River, Choptank River, and other key spots down the Bay.

In the Choptank, Dr. Eric May already found that stripers caught and released in highly saline waters of the Choptank River survived nearly 100 percent. Not so in the fresher water up the Bay. High water and air temperatures, along with no salinity caused very high mortality of hook and released stripers.

When the striper fishery reopens, the DNR will have enough data to regulate the catch, Early said.

Captain Earl pointed out some familiar rocks as we trolled upriver in the "Susquehanna Skiff" he designed. (It is all mahogany, 16 feet long, and beamy enough for two anglers to sit side-by-side facing backward on the middle seat. It is powered by a 15 HP Johnson).

"Dale, I believe the water is up in the Hog Back, and don't forget, we have to try the Fish Pot," Captain Earl said as we trolled two bucktails, one from each side of the boat.

"I guess I've caught 250,000 pounds of rock in my time," Captain Earl said. "My biggest rock ever was a 33-pounder. I fought it on a Pflueger Supreme [bass-sized] reel. We were rowing a skiff trolling for walleye when it hit near a rock called Wagontop."

The water was rushing past the rocks at a furious clip. Captain Earl talked about the danger of wade-fishing here. "I've picked up a lot of people drowning in their waders," he said.

He has the only Coast Guard license of its kind, he said. No other guides have a license particular only to the Susquehanna River.

At Lee's Ferry, a 3-pound striper hybrid hit like 20 pounds of any other fish. The hybrids are white bass x striped bass crosses and have a deep stomach that gives them more purchase on the water. They gave us a fit. Dale took statistics of hybrids and released them as quickly as possible. We only kept pure stripers.

A 6-pound striper was next, on my line again. Dale took the water temperature. It was 78 degrees. Too hot for good fish survival. We would only take the 10 stripers Dale needed, and quit.

We trolled past "The Pipe." I caught a couple more stripers. I got cocky about it, kidding Dale who was up to then fishless. Captain Earl said Dale's turn would come. Good captains like Earl, as you know, can put the other guy's lure in any pocket they want. My luck began to change. Dale was polite enough not to mention it.

"Cap'n Earl, these fish are really thin," Dale remarked. Earl replied that the gizzard shad had been in short supply. "Too much water this year," he said.

Captain Earl Ashenfelter with a Susquehanna striper.

Captain Earl explained his system for trolling these waters. He used two level-wind reels on 7-foot rods. His leader was about two feet long, of the

Angler-Induced Mortality Rates for Striped Bass Less Than and Greater Than 18-Inches, Taken During 1989 Study at Oxford, Upper Bay, and Susquehanna River, MD

Location	Salinity	Length	% Mortality
Oxford	8.0 ppt	Less Than 18"	1.25
		Greater Than 18"	4.16
Upper Bay	3.0 ppt	Less Than 18"	23.81
		Greater Than 18"	38.39
Susquehanna	0.0 ppt	Less Than 18"	50.00
		Greater Than 18"	78.69

What the above chart of Dr. May's indicates, fishin' fans, is that you are going to kill *four out of every five* stripers over 18 inches that you catch and release in the Susquehanna, and about *one out of every three* you catch and release in the Upper Bay. Down the Bay, there is high survival. Up the Bay, catching-and-releasing stripers could result in dead stripers floating everywhere. A bad press for recreational anglers.

What can be done about the high kill in fresh water?

1. No fishing in the upper Bay.

2. Ben Florence had a good suggestion: No size limits. You keep every striper you catch until you fill out your limit. Just like duck hunting. If your stripers are six inches or 25 pounds, you keep them and stop fishing when you fill your creel limit. That way, you won't continue killing fish you can't keep.

3. On some Canadian rivers, even the salmon you release are counted as part of your creel limit. Whether you keep your salmon or not, when you catch your limit you must stop fishing.

Which system would work in the Chesapeake striper fishery? Probably number 1. Too many anglers, too much water, and too few police to enforce anything else.

---

same 14-pound test line that filled the reel. Split shot were added as necessary. A small 1/0 bucktail was decorated with half a plastic bass worm in Earl's secret color.

"Keep that bucktail inside the boat," Captain Earl kidded me, "that thing's so good rockfish will jump into the boat to get it."

Nearing a hotspot, Captain Earl let out one line "until it felt right" and handed the rod to the angler on the port side. Then he let the other line out, and handed it to the starboard angler. Next, he took the port rod back and let its line out "a little more."

It seemed Captain Earl ran his motor at so many different speeds it would be hard for a rockfish to gauge lure speed and grab it, but such was not the case. Grab it they did, with amazing regularity.

When we had our 10 stripers in the cooler, we gave up. A storm was rolling in. Thunder boomed above the sound of the motor. Captain Earl set a course over the tops of the same rocks that were showing on low water. He glanced back over his shoulder frequently at the approaching thunderstorm.

"Helluva buster coming," he mumbled at the storm.

Back at Townsend's Marina, Dale and I worked hard to beat the storm. He gutted the stripers to sex them and determine stomach contents, while I wrote the data on scale envelopes.

Fish scales have annual rings like the cross-section of a tree. Biologists count the rings to determine how old the fish is. The stripers this day measured from 18½ to 29 inches. You can guess who was lucky enough to catch the big one, and is now bragging about it. Their guts were all empty, either because of the lack of shad or because fish digest food rapidly in hot water.

As Maryland anglers know only too well, the striped bass we caught were under a moratorium. The ones we caught in the study were iced down and given to a local nursing home, and believe me, the tons of DNR paper work that followed this threatened fish through the system precluded any hanky-panky.

Besides, I have developed quite a taste for (legal) white perch since the 1985 striper moratorium.

Bedlam on the Choptank
... October, 1989

Halloween Day rain showers marked the end of Indian summer. In the week of perfect weather before Halloween Choptank River rockfish were breaking from the mouth of the Tred Avon River across the Choptank to Buoy 13.

It was bedlam. Anglers fished in the midst of hundreds of seagulls. Hundreds of fishermen who had refrained from rockfishing since 1985 stood in awe as big fish tossed hundreds of baitfish into the air amid flying spray.

Those anglers soon found out that there were no bluefish. Only rockfish that ran from five to 10 pounds. They kept fishing anyway. Dozens of boats chased after the concentrations of gulls as the fish moved. Some fished with lures armed with single barbless hooks to make it easier to release rockfish.

Like bluefish in a feeding frenzy, the Choptank rockfish anglers continued to catch and release, catch and release.

And therein lay a controversial problem. Weren't striped bass considered a threatened species? Wasn't it illegal to fish for them in Maryland? It was illegal, according to Woodland "Woody" Willing, Chief of Field Operations for the Natural Resources Police, "Our goal is to ensure compliance with the law. We issued warnings, and citations for the second violation."

"What's the difference between a warning and a citation?," I asked DNR Police Sergeant Joe Jones, who patrols the Choptank area.

"A warning doesn't cost you anything. A citation is $500," Jones said. He told of a western shore charterboat captain who brought a party to the Choptank to fish for stripers. "We caught over a hundred rockfish," the captain bragged to Sergeant Jones.

From the point of view of DNR officers who were already stretched pretty thin over a lot of water, catch-and-release rockfishing by recreational anglers did not have top priority. DNR police already had a pretty full plate, what with checking boating violations, crabbers, clammers, oystermen, fishermen, and ever-growing numbers of sea duck hunters.

From the point of view of anglers who hadn't seen good rockfishing for several years, it would be hard to stay home and not go striper fishing. They had heard Governor Schaefer say fishing would be allowed in 1990. Newspaper accounts quoted DNR officials: "It's pretty clear that the populations of rockfish have recovered."

If the guvmint says it's true, many fishermen figured, it must be. Let's go fishing, even if we have to release them.

Have the striped bass recovered? It depends on who you talk to. People who actually fish have a much different viewpoint from fisheries scientists and managers.

Along the Atlantic coast, Bob Pond striper fished really hard for a solid month in autumn. He worked hot spots he had fished since the 1940s. He did not catch a single striper! If anyone knows how to striper fish the Atlantic shore, it is Pond. He said many of the places that used to hold tons of stripers in the good times were no longer good.

"Where all three or four tidal rips in an area once all held striped bass, the fish that were there were together in one rip," Pond said. "It was strange. They were not spread out as you might expect."

Bob Pond loves to cast Atom plugs.

Captain Jim Price found much the same thing. As he caught rockfish for Dr. May's hook-and-release mortality study, he found Choptank River stripers were not spread out evenly in many locations as they once were, but in small pods in one or two places.

Neither were Choptank stripers as plentiful as one might expect, considering the striper fishery had been closed for five years. Price's goal was 30 stripers a day, and he had to work hard to catch that many in the summers of 1988 and 1989. In the halcyon years of rockfishing, his parties normally caught 100 stripers on a day trip.

In the summer of 1988, I accompanied Price on the Choptank as he caught stripers for the DNR. It was a tough pick. We finally caught fish, but way upriver. Another captain fishing for the DNR came all the way from the western shore, and trolled up the Choptank River in likely spots where anyone would expect to find rockfish. He caught nothing until Price put him on fish way upriver above Chancellor Point. If rockfish were plentiful, why couldn't this experienced captain catch them downriver?

Jim Price also questioned the total numbers of stripers available in the Choptank River. The fishery has been closed since January, 1985. The 1982 Choptank River juvenile index was a whopping 13.0. There were rockfish breaking all over the river and spilling out into the Bay for several autumns following 1982, Price says—even though there was heavy pressure on the '82s in an open fishery. But, the 1987 Choptank index at 12.1 was nearly as good as the 1982 index at 13.0, and the fishery was closed. "Where are all the 1987 fish?," he asks, "They are not here."

The breaking stripers mentioned at the beginning of this chapter were only in a narrow band extending across the Choptank near Oxford. We

Casting and trolling are favorite methods of catching Chesapeake stripers.

saw no breaking fish downriver nearer the Bay. Where were the endless schools of stripers you would expect to find after five years of a closed fishery? With no fishing pressure and a high 1987 index, rock should have been tearing up the water the entire length of the Choptank River, and out across the Bay.

A "Conservation Ethic"

It was gratifying to hear officials from National Marine Fisheries Service (NMFS) and the Maryland DNR in a press conference make warm and fuzzy statements that the adoption of a conservation ethic by sport-fishermen would help stripers. Catch and release was good, said the officials. We want to see sportfishermen keeping only the fish they want to eat, they added.

But, since we were attending a combined DNR and NMFS press conference for outdoor writers, no mention was made of a conservation ethic for commercial fishermen.

"Keeping Score" Video

A catch and release video was premiered at the April, 1990 press conference. Titled "Keeping Score," the video starred famous angler and outdoor writer, Lefty Kreh, and Dr. Robert Lippson of the NMFS, fishing at the Bay Bridges for stripers from a charterboat.

"Unfortunately, we always kept score by counting our catch," Dr. Lippson said in the video, "now we need to count how many we release."

Lefty said about the past, "Those were the days of the big scores. We thought it would never end."

Lefty demonstrated how to handle and release rockfish that they caught chumming with grass shrimp at a Bay Bridge piling. He showed how to use a long-handled de-hooker.

Lefty held a striper upside down which seemed to tranquilize it as he removed the hook, then he turned it right-side up for release. Lefty recommended cutting the leader and leaving the bronzed hook to rust out in a gut-hooked fish.

When the "Keeping Score" video was shown in an MSSA meeting at the Talbot County Free Library later, Charter Captain Bobby Marshall objected to striper catch and release fishing with grass shrimp.

"If you want to kill as many rockfish as you can," Captain Marshall said, "catch them on grass shrimp so they'll swallow the hook."

The video left some questions unanswered. It showed the "actors" catching and releasing a lot of stripers. Seen by the average angler, the video seemed to convey the impression that catching and releasing stripers would be allowed.

"No," said James Peck, Assistant DNR Secretary, "Not while the moratorium is in force."

Can we tie our boats to the Bay Bridge like they did in the video? "No," said DNR Fisheries Director, Pete Jensen, "This was experimental."

I had always believed it was illegal to tie up to the Bay Bridges, so I never did it. Charter Captain and *Arundel Sunpapers* outdoors columnist Bob Spore spoke up: He said it *was* legal to tie to the bridges, but illegal to tie to navigation aids like buoys. I won't tie up to a bridge or a buoy. I don't want to get a ticket on Spore's say-so.

How Many Sport Anglers?

In that April, 1990 press conference, DNR Director of Fisheries, Pete Jensen referred to 200,000 Chesapeake Bay Sport Fishing Licenses (CBSFLs) sold, plus 200,000 fresh water licenses. Bill Perry said the correct number of CBSFLs actually sold was 152,000, but several anglers can fish for each Pleasure Boat Decal and each charterboat license, so there is a multiplier effect.

I asked Jensen if the number given me six months before by the DNR's Howard King of 538,000 [estimated] anglers fishing under the CBSFL was correct. Jensen said 230,000 would be closer.

There are three reasons it is almost impossible to get an accurate count of Chesapeake Bay anglers fishing under the CBSFL: First, every angler doesn't have a separate license. Second, holders of the Tidewater Fishing License (commercial fishermen, oyster tongers, crabbers, etc.) can sportfish under that license without buying a CBSFL. Third, CBSFL data was not entered into the computer as is every other license in Maryland; i.e., barbers, hunters, boat and auto registrations, drivers, food service, etc. CBSFLs were not computerized for ready reference. From its beginning, CBSFL data was stored in the DNR's equivalent of shoeboxes.

Harley Speir of the DNR later gave me a copy of a letter titled in the best bureaucratic style, "Revision to the revision on the number of sport-fishermen in Chesapeake Bay." Changes had been made to previous estimates because of an incorrect number of Pleasure Boat Decals that had been supplied. In the letter, the most recent low estimate had been changed to 432,500 and the high guess was 546,500 anglers. Pinned down, Speir said he'd "go with a half-million."

Gene Mueller of *The Washington Times* had a final comment for DNR and NMFS officials: "The day will come when the Bay will not support a commercial fishery. Get used to seeing a LOT more of us recreational fishermen."

19

GAMEFISH?

Og Hauls in a Big One

One might imagine the first discussion of striped bass as a gamefish began about 3,000 B.C., when Og hauled in a big Chesapeake striper. He used a line made of monkeyvine. His "hook" was a bone gorge deftly concealed inside a soft crab. When Og's fish picked up the bait, Og hauled like crazy on the monkeyvine to get the fish ashore before it could spit out the gorge.

After quite a tussle, Og sat on the beach admiring the big silver fish flopping on the sand at his side. He guessed it weighed over 200-stone, setting a possible new record in his cave.

"Why do you go to all that trouble?" asked Og's commercial fisherman cousin, Boog, as he approached the panting gamefisherman. "I have a bunch of those *Roccus lineatus* in my weir just upstream."

"It's fun," Og replied. "I get a big kick out of outsmarting fish. And they are a whale of a lot of fun on light monkeyvines."

"You're wasting your time," Boog said, "I can get 300 clams for my mess of *Roccus* right now. Your fishing outfit cost you that much."

"I just feel that more of our cave people benefit from sportfishing for these *Roccus*," Og said. "I think it would be a more even distribution of the resource among the people if it's a gamefish."

There! Og had said the dreaded word: "Gamefish." Boog didn't want to hear it. His side of the family had commercial-fished weirs on the Chesapeake Bay since time immemorial. It was traditional.

"Think of all the little old ladies in the caves upstream," Boog countered, "They never get a chance to fish monkeyvines. They should have a right to eat some *Roccus* too. And, if I can make a few clams at the same time, what's the harm?"

"Economics," Og replied. "In another 5,000 years, a University of Maryland study will show that *Roccus* is worth 10.7 times more as a gamefish than it is as a commercial fish. By then, there will only be 365 weir fishermen, but 500,000 vine anglers. There will be log canoes out on the Bay everywhere, carrying vinefishermen willing to pay big clams to catch *Roccus*. And, think of the additional clams generated by the tourism industry: Cave motels, vine-rigging shops, restaurants. . . ."

"Wait!" Boog interrupted, "Who will supply the restaurants with *Roccus* if it's a gamefish? And, what about our historic tradition of weir fishing?"

"We'll raise *Roccus* hybrids in ponds for the restaurants," Og said, "Of course, we have to invent hybrids first. Then, you weir fishermen can hack out log canoes to carry vinefishermen. You certainly know where to find *Roccus*. You'll make a lot of clams carrying sports in the summer. You won't have to pick fish out of your weirs with frozen fingers in the wintertime, either. You'd trade the boom-and-bust of commercial fishing for comfort and a steady income all year. You could call it charter-log-fishing."

Boog was not convinced. He couldn't imagine not fishing his weirs during the spring spawning season. He once made enough clams, tax free, in two days to pay off the mortgage on the cave. And, he got just as big a thrill feeling a bunch of big *Roccus* bump against his weir as Og did wrestling his single fish in on a monkeyvine. Imagine, Boog thought, doing all that work for just a single fish!

"How will you vine anglers get gamefish status for *Roccus* when we weir fishermen own the legislature?" Boog asked. (Maryland wasn't invented yet, but the Eastern Shore Delegation was). "We can get a gamefish bill killed with only a single smoke signal."

"Numbers," Og said. "Pure and simple numbers. We will form organizations. We will work to vote your legislators out and ours in. After all, you will only be 365 weirmen against 500,000 vine anglers. We'll get it done, you'll see."

"I don't think *Roccus* will ever be a gamefish," Boog said, but his conviction was fading. "*Roccus* will always be worth a lot of clams. Besides, there are plenty of *Roccus* out there. If I don't clean them out, they'll soon clog up the Bay."

"We WILL make *Roccus* a gamefish," Og said, determined, "Even if it takes 5,000 years!"

And that, Chesapeake Striper fans, is how it all began.

An Early Rockfish/Gamefish Bill

George Gambrill and his Maryland Rockfish Protective Association (MRPA) tried to get a rockfish gamefish status bill through the Maryland Legislature for years. He was one dedicated man. I didn't know him, but years later I heard from his son. At boat and fishing shows, I talked to folks at the MRPA table, but never joined. They didn't have a good press in those days. I remember they were treated like second class citizens; many people had been convinced by the commercials that there was no reason for gamefish status when there were "plenty of rockfish." I heard that same song for years.

The perennial MRPA rockfish/gamefish bill was to be heard by a Maryland Senate Committee at 10 a.m., we thought. We were too wet behind the ears to realize the games that legislators play when they want to scuttle a bill. Carole and I took a day off from work and went to Annapolis to hear all about the benefits of striped bass being declared gamefish. We thought it was locked in concrete. What did we know?

At 10 a.m., a hearing on slot machines started. Recess for lunch. More about slots. Looking around, we saw no anglers, no commercial fishermen. What was going on? In mid-afternoon it was announced the rockfish bill hearing had been rescheduled for 7 p.m. Everyone knew about the new time but us.

Carole and I had dinner at a local restaurant. Back to the hearing room, which by then was packed with commercial fishermen. Now, I understood the delay. Delegate Randolph Harrison, then Chairman of the committee that would hear the bill, supported commercial fishing on rockfish. He was from Tilghman Island.

Testimony was taken from both sides. The commercial testimony was cheered by the 200 or so commercials, who loudly booed George Gambrill's rationale for gamefish status.

After the testimony, Delegate Harrison called for all who supported the gamefish bill to stand. Carole and I stood. We looked around at a sea of hostile faces. In the entire hearing room, there were only a half-dozen people standing. I saw no outdoor writers I knew, which I thought was strange, considering the importance of this bill to recreational fishermen. It was a tense moment for us. I began to wonder if we could get to our car without coping with a hostile mob outside. These boys were angry. And healthy-looking. I weighed about 145 pounds then, no match for even one of them.

"All not in favor of this bill, please stand," Harrison said. At least 200 cheering, clapping commercial fishermen stood up. We were still sitting amid what seemed like a jillion hostile commercials standing up, glaring down at us.

"Mr. Gambrill," Harrison said with some glee, "You have had your day in court!"

Many years later, Randolph Harrison's nephew, Levin F. "Buddy" Harrison, Jr., and his son, Bud, were to testify in favor of a $25 "rockfish stamp" that would provide funds for a commercial buyout and make the striped bass a gamefish in Maryland.

What goes around, comes around.

MSSA Begins to Learn the Gamefish Ropes
... May, 1983

When the Maryland Saltwater Sportfishermen's Association (MSSA) was formed in the early 1980s, I joined. MSSA President Mike Pivec and Vice President, Tim Fisher wisely chose rockfish conservation as their top priority. That's why many of us joined MSSA. Rockfish were in decline, and something needed to be done about that. Early discussions centered on gamefish status and an outright closure.

MSSA President Mike Pivec handed out prizes at an early bluefish tournament. Left to right: Pivec, Lyle McLaughlin, John Schuelling, Tim Fisher, and Rich Novotny (behind Fisher).

Pivec commented on the failure of House Bill 490—"Making the Bluefish a Sportfish in the Chesapeake Bay," in Volume 1, No. 1 of MSSA's *Tidelines* (May, 1983): "The wishes of the people don't count. It seems that no matter how many people your particular elected official represents, you can still be sold out." Pivec told how he testified with "good, sound biological and statistical information . . . yet we were ignored."

Then, the watermen testified. Pivec had nothing good to say about the watermen's presentation. "However, they were successful in getting this bill defeated," Pivec said, "The fix was in."

After this sobering experience, MSSA officers zeroed in on a striped bass moratorium. A gamefish attempt would come later.

New Zealand's System: The Future of Fishing?
. . . December, 1987

"SPORTFISHERMEN WANT ROCKFISH FOR THEMSELVES" read a headline in the Easton *Star-Democrat* about the Easton meeting of the Sports Fisheries Advisory Commission (SFAC). The article itself, written by Meredith Goad, was a well-balanced account of the meeting, but the headline writer didn't take the time to read her article. Scare headlines like this worsened the recreational/commercial rift that promised to be wide enough anyway when the striped bass fishery is reopened.

Most recreational anglers already feel there is no reason for a net fishery on stripers. Others say gillnets and modern fishing methods are so efficient that the resource can be destroyed overnight.

The system that may prove most acceptable to everyone—but, far in our future—is New Zealand's: Their fishing philosophy is based on natural resources belonging to *all* of the people equally. New Zealand's recreational anglers get first crack at the fish. The unharvested surplus is available to commercial harvesters who *pay for the right* to harvest those fish. Money collected from the commercial harvesters is used to manage the fishery.

"Since the fish belong to all of the citizens of New Zealand, there is no cost to those who harvest for their own pleasure," according to the Sport Fishing Institute.

Recreational fishing organizations everywhere: Take note. New Zealanders may have the best way to manage natural resources that belong to all people equally.

Fisherman Readers Said "Ban the Nets"
... March, 1988

A report in *The Fisherman* magazine about commercial bias on the Governor's White Paper Committee brought in many thoughtful, articulate letters from recreational anglers.

In the Maryland Legislature and among many hook-and-line anglers, there was support for a permanent buy-out of commercial nets using funds from the Chesapeake Bay Sportfishing License, or from the special $25 rockfish stamp proposed by Buddy Harrison.

Almost every letter to *The Fisherman* said, "Ban the nets." Most voiced their concern for the fish by stating that it would be better to leave the moratorium in place than to reopen commercial fishing. Creel limits for private boat, charter boat, and commercial fishermen should be the same for all, said many.

(Note: In editing this article that appeared in *The Fisherman*, I took out the names of many anglers who wrote in originally. They may have changed their minds—but I doubt it. They were really upset. But, mentioning their names years later might embarrass them. I'd rather avoid that).

There were too many letters to include every good idea from all of them, but some of the highlights are listed below, all from Marylanders except where noted, leading off with one of the zippiest:

"I've seen rockfish netted all through the moratorium," said one reader who lives in a commercial fishing town on the Eastern Shore. He mentioned some of his hard-working friends who made a good living on the water without catching a fish, and added:

"It's the lazy-ass commercials [fishermen] that want to set their nets and go home and watch the soap operas on TV. These people don't want to work. That's the reason they are raising so much hell. The more hell they raise, the more money they get to give up their nets."

Paul Gambrill wrote, "There should not be any gill nets allowed in the Chesapeake Bay at any time. My father was President of the Maryland Rockfish Protective Association from day one, for about 30 years, until his death. We wanted seasonal control of gill nets to give the rockfish a chance to spawn, but our great politicians sided with the commercial boys every time." (I know. We witnessed such a hearing).

ON COMMERCIAL ROCKFISHING: "The [commercials] basic objective is to make the most money in the shortest period of time. Again, the root of all evil is money," said one angler.

"No sale of rockfish at all," said another, "They [commercials] have survived since the moratorium. Don't allow commercial fishing for rockfish in the Chesapeake, or we'll be right back where we started— no rockfish."

And, "If a commercial fishery could not be sustained with the numbers of fish we had in the 1970s, how can we possibly sustain a commercial fishery now?" asked one man.

Another told of having some good rockfishing many years ago in the Potomac until a netter made a set across his anchor line. The next day, he could catch no rockfish there—nor could the same netter!

The lack of consideration that was shown to this angler by the Potomac netter echoes a similar experience I had at the Bay Bridges: I was casting a bucktail to a Bay Bridge piling just 20 feet away when a netter came between me and the piling, setting his net—and *gave me a dirty look!*

ON THE STRIPED BASS WHITE PAPER COMMITTEE: "Each group [on the Committee] should have an equal number of supporters to relay information from the group they represent," said one man who also voted for aquaculture and watermen's assistance. He knew how much people hate to write letters, so he composed a letter his Dorchester County friends agreed with, and they signed it, saying: "No more gillnets for rockfish, hook-and-line commercial fishing only, and under no circumstances should the commercial fisherman or charterboat angler be allowed to take more rockfish than the sportfisherman."

Many letters expressed the same dismay as the 75-member fishing club chaired by Al Smith and Frank Shaffer, quote: "We protest the biased attitude of the Whitepaper Committee toward commercial interests."

ON GAMEFISH: "It is difficult to imagine any business in Maryland that is not somehow benefitted by sportfishing," said one DNR official.

The potential for additional tourism should give the Maryland Department of Economic and Employment Development the best incentive to jump on the "Striped bass/gamefish" bandwagon (behind Governor Schaefer, of course).

"My out of state friends no longer come here to fish," one Maryland resident said. He was one of many to echo that statement, including several out-of-staters: "The money is spent where the fish are," said one Pittsburgher, "Look at the western basin of Lake Erie [walleye] or the latest hotspot, western lake Ontario [salmon]—to see what happens when sport fishermen get priority on fish stocks. Should there be any question concerning economic rationing of the rockfish stock?"

And, "I'm for whatever it takes to restore the King of the Chesapeake Bay to his throne," said a New York resident who fishes in the Bay, "Commercial fishermen cannot be allowed to ravage this precious natural resource and deprive millions of people from their favorite sport."

A Delaware angler who owned property on the Bay and fished here, feels that the reason he caught [and released] so many rockfish in 1987 was the absence of nets. Many folks outside Maryland had a proprietary feeling about Chesapeake Bay stripers!

"What kind of revenue does the sportfisherman generate for the State [of Maryland] as compared to 425 commercial netters?" asked another angler. "And, how many more Chesapeake Bay Sport Fishing Licenses would be sold if the striper was a gamefish?"

Could striped bass/gamefish happen? Sure, the letter writers said. Governor Schaefer has said he will support gamefish status. Then, the legislature must be convinced (by 500,000 Chesapeake anglers) that gamefish status for the striped bass will provide the most economic benefit for Maryland. Legislators must hear from a half-million sportfishermen instead of 400 commercial fishermen.

Governor Schaefer successfully promoted the Baltimore waterfront as a tourist attraction when he was mayor. Imagine the benefits to the state if he could say Maryland is the:

"ROCKFISH CAPITAL OF THE WORLD"

A Rockfish/Gamefish Attempt
... Fall, 1988

Maryland Governor William Donald Schaefer announced that he felt gamefish status for striped bass (rockfish) was possible, and that commercial rockfishing should remain closed "because we'll be back to where we were four years ago, when rockfish were being depleted so dramatically."

His statement was the first time anyone could remember a Maryland Governor saying rockfish should be a gamefish, and that the commercial fishery should remain closed.

Rich Novotny, then President of the 4,000-member MSSA said he would never allow the "rape of the rockfish" again.

The MSSA retained Maryland lobbyist, Bruce Bereano, to help in the 1988 legislative battle to attain gamefish status and ban the commercial sale of striped bass. Bereano helped organize the MSSA's Political Action Committee (MSSA-PAC).

MSSA members began to gather support for their rockfish/game-fish bill (S.B. 603). They tried to convince legislators that gamefish status for rockfish is the highest and best use of rockfish for the greatest number of Marylanders.

Seventy-two commercial fishermen and 62 charterboat captains working under the Watermen's Compensation Program were paid annually between $2,000 and $10,000 each since the moratorium, according to Novotny, who favored some financial support for the commercials—but "not forever." He did not agree to a buyout of all nets, but preferred a compensation program with a definite sunset, possibly paid for by a rockfish stamp that would be required for anglers when the fishery reopens.

Buddy Harrison of Tilghman Island, who has fished Governor Schaefer, had proposed a $25 Rockfish Stamp for anglers who wanted to fish for stripers when the fishery reopened.

Buddy figured, conservatively, that if 100,000 recreational fishermen bought the $25 stamp it would generate $2.5 million to buy out netters who once fished for rockfish. Buddy found support for his proposal, even from some members of the Eastern Shore Delegation, who told him their commercial fishing constituents would not be hurt by the proposal.

Also suggested was that the rockfish stamp be continued and stamp monies be used for hatcheries or rockfish research after the commercial fishing buyout. The Rockfish Stamp Bill did not pass.

Back to S.B. 603: "We do not want the moratorium lifted until the DNR says we have a viable fishery," said Novotny, "we don't want to harm the species." Novotny also wanted the DNR to have the power to set realistic size and creel limits if and when the fishery is reopened: "Let the profession-als manage the fish."

DNR Secretary Brown seemed to wield more power under Governor Schaefer (witness the Gov's backing of the DNR's one-goose limit in spite of heavy pressure from commercial hunting outfitters). It seemed that Governor Schaefer listened more to the DNR than to commercial interests.

Aquaculture, particularly the pond raising of rockfish hybrids, had been suggested to supply commercial markets, and Novotny saw this as the "only future for a commercial rockfishery in Maryland." He cited the successful commercial pond-raising of catfish throughout the south as a model for the future of rockfish aquaculture.

Commercial fishing advocates often alluded to large amounts of money generated in the marketplace by rockfish sales, but a 1980 survey by the University of Maryland showed that sportfishing generates 10.7 times more money per pound of fish than a commercial fishery.

"We want to make two things clear," said Tim Fisher, MSSA Vice President and Chairman of the MSSA's Legislative Committee working with Bereano, "First, we don't want to control the fishery—that's the DNR's job. Second, the climate is right this year to make the rockfish a gamefish—but, we need grass roots support in the form of letters and phone calls to Legislators. It only costs 25 cents to call or write, and we need to show the legislators that there is a tremendous voter base that they need to be aware of."

The MSSA took additional steps to gather support for matters of concern to recreational anglers and boaters: The MSSA joined with the Chesapeake Bay Yacht Racing Association (CBYRC) and the Chesapeake Bay Yacht Club Association (CBYCA) in an umbrella group called The Chesapeake Bay Recreational Boating Council (CBRBC). If that seems like a lot of letters to digest, the reader only has to remember one fact: The umbrella group (CBRBC) has a total of 50,000 members. That is a lot of votes!

Lobbyist Bereano felt that the rockfish/gamefish bill would be a "hot potato" in the 1989 Maryland Legislature, said Fisher. It was.

The watermen had always been on the offensive, and disorganized recreational anglers always lost the battle to protect the rockfish resource, but: "Now we are on the offensive for the first time in memory," said Fisher.

"This is a war to save the rockfish," said Novotny, "The timing is right, and it's a battle we can win. We want to get the rockfish/gamefish bill passed this year. But, if our bill does not pass, we will fight to keep the fishery closed until it does pass."

A Surprise from Dr. Brown
... March 7, 1989

"I favor the rockfish as a gamefish idea," Governor Schaefer said, "In the interim we need to do what we can to help the true watermen who have been hurt by the loss of the rockfish." This statement preceded a joint hearing by the Maryland Legislature on S.B. 603, the Rockfish/Gamefish bill.

Maryland DNR Secretary Dr. Torrey C. Brown was in a bind. He was on the "Schaefer Team," which meant he'd better stand up and salute the Governor's Rockfish/Gamefish plan. But, he usually supported commercial rockfishing. How would he handle that?

The joint hearing room was packed with commercial and recreational fishermen. If the ice storm outside had deterred anyone from attending, it wasn't evident from the crowd. Chairman Clarence Blount said it was the largest crowd that he had seen for a hearing in 18 years. The MSSA had taken a page from the watermen's book and hired busses, and organized car pools.

Senator Gerald W. Winegrad stated the bill was premature, that cleaning up the Bay had precedence, not who is going to get what share of the fish.

Watermen said rockfish should be evenly divided between commercial and recreational fishermen, and asked for a chance to show that a limited fishery could work. It would be easier to regulate 3,000 watermen, they said, than 500,000 sportfishermen.

MSSA lobbyist, Bruce Bereano, said bill drafters had made provision for the watermen with a $1 million compensation program.

Dr. David Rockland, then the Sport Fishing Institute's fisheries economist, stressed the economic benefits of a recreational striped bass fishery at $51.4 million versus a commercial fishery at $2 million, where the commercial catch in pounds was almost five times higher.

"With only 17 percent of the [1980] total catch in the Maryland Chesapeake Bay, sport fishing generated 96 percent of the economic value," Dr. Rockland testified. "Comparatively, the commercial fishery took 83 percent of the fish, but generated only 4 percent of the value."

Then, Dr. Brown surprised attendees by asking for an amendment that would not make rockfish a gamefish unless all other coastal states did the same, saying it was not fair for other states' commercials to be able to harvest rockfish when Maryland watermen could not. It seemed to me that amendment was Dr. Brown's way of squeezing out from between the Schaefer gamefish rock, and the commercial fishing hard place. His proposal had a chilling effect on S.B. 603, which was referred for summer study, and died there.

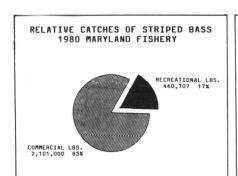

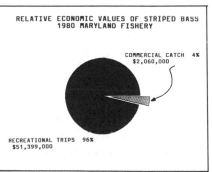

Courtesy of Sport Fishing Institute.

Buster Said, "Buy Up the Net"
... August 22, 1987

"We made one mistake when we closed the rockfishery," said Louis N. "Buster" Phipps, Jr., "Right then we should have bought up all the net." Buster Phipps was Deputy DNR Secretary under James Coulter in the early 1980s, but retired before the 1985 striper moratorium.

I had mentioned striped bass gamefish status to Buster at Clay Katski's West Ocean City Blue Marlin Invitational Tournament banquet, and he surprised me with the quote above.

"It wasn't the first time we closed rockfishing," Buster said. "Jim Coulter was in the hospital. Ben Florence and Joe Boone recommended we close it [in the spawning season], and I did. They knew more about rockfish than anybody. When Coulter came out of the hospital, he reversed my decision, but the [net] fishery was closed for about six months."

"I think we should have bought all the net for several reasons: First, I think we should eliminate all net fishing in the Bay and fish with hooks only—the resource will not stand the pressure of a net fishery. And, most of the net was twine then—it was going to rot anyway. I have a lot of respect for watermen and their way of life. They are a proud people. They didn't want charity. Buying the net would have been a way of compensating them. They are all skilled fishermen, and I think they can make a better living with hooks, taking people fishing."

"Rockfish will be gamefish sooner or later. Just keep putting in that bill, and sooner or later it will pass. I don't think MSSA needed that lobbyist. Sometimes they hurt you. A lot of legislators don't trust them. What you have to do is get all those sportfishermen to put public pressure on the legislators. Grass roots works best."

"I didn't mean to unload both barrels on you," Buster said, almost apologetically. No problem, Buster. I can dig it. I wish you hadn't retired.

A Federal Gamefish?
... January, 1990

Congressman Frank Pallone, Jr. (NJ) earned the undying respect of the Jersey Coast Anglers Association (JCAA) with his January, 1990 bill to make Atlantic coast striped bass gamefish. Pallone's bill (H.R. 3903), co-sponsored by Congressman H. James Saxton (NJ), would make it unlawful to commercially harvest striped bass in coastal waters or in federal waters offshore. The federal bill was announced at a combined press conference with JCAA President, Tom Fote, at Toms River.

"When the ASMFC decided to open the waters of the Chesapeake to commercial netting and reduced the minimum allowable size limit, they completely turned their back on nearly a decade of stringent conservation measures," Pallone said in announcing H.R. 3903. "The only conclusions I could draw from that decision were that either the ASMFC is not serious about responsible conservation and management of a threatened species, or that they are more sympathetic toward commercial fishing interests than recreational, or both."

"Commercial fishing, particularly netting operations, have a much more severe impact on the resource than recreational rod and reel fishing," Pallone added, "The very nature of commercial netting, which is capable of snaring huge numbers of fish in a completely undiscriminating way, is at odds with the goals of protecting a severely depleted fishery."

One of the main reasons for the federal gamefish bill, Fote said, was that the ASMFC opened the fishery using questionable data. Data questioned, Fote added, by many newspapers, magazines, and most recreational fishing organizations along the Atlantic coast. Fote also mentioned that New Jersey had banned commercial netting of stripers and had a 10-striper bag limit. "Had other states followed suit," Fote said, "we would not have this problem." He said New Jersey anglers suffered due to mismanagement of [striper] stocks by other Atlantic coast states.

What are the chances that H.R. 3903 will pass? Slim to none. Sitting on the House Merchant Marine and Fisheries Committee with Pallone, Saxton, and Claudine Schneider (pro-recreational) are Representatives Gerry Studds (MA), Roy Dyson (MD), and Helen Bentley (MD). Representative Studds wrote me that commercial hook-and-liners in his home state have a right to participate in the fishery, too. Rep. Dyson has always supported commercial fishing for stripers. Rep. Bentley never replied to my letter.

More than the opposition of these politicos, says Dallas Miner of the American Fishing Tackle Manufacturers Association (AFTMA), is the fact that H.R. 3903 would manage a species, something congress has historically shied away from.

Striped Bass Conservation Coalition
... June 2, 1990

Dr. David Rockland, Executive Director of the *Times-Mirror* Conservation Council, convened a meeting at the Vista Hotel in Washington, D.C.

Present were representatives of large sportfishing organizations from Maine to Texas.

Dr. Rockland stated it is the policy of the *Times-Mirror* publishing group to be a positive influence on conservation through its numerous magazines and newspapers that reach 33 million readers.

The purpose of the conference was to discuss the possibility of game-fish (no-sale) status for striped bass on a state-by-state basis. Congressman Pallone's federal gamefish bill, H.R. 3903, though it has nine sponsors, is not given much chance of passage since it preempts states' rights. Eric Burnley reminded us that the Studds Amendment [that forces Atlantic coast states to comply with ASMFC management recommendations] *also* preempted states' rights. Dr. Rockland added that the two committees that would hear the bill are chaired by Congressmen with strong commercial fisheries constituencies, and they are unlikely to bring the bill up for a hearing.

There was a general consensus that the ASMFC has failed to manage the striped bass resource. The hodge-podge of regulations the ASMFC approved under Amendment #4 for coastal states was cited.

Bob Pond of Stripers Unlimited said southern states with stripers in reservoirs would probably agree on national gamefish status for stripers. Someone said there was no precedent.

Bob Lick of New Jersey said the precedent was migratory water-fowl management. Lick compared the striper's migrations with those of waterfowl.

Dick Russell of the Striped Bass Emergency Council listed the reasons he thought the ASMFC had failed to regulate striped bass:

• The YOY anomaly used as a trigger to reopen.
• Illegal fishing along the coast.
• Lack of enforcement.
• The bycatch of coastal stripers is now at MSY (Maximum Sustainable Yield), even before reopening.

Andy Loftus of the Sport Fishing Institute (SFI) took it one step further, "It looks like the opened fishery will be at the 'Recovered Fishery' rate, not at the 'Transitional Fishery' rate." Loftus cited the high rate of bycatch and hook-and-release mortality.

Les Smith of the 30,000 member Atlantic Sportfishing Association (ASA) agreed the ASMFC had failed on striper management: "I've even seen [ASMFC] commissioners argue with their own biologists."

One representative said the ASMFC lost credibility when they allowed adjustments in mortality from Amendment #4—"Too many exceptions," he said. "Most of us feel Amendment #4 will fail," he added, "even our limited quota can't be enforced."

Dr. Rockland swung the meeting back to Gamefish Status: "Let's talk 'Prohibition of Sale' for striped bass instead of 'Gamefish,' which conjures up an image of rich sportfishermen vs. the poor watermen."

Tom Fote of the 50,000 member Jersey Coast Anglers Association (JCAA) reported that he expected to have "most of Congress on his bill [H.R. 3903, gamefish] by the end of the year." Fote felt the President, Congress, and most of the ASMFC was for no-sale. Fote added that a 1,600 member Delaware fishing club had joined the JCCA.

Eric Burnley of the ACCA of Virginia (ACCA/VA) said he must work with Virginia watermen. He also said Virginia's five stripers for charterboat anglers was approved by the ASMFC, and "Now Travelstead [Virginia Marine Resources Commissioner] is back with a two-fish limit for everyone."

New York resisted endorsement of gamefish status at this time (they felt lucky to have outlawed haul seines—a "dirty fishery"), although they would not "oppose the idea."

I attempted to come up with wording all would agree with:

"How about 'We support the management of coastal striped bass for the best and highest uses of the greatest number of U.S. citizens?'" New York did not oppose, but did not support. One New York representative who previously spoke in favor of commercial fishing said, "That means commercial fishing!"

"Not so," said Walter Fondren III, Director of the Coastal Conservation Association, "We have the statistics to prove otherwise."

Fondren continued: "We have to do away with the perception that 'Equal Access' means that 400,000 anglers get the same amount of fish as 11 commercials. We must also do away with the [commercial] perception that sport fishermen are 'elitists.' Particularly since one-third of *all* Americans fish. That's a lot of elitists."

Reports as to the possibility of no-sale in Atlantic coast states included the information that six states did not allow sale; eight would allow sale, but two of those had no commercial fisheries.

Rich Novotny of the 6,000 member MSSA reported they would be back to the Maryland Legislature in 1991 with a no-sale bill. He said, "The MSSA supports Congressman Pallone's H.R. 3903 federal no-sale bill, and companion bills by Senator Roth and Representative Saxton to eliminate striped bass possession in the EEZ (Exclusive Economic Zone, or federal waters from 3 to 200 miles offshore)."

The meeting ended on the positive note that striped bass as a gamefish (no-sale) is possible, and highly probable.

Prohibition of Sale

Prohibition of sale is an alternative to legislation that would not allow commercial fishing for striped bass, according to Dr. Dave Rockland.

"Try to regulate the gear and there is always a way around it," said Dr. Rockland. "If you say 'hook-and-line only' they longline. As long as there exists a market incentive to take wild things and the access to those wild things is open, people will overharvest."

20

STRIPER TACKLE AND TECHNIQUES

Tackle

BAY TROLLING TACKLE: For deep trolling, I use old True Temper beryllium copper step-tapered rods with roller tips made in the 1950s. The reels are from the same era: Either a Pflueger Akerite model 2068 with star drag, or a similar Ocean City "Bay City" trolling reel. These reels are no longer available, except at garage sales. One trolling outfit has modern 40-pound test Berkley Nicro wire line on it, and one has 30-pound test Berkley Dacron line. If it sounds like I'm in the antique tackle business, so be it. Collecting old tackle was once a hobby. We will look at modern Bay trolling tackle when we go fishing on a charterboat in another chapter.

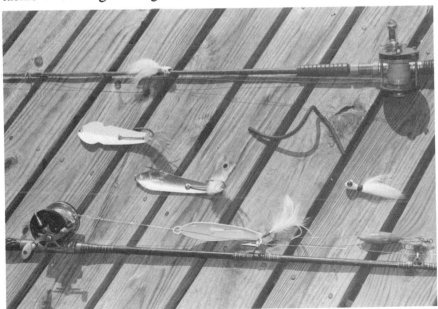

The author's bay trolling tackle: Top rod with Akerite reel is rigged with a 7/0 ruby-lips bucktail. The old "Bay City" outfit on the bottom is rigged with an 8-ounce in-line sinker and an 11/0 Crippled Alewive spoon. Between the rods from the left: #21 Tony and #34¹/₂ Drone, a red surgical hose eel, and a 9/0 banjo-eye bucktail.

Over the years, I have refined my striper tackle to three (well, maybe four or five) basic outfits. But, every time I think I have the ideal outfit something else comes along to distract me.

If brand names and model numbers are mentioned, it is only for example. Some of my newer stuff is a bit pricey, but there is a lot of striper tackle in the moderate price range that will do the same job. Much of my tackle is old and long since out of production, but I like to use classic and collectable tackle and I haven't worn it out yet.

ULTRALIGHT SPINNING TACKLE: My ultralight spinning outfits are a bit too light for the average angler's striper fishing. If the drag is not set exactly right, the four-pound test line snaps too easily when a striper over two pounds hits. A Berkley model LR20-5'F Lightning Rod and a Penn 220GR spinning reel make a balanced ultralight outfit to cast four-pound TriMax line. This combination is balanced for casting small bucktails and spinner-and-grub lures that take rockfish big enough to make you wish you had used heavier gear.

Lures balanced for ultralight spinning tackle. Left board: ⅛-ounce jigs include a shad dart, Meushaw jigs tied with bucktail hair (top) and feathers (bottom). Middle board: Spinner-and-grub (top) and a pony head jig with swimmer tail grub. Right board: #13 Tony (top), and #0 Drone (bottom).

MEDIUM SPINNING TACKLE: My medium spinning outfits include Berkley Bionix Pulse model X27-6' rods in medium-heavy action. I also use these rods for bass plugging and worming. Reels are 1950s-era Luxor 1-S models loaded with eight-pound test TriMax. There are many modern spinning reels that may be better and lighter, but I wound up with a drawer full of high-quality Luxors when I was collecting. I hate to give them up, and they won't wear out. Luxors had the first silent anti-reverse, a smooth drag, and machine-cut gears that run as quietly and smoothly as a Rolls Royce. These medium spinning outfits can cast bucktails from ¼-ounce to ¾-ounce. And, this medium size outfit will tame stripers of 15 to 20 pounds and beyond if one suddenly surprises you.

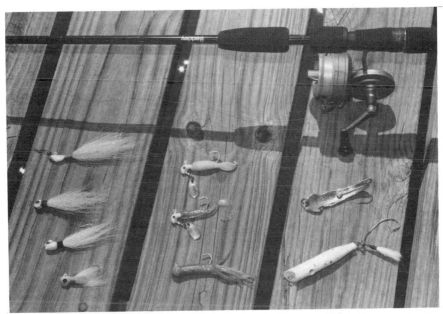

Striper lures for medium spinning tackle. Left board: All ¼-ounce bucktails, from top to bottom – potgut, round head, ruby-lips, and a glass-eyed with green skirt. Middle board: All with ¼-ounce jig heads. From top to bottom – pony head with grub, pony head with chartreuse swimmer tail, and a round head jig inside a soft tube lure. Right board: #14 Tony and a ⅝-ounce Atom popper.

MEDIUM-HEAVY SPINNING AND CONVENTIONAL TACKLE: Longer casting distances can be had with a medium-heavy spinning outfit. My choice for casting plugs all day is a graphite Berkley Series One Steelhead rod, model S94-7'8"MT medium action, designed for 8- to 14-pound test line and lure weights from ⅜ to 2 ounces. It is a slender rod that looks incapable of casting the heavier plugs, but it will fool you. The companion spinning reel is a Penn 250GR loaded with 14-pound test TriMax monofilament line.

The sister casting rod to these medium-heavy spinners is made for conventional level-wind casting reels. It is a Berkley Series One model S92-8'2"MT trigger stick in medium action. I use two different reels on these casting rods, a Ryobi T-2 and an Ambassaduer Mag II. Both of these gorilla-sized level-winders are loaded with 14-pound TriMax line. Most new level-wind reels have adjustable magnetic drags to allow long casts without backlashing.

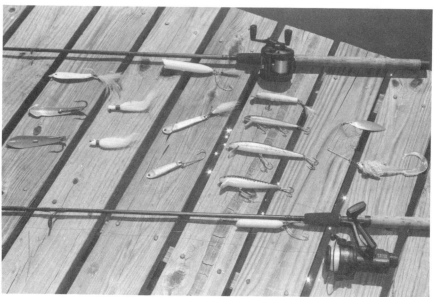

Lures for medium-heavy tackle previously described include a 1½-ounce single-hook Atom popper alongside each rod. Left board: Spoons from top to bottom – 7/0 Crippled Alewive, #18 Tony and a #3½ Drone. Second board: Homemade 1-ounce popeye and ruby-lips bucktails. Third board: Knife-handle lures – Drone SD3 (top) and a Hopkins Shorty. Fourth board: All swimming plugs from one to two ounces. Top to bottom – Atom, Redfin, Rebel, and Shallomac. Far right board: A giant spinnerbait, 12" overall length, that was made up as a joke. Someone caught big stripers on it, ending the joke.

Medium-heavy outfits will cast my favorite 1¹/₂ ounce Atom popping plugs an Eastern Shore mile. Rods in this class have long butt sections that allow the angler to use both hands when casting, and give more leverage when fighting a fish. These spinning and conventional outfits are about equal in distance casting, at least for me. I switch back and forth, as each type of casting tires different muscles.

HEAVY SPINNING AND CONVENTIONAL SURF CASTING TACKLE: Included here are reels that carry 300 yards of 30- or 40-pound test mono or dacron line for surf casting. Along the Atlantic coast where stripers up to 60 or 70 pounds are possible, this heavy tackle is recommended. This equipment can be used from beaches like Sandy Point in the Chesapeake, but it is a bit too heavy for the size of striper that might be expected there. Spinning reels include huge old Luxors only slightly smaller than a boat winch, and huge modern spinners that carry 250 yards of 25-pound test. Any mention of conventional surf reels must include the old classic Penn Squidder, but modern anglers use the Garcia Ambassadeur Nine or Ten with centrifugal brakes to avoid the monumental

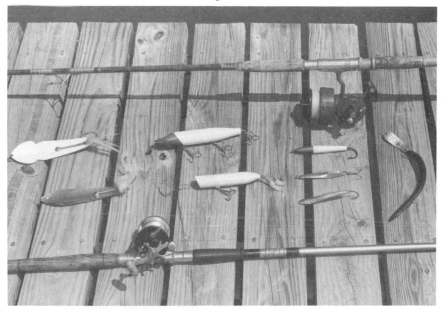

Lures grouped between the heavy surf-casting Luxor spinning outfit on top and the conventional Squidder outfit below, starting from the left, include: #21 Tony spoon and a #34¹/₂ Drone spoon; an 8-ounce homemade swimming plug and a 3-ounce Atom popper; three squids – cedar, Lujon, and sand eel; and a 3¹/₄-ounce, 13-inch long rigged ALOU Bass Eel.

backlashes possible with the old Squidder. Rods are beefy and run from 9 to 11 feet or more. While these outfits are a bit too heavy for average Chesapeake striper fishing, I used a Squidder on a beefy 8-foot surf stick to troll (and cast) humungous 14-inch Creek Chub swimming plugs for 30-pound stripers around the Bay Bridges. A lighter outfit would not have handled lures that big.

What to Buy?

Perhaps the most versatile all-around combination for Chesapeake striper fishing is the medium-heavy spinning outfit described above. It can be used for casting bucktail jigs, plugs, and spoons. It is ideal for bait fishing with eels, crabs, or clam chumming. Trolling in rivers without weight, or along the shoreline is suitable with this gear. A #10 Romer interlock snap swivel on the end of the line makes quick lure changes a snap. While I call it a "medium-heavy" outfit, the heaviest line I use is 14-pound test. I have caught stripers over 30 pounds with a similar outfit.

Around the Bay Bridges where stripers run around pilings and cut the line on barnacles, many anglers use 20- and 30-pound test line, but I still use 14-pound test.

The medium-heavy spinning and casting outfits I mentioned are really very light in weight because of their graphite construction—light enough to cast with all day without undue fatigue. It's a good thing. Sometimes it takes all day to find the stripers.

Romer #10 interlock snap swivel. Three times actual size.

Spots or Stripes, They Act the Same

Spotted seatrout (*Cynoscion nebulosus*), called "speckled trout" or "specs" by Virginians to our south, took the Eastern Shore by storm recently. This is not the same fish as the weakfish (*Cynoscion regalis*) that we call "trout," but a spotted cousin that sometimes hangs out with his bottom-feeding weakfish relatives.

A spec's best quality, besides being great table fare, is that he can be caught on bass tackle by casting Rat-L-Traps, grubs, and bucktails in shallow water. In that regard, specs are like stripers, who also hang around shallow water obstructions and compete with specs for lures that resemble dinner.

Rat-L-Trap plug and a bucktail tied with flashabou will take spotted seatrout as well as stripers.

The first word I had that specs were in the Choptank River came from charterboat captain Jim Price. Jim caught a few spotted seatrout mixed in with the rockfish he was under contract to catch for the DNR. Jim trolls with dacron line, a drop sinker, and a small bucktail around "rocks" or "lumps" near Oxford.

Specs like the same habitat as rockfish. They both hang around structure. If Jim had caught them upriver trolling, maybe I could catch some downriver, and closer to shore on light tackle.

Bill Perry and I explored Cook Point at the mouth of the Choptank for specs one summer Sunday. Nothing. We cast Rat-L-Traps and bucktails into the rip that forms when the tide flows past Cook Point.

Since we found no action there, we ran to the north end of James Island, and began to cast our lures into shallow water on the east side of the island. Erosion is rampant there, and downed trees near shore provide excellent cover for specs.

Several anglers trolled past in about four feet of water, off the northern end of James Island. We didn't see them catch any fish, so we continued casting lures in the shallows. Something grabbed Bill's silver Storm Shallomac swimmer in a shower of spray and gave him quite a tussle on his 12-pound test spinning gear. As it neared the boat—bad news! The fish wore stripes. No spots. No keeper. Bill released the fish.

Near the center of the island, there is a pass deep enough for my 20-foot Mako. We tossed our bucktails and plugs near the shore. No luck.

With all that good spec habitat, we were surprised we didn't catch specs there. The sun was low. It was time to run toward home.

On the way back Jim Walker, fishing from his 20-foot Aquasport, held up a Cook Point spec for us to admire. He had caught it on a $^1/_4$-ounce chrome Rat-L-Trap. All I had was $^1/_2$-ounce Traps.

"Cast into that ruffled water," Jim advised. Bill and I did as we were told. Something slammed my lure and gave me a good fight. Near the boat, the fish's size was magnified by the water. The fish was a little smaller in the net, but a $4^1/_2$ pound spec is a keeper.

On a flood tide at Cook Point, the rip forms a bit strangely, but it can be productive. On this day, there was a definite line between the dirty water caused by erosion from the point, and the cleaner incoming water from the Bay. The fish were hanging on the clean side of the "mud line."

The secret was to fish the lure low and slow, just as you would for stripers. The specs were as close to the bottom in seven feet of water as a lure could be fished. Bill tried a small white bucktail and caught a nice spec. It hit right near the edge of the clean water, and fought like a bigger fish than the one I netted.

We have had specs jump out of the water like tarpon when hooked in the shallows. On light spinning or bass-sized level wind reels, the speckled trout is a gamester worthy of much admiration. Ask any angler from the Gulf of Mexico states. Gulf anglers get misty-eyed and emotional about specs the way we do about stripers.

Friday the 13th seemed like a lucky day for spec fishing. Jim Walker joined me for an expedition to James Island. Jim used a plain white bucktail with a white head and red thread. Cook Point was crowded with anglers, so we passed it up and ran south looking for a similar place to try.

At Hills Point the tide was coming in. Jim cast bucktails and I tried a Rat-L-Trap in "Tequila Sunrise" color. My fancy rattling plug got itself hung on a submerged rock and stayed there. Jim's bucktail got itself hung in the mouth of a two-pound spec. I changed lures.

I caught a nice spec on a "potgut" bucktail made by Jack Stovall. He combines "flashabou" and bucktail hair as recommended to him by Lefty Kreh.

Jim and I talked about how fickle fish are in selecting lures.

"We'll sit around all winter tying flashabou bucktails," Jim said, "then next summer they'll be hitting something else."

I tried a popping cork/small jig rig. In Florida, spotted seatrout anglers use a molded polystyrene "cork" above a live shrimp for Banana River specs. I once caught a nine-pound spec in a canal near Cape Canaveral, Florida on that rig. We filleted the fish and ate it for dinner. The carcass was buried under a rose bush. If I had that fish now, it would be enshrined on a piece of driftwood on my rec room wall.

I mentioned to Jim that an angler told Chuck Prahl at Tommy's Sporting Goods in Cambridge that he had caught 23 specs right here.

"Never believe what you hear in a tackle store," was Jim's comment.

We ventured south to James Island. "This is prime spec habitat," Jim observed. "Cut away sod banks, fallen trees, a great spot for specs. I don't want to see any rockfish, though."

We did see rockfish, though not as many as should be there, if one believes restoration rumors. Jim got hung up in tree stumps several times, and we used a trick I learned from lady bass anglers—wind the lure right to the rod tip. The rod will be straight down into the water. Jiggle the rod tip until the lure comes lose.

The downed trees and other debris behind Jim Walker are great spotted seatrout and striper habitat.

"I want this lure back," Jim said as he lifted a huge tree limb with his flashabou bucktail attached.

"What we'll do to save a flashabou," he joked.

We motored back to Cook Point. The tide was outgoing, and there was a sharp line between silty and clear water. I cast the flashbou potgut bucktail and caught a spec. The secret? Deep and slow in eight feet of water.

Spotted seatrout can inhabit really shallow water, as Jim Walker found out. He caught several specs in less than two feet of water next to shore on peeler crab. But, Clarke Reed of Trappe, Maryland did better than that. He caught a 6½ pound spotted seatrout on an Atom popping plug in the Choptank River shallows at Castle Haven in September!

Charter Captain Chris Rosendale told MSSA/ACCA members he caught good numbers of specs trolling slowly with small bucktails, the same way we always did for rockfish. He was a bit sketchy about the exact location, but said "fish always come back to the same places every year."

If spotted seatrout inhabit the Chesapeake in the numbers they have recently, I would expect to catch them almost one-for-one with stripers. Whatever you do for stripers, try for specs, and vice-versa. Remember to release the striped ones (unless the law allows otherwise), and keep only as many spotted ones over 12 inches as you need. Take it easy on the specs. They could be the next fish to go.

Charterboat Stripers

Every striper angler should try a charterboat trolling trip for stripers or blues. Come along with us on a typical May trip out of Buddy Harrison's Chesapeake House on Tilghman Island, Maryland.

Buddy's annual Pro-Am Bluefish Tournament is held in May, at a time when the bluefish are normally in good supply. It is composed of a mixture on each boat of businessmen (Ams) and outdoor writers (the "Pros").

After a hearty breakfast at Chesapeake House, our Pro-Ams checked the daily roster for boat assignments. I was to fish on the *Tradition* with Captain Glenn Foster. Our "Pros" on the *Tradition* were Bill Perry and me. Our "Ams" were Jim Proutt and Charlie Luthardt of Arundel Corporation in Baltimore; and Dave Karns and Bruce Rudderow of Karns Food, Ltd. in Mechanicsburg, PA. Several of Buddy's boats fished that day; also the 55-foot offshore sportfisherman, *Hunter*, owned and operated by Captain Clay Katski of Bozman, Maryland.

A parade of charterboats motored under the opened Knapps Narrows Bridge toward the open Bay. Three-foot waves were rolling in just outside the inlet, pushed by a strong southwest wind. It would have been a bit rough in my 20-foot Mako, but the 37-foot diesel-powered *Tradition* took the waves well. We were comfortable.

Leaving Knapps Narrows Charlie and Jim of Arundel Corporation noticed the rip rap protecting the shoreline. "We sold that rock," Charlie said. "They sure did a neat job with it, too," Jim replied. We headed across Chesapeake Bay to the western shore.

"They changed the buoy numbers over the winter," Captain Foster said, "I came out here and thought I was lost." Buoy #71 had been changed to #83. It was like reading a street map where all the street names were changed.

Captain Foster put out all seven trolling lines himself. Most charter captains use Penn 309 level wind reels on 7-foot roller tip trolling rods with long hypalon grips and rubber butt caps. The 309 reels are loaded with either monofilament or wire line depending on depth desired. Level wind reels are easier for inexperienced anglers on charterboats to use. Each traverse of the level wind's line guide is about 10-feet, so captains tell their anglers to let out 14 traverses to get their lure 140-feet behind the boat. Each line goes out a different distance. This day, every line had a Crippled Alewive spoon on. In fact, after a few fish were caught, the anglers were anxious to use the "hot" lure, a 9/0 "Rechargeable" chartreuse spoon.

"If it ain't chartreuse, it ain't no use" Bill Perry said about favored Bay lure colors.

Fred Meers' Crippled Alewives are charged in sunlight and glow in the dark, deep Chesapeake waters. If I were a fish, and something that glowed swam through my living room, I'd wonder if it had spent too much time near the Calvert Cliffs nuclear power plant.

We started trolling in 60-feet of water west of buoy #83.

"Fish on," someone yelled. Bruce grabbed the rod and fought the fish, alternately pumping the rod tip backward, then reeling as he moved the rod tip toward the fish. To help him gain line, the captain took the engine in and out of gear to slow forward progress.

When the fish neared the boat, we realized it was a rockfish. The captain swung it aboard while the outdoor writers took pictures. It measured 22 inches, which would have been over the 18-inch minimum if the fishery was open. It wasn't. The fish was gently released by our captain.

Everyone but me took a turn bringing in a rockfish. Not a single blue was boated, although one got off at the transom. "A long-line release," said one wag. I was too busy getting pictures to crank in rockfish.

We had three "get-offs" near the transom, most likely rockfish. One rockfish threw up a gob of mayworms before it was released. Mayworms

Bill Perry released this 12-pound striper he caught on a chartreuse spoon.

look like a cross between garden and bloodworms. They spawn in the Bay every month, but the May full moon is their most prolific time. I caught big blues that were loaded with Mayworms in May, 1988.

"I don't care what he eats," Captain Foster said, "as long as he eats what we've got."

It seemed that one of the most productive rods had a 12-ounce drop sinker and a 30-foot leader. "They are leader shy at this time of year," said our captain. Another top rod was the center one, way back behind the boat with a 3-ounce sinker, just enough weight to keep the lure from surfacing. Some call this shallow-running line a "floater," and consistently catch big spring spawning rockfish on it.

An old Bay charterboat went slowly past, and we commented on the lack of activity aboard it. "That captain couldn't catch fish in an aquarium," our captain said.

Charlie caught a 28-inch rock that weighed 13 pounds on a line with a 20-ounce sinker, "Right on the bottom," he said.

It seemed that we were catching a striper every 10 minutes. We started to time the catches. What was most likely happening was that the boat was slowly circling through a school of fish every 10 minutes.

The *Tradition* had no Loran-C aboard, so the captain must have had some pretty good shoreline marks to steer by. By lining up a nearby buoy with some object on the far shore old time captains get a "line of position," or LOP. Two different LOPs that cross will put you within yards of any structure or a stationary school of fish.

Catching rockfish developed into an efficient pattern. When the captain let out each line to suit him, he set a light drag with the reel's clicker on. When a fish hit, the rod would bow, and the reel clicker screamed.

"Tighten the drag," the captain yelled. The angler tightened the star drag and took the clicker off if it was on, then started to pump and reel, pump and reel, gaining line. When the leader was near the boat, the angler walked backward until the captain could grab the leader and hand-over-hand it until the fish was close. If it was a small rock, less then 24 inches or so, he swung it aboard by the 50-pound test leader. If the fish was bigger, he called for the net.

Using this system, Dave caught a 30-inch rock that he released before it was weighed.

"How did you do that?" he was asked about the biggest fish of the day.

"Clean living," Dave laughed.

The question of pursuing rockfish will soon surface. *Tradition* was not the only boat that caught a lot of rock, but no blues. The consensus of opinion from outdoor writers I have interviewed is that, yes, it is illegal, but how do you determine if the anglers are trying for bluefish or participating in a "directed" fishery for stripers? It's a tough call, and I will not moralize

Dave Karns releases a striper.

on the subject. There is a considerable amount of catch-and-release rock-fishing going on, but I have heard of no tickets given.

The captains got together on the radio frequently to discuss the lack of bluefish action. "Neither boat has caught either bluefish," our captain said in Eastern Shore vernacular. Since I've lived on the 'Shore, I've heard the use of "either" and "neither" applied to fish and crabs, but I could never figure the rules of grammar for them.

"I caught neither crab today," one waterman told another on VHF radio. "I ain't caught either one, neither," replied his buddy. The words seem to be interchangeable, but I expect if you, a "foreigner," used them improperly or made fun of a 'Shoreman's grammar, you would soon find yourself outside covered with dust and bruises.

"No more bluefish than I've caught today, I can clean them myself," radioed Captain Jo-Jo. Captain Foster agreed.

Our final score was rockfish-27, bluefish-0. Our captain handled the fish to be released with care, and our anglers likewise. I have seen slob anglers do otherwise, slamming the rockfish down on the transom to tear out the hook, then throwing the fish back with enough force to stun or kill it—all in a childish fit of rage because they can't keep stripers. Immature slobs are still slobs.

How to Find Chesapeake Stripers (and Catch a Few)

Let's go on a typical striper fishing trip in my imaginary river. You should watch for things I've learned that can be applied to your creek or river. Similarities in my fictitious river, bottom types or structure, will apply to any area where stripers hang out.

First, you have to think like a rockfish. Well, maybe not in spawning season. But, you can see what I mean.

Stripers have needs not too different from ours: Food, shelter, and a place to hang out with the gang. Food and shelter can be found in the same place—near structure.

Fishing guide Ken Penrod's study of a single largemouth bass in an aquarium applies to stripers, too. If there was a single stick or stone in the aquarium, Ken said, the bass would be hanging next to it. If he moved the object, the bass would soon be next to it again. Plain sand bottom gave the bass the heebie-jeebies.

Stripers can be found hanging around pier and bridge pilings, oyster shell bottom, fallen trees or submerged stumps, along edges where the bottom contour changes rapidly, sunken wrecks, rocks, you name the object. At some time a striper will be there. You have to figure out how to be there at the same time with whatever is on the striper's menu at that exact minute. No problem.

Structure attracts marine growth that hides small edible things. It provides security for things the striper eats, and a place to hang out with his buddies who eat the same things he does. Usually, in a strong tidal flow, stripers will be just out of the fast current, waiting for something edible to be swept past. In most cases, they will be on the downtide side—but don't depend on that. Fish all sides of structure. In deep water, fish all depths—top to bottom.

Once you get used to looking for striper spots, you'll see them everywhere. It doesn't cost anything to cast a few lures to find out if you are properly reading the water. Come with me for a trip on my imaginary Oldman River, just off Chesapeake Bay.

Points and Drop-Offs

Coming into Oldman River, we pass near Moot Point. Shallow near shore, Moot Point is only six feet deep for about a mile out. Strong tides cross Moot Bar. A steep drop-off is on the river side. A few rocks are just under the surface. Erosion has taken its toll, and a "mud line" is sharply defined on an outgoing tide. Water is clean on the bar on the incoming tide. Where can we find a striper here? Nearly anywhere, except in the muddy water.

Start by casting surface poppers over the shallow bar near shore and drift outward along the mud line. Next, troll a bucktail or small spoon with no added weight along the dropoff—but in the clear water. If that doesn't work, cast a bucktail jig or jig-and-grub; first into shallow water on the bar, then reel it slowly so it bounces along bottom on the drop-off. If you felt a nip at the lure, speed it up and slow it down with a "Florida twitch." Cast lures right to the eroded bank on both sides of Moot Point. Let them land on the beach and pull them off into the water. Many times a striper will be right on the water's edge. Sometimes, depending on your mood, do a change-up in the sequence of events above. Work the area over. Nothing? O.K. Let's move on.

Wrecks

The Hesperus is a WW II airplane wreck in midriver. Rumor has it that some of the good 'ol boys snuck out at night in past years and added things like refrigerators and car bodies to it. It must be a tackle emporium down there with so many snags. How to fish the Hesperus? Anchor near, but not directly on it, and dunk bait. Careful. There are a lot of anchors down there, too, according to Navy divers. It would probably be a good place to chum with clams or grass shrimp. A bushel of clams would do it. Smash up some clams in a bucket with a ball bat and ladle them overboard, a little at a time. Bait your 2/0 hooks with clam snouts. Peeler crab on double-hook bottom rigs would likely be good here,too. Fish as close to the wreck as possible without hanging your rig in it. You brought extra tackle, didn't you?

Shallow Rocks, Plug Casting

Just upriver off Pin Point, there is a productive bottom locals call Dingprop Rocks. A great place to try surface plugs and small bucktail jigs. We should try our poppers first, because we like to see stripers bust plugs on top. If that doesn't work, cast a small bucktail adorned with pork rind and reel it in slowly with the rod tip pointed up to keep the lure running near the surface. A hookless broomstick popping plug with a small jig tied behind it on an 18-inch piece of monofilament is called a "pollock rig" around the Cape Cod Canal. It works in Oldman River shallows, sometimes. Be careful casting this rig, as it will occasionally get tangled. Pop the plug on the surface to attract a striper that will grab the bucktail jig. Slowly drift along the shoreline, casting in shallow water—right next to the beach! Next to rock riprap is best. Rockfish like rocks.

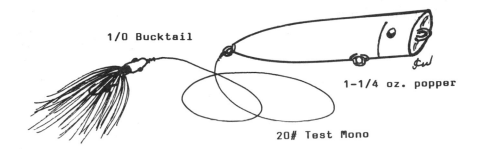

Pollock rig.

Shallow Rocky Shoreline, Trolling

Let's try a little shallow trolling. Remember, they call this place Dingprop Rocks. You have to troll here at high water, and with a stainless steel prop. Aluminum props last only seconds here. Our medium-heavy spinning gear will be fine. Use a 1/0 bucktail, with or without pork rind. Some like split tail rind, others swear by ripple rind. Take your choice. Put the outboard motor in gear and idle along about 50 to 100 feet out from the shoreline, water depth and rocks permitting. Let your line out at least 100 feet behind the boat. Small spoons are good lures, too. You say the tide is too low? Your prop is wearing out? O.K., we'll come back at high tide.

Bucktail with ripple rind.

Bottom Bumping the Lumps

Get out the heavy trolling gear. We're going to look for a new hotspot called Taikyur Lumps. Our Loran-C knows the location, but we'll have to use the depthfinder to pinpoint the lumps—and see if there are any fish on them.

The Loran-C says we are right on the lumps. Watch that depthfinder. The 14-foot bottom will suddenly go up to 10 feet. That's a good lump. See if there are any fish showing. Have your marker buoy ready! There they are! Small blips just above the lump. Toss the buoy. Now, get out your trolling tackle.

The dacron line outfit is best here, but we like wire line over oyster-shell bottom so we can feel the shells better. A 12-ounce drop sinker is fine. Use an 18-foot leader with a ¼-ounce bucktail or #14 Tony spoon tied to the end. Let your bottom rig out until the sinker bounces once, then wait for boat speed to pick it up off bottom. Then let it out to bump bottom again. Two bumps, very scientific. Hold your rod so you can bump bottom intermittently.

Troll slowly around your marker buoy, and bring your lures past the lolling stripers noses. A hit! Bring it in slowly, now, right up to the leader. Now, hand-over-hand up the leader to the lure. We net our stripers so they can be released easily if not legal to keep.

This type of trolling is also productive around day markers in Oldman River. Look for day markers in 10 feet of water or deeper. Stripers are usually there, close to the marker. Floating buoys are anchored by chains or cables, and hang-ups are possible.

Arstershell Ups-and-Downs is a good place to bottom bump bucktail lures, too. Not far upriver from Taikyur Lumps, we find Arstershell Ups-and-Downs with our flasher depthfinder. We learned this from our old friend, Chuck Prahl. Chuck sets his depthfinder gain until the second reflection is just barely tuned out.

In 20 feet of water on sand bottom, turn up the gain until there is a second blip showing at 40 feet. This is called "doubling." Just barely tune the second blip out. When you go over rock or oyster shell bottom, the second blip will show again, and be slightly "raggedy." Toss your marker if you think you see fish. Re-read the paragraphs above for what to do.

Strange Structure

Now, we'll take you to a secret place. Hickory Dickory's Dock. What's that? No rockfish here? Don't you believe it. Look at the signs. Structure (dock pilings) extending into at least six feet of water. An ósprey nest nearby. That bird guarantees there are enough fish around to feed a hungry bird—and you, if you pay attention. Then, think about this: For years the Dickorys have walked to the end of the dock and tossed their empty oyster shells overboard. There is a ready-made shell pile so stripers can feed on oyster worms and other smaller things that feed on oyster worms. The pier pilings harbor minnows, silversides, grass shrimp, and sometimes a piling clinging soft crab. If you were a striper, would you live here? Even if your address had a silly name like Hickory Dickory? Darn right, you would.

Now, how to fish this striper structure? Just like you would fish a dock in largemouth bass country. Well, almost. Accurate casting is necessary. Lay that 'ol bucktail right alongside the pilings. Not 10 feet away. Right alongside. Let it sink against a taut line with a closed spinning reel bail, just like worming for bass. Watch your line like a hawk. If it moves to the side or even twitches, strike. Also, try skipping your lure like a stone right up under the dock. See how easy that was? Off the end of the dock, try a bucktail fished over the oystershells might pay off. Spinnerbaits and rattle plugs would likely work, too, but they are more expensive than jigs you can make yourself. You'll lose some lures.

Medium spinning tackle with 10-pound test line is ideal for bucktailing around Dickory's dock, and around the day marker at Gun Point. Day marker? Sitting out in the middle of a river with noisy boats passing? Yes. Remember, the striper likes structure. Stripers may be hanging around each day marker. Depending on tide flow and other factors, they may be on either side, near the surface or bottom, or even several feet downtide from the navigation aid, or even along the dropoff the day marker marks. If you get hits here, remember it. There will be stripers in those same places year after year.

Grass Beds

The Bay had a lot of grass at one time. In my area, there is very little. But, if you find a nice grass bed in rockfish country, fish there. It is like a smorgasbord restaurant to a striper. Minnows, grass shrimp, silversides, soft crabs, perch, and the fun of rooting around in the grass to find these snacks. What hungry striper could ask for more? You can almost hear them belch happily.

Grass bed striper fishing is retold from memory, but who knows? Maybe the grass will return one day.

We slowly idle up to the edge of Grasschoke Flats and cut the motor. The drill is to drift until we get a bite or follow, then slide a small anchor overboard to fish the area completely, casting all around the "clock."

At high tide, surface running swimmers like Redfins might be best, but we can start with surface poppers if you like. At low tide, look for holes between the grass beds and toss regular bass spinnerbaits or other weedless bass lures in there. Also, at any tide, fish peeler crab or grass shrimp baits on the outer edge of the grass. Bottom rigs or floats both work well.

Bridge Pilings

We have worked our way upriver to the town of Troubled Water. There is a bridge there. Hundreds of pilings to try here, but not all of them hold fish. Usually, we would find more stripers alongside pilings in 10 feet or more of water, but at certain times of the year, shallow water pilings near shore are better. Casting 6/0 or so sized bucktail jigs adorned with split pork rind right next to the pilings would be a good place to start. Here, we keep the motor running to maneuver the boat. We usually cast uptide and bring the lure directly past the piling at some mid-level. Next time cast the lure further so it will sink a little deeper as it swims near the piling, and so on until you have covered all of the vertical water column. Then move the boat and start over on the other side of the piling. Move from piling to piling until you find fish. Some anglers fish their bucktails against the tide.

Bait can be fished here, too. Float peeler, soft crab, or grass shrimp baits at mid-levels with varying amounts of sinker weight to find the feeding level. Here, the boat is anchored and baits are floated in the tide, near pilings or in eddy currents around them.

If big stripers are present at Troubled Waters Bridge, lip-hooked live eels are a good bait. Eels are fished on 2/0 Eagle Claw hooks on 18-inch leaders of 30-pound test. Pinch-on sinkers to provide weight. Again, the stripers are right alongside the pilings—hardly ever more than a few feet away.

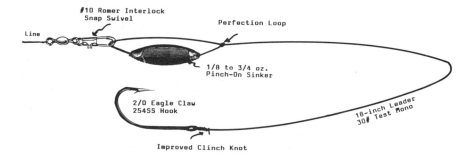

Live eel (or soft crab) rig.

Occasionally, trolling past the pilings can be productive. This is tricky on the uptide side, because the tide can wash your lure right into the piling. Hangups are frequent. Better to troll on the downtide side, or parallel to the tide, passing alongside the piling.

Jigging Stripers Up to the Surface

We haven't tried this system upriver at Flatulent Flats, but we heard it works. If a pod of stripers can be found, a multiple jig rig can be used. Tie several small jigs on a three-foot long leader at intervals. Lower the jig rig to the bottom, and jig it around a bit. If a striper hits, hold the rig there while the first fish tows it around, and see if another fish gets on. Watch the depth finder. Sometimes after jigging a few stripers up from the bottom, the fish will slowly rise until they are right under the boat.

Breaking Stripers

Once, we were lucky enough to find endless schools of breaking rockfish and blues mixed in Oldman River. Here, in the mid-1970s, we were able to go from school to school until we found the exact size of striper we wanted for the freezer, then stop and catch as many as we wanted. Striper populations won't support that much fishing now.

Each autumn, though, breaking stripers will be found somewhere in Oldman River. In some Octobers they were mixed with blues in a ratio of five blues to one striper. With the first cold snap, the blues moved out, and the striper/bluefish ratio reversed.

If stripers are breaking, they are easy to find. There will be clouds of screaming gulls swirling everywhere above the breaking fish. Frantic bait

Screaming flocks of seagulls pinpoint feeding stripers.

fish will be driven almost out of the water. Huge swirls surround your boat where stripers and blues are chasing bait fish. It is pandemonium. Boats converge from all directions. Screaming reel drags protest the hard work of taming big stripers. Boats are sometimes close enough for the anglers to shake hands, but friendly conversation is the last thing on their minds. Anglers go into a fishing frenzy, much like bluefish in a feeding frenzy.

How should we fish for these breaking fish? Medium-heavy spinning tackle with 14-pound test line is our preference. Surface plugs with a single hook instead of two trebles have come into favor. We file or mash down the hook's barb so it is easier to release fish we will not keep. It is more of a thrill to catch fish that will hit a plug on the surface, but sometimes the fish go down. They play hard to get.

When stripers sound and get lockjaw, it is sometimes possible to find them with the depth finder. Look for a concentration of gulls sitting on the water. They are waiting for the fish to begin feeding again. Gulls won't be very far away from their next meal. Then, run the boat slowly in large circles and watch the depth finder. If stripers show on the finder, try jigging with bucktails or knife-handle lures like the single-hook hammered Hopkins Shorty.

Oldman River is Your River

Well, we have fished for stripers up and down Oldman River. I hope there are places in your river that are enough like those in Oldman to be a guide in your striper search. You can expect to find stripers in the kinds of places I told you about, but not every time. If you did, fishing wouldn't be called fishing. It would be called catching. And, it would soon cease to be fun.

Keep the fun in fishing. Do what I do. Get skunked occasionally.

21

WINTER WORKSHOP

Tackle Tinkering Techniques to Terminate Tedium

Once, in a local establishment, I commented on some anti-social behavior to the gent behind the polished mahogany. He held a spotless glass up to the light, examining it.

"Yeah," he sighed, "the full moon brings them all out."

The full moon is nearly always out for a real, rabid, foaming-at-the-mouth striper fisherman. His strange behavior begins in early winter, about the time it gets cold enough to freeze your hand to a reel handle. His unusual conduct continues to worsen through the winter and does not abate until the ice in the bird bath melts.

A word of caution to family members, though: The worst time is during the full moon. Watch for the first clues that the angler is coming down with Piscatorial Cabin Fever (PCF, something like PMS, only a thousand times worse).

PCF anglers snarl at the breakfast table. Grow beards and sharply pointed canine teeth. Have flecks of foam near the corners of the mouth. A 500-mile stare. If you see any of these clues, it is time for immediate corrective action!

The concerned family must instantly rechannel this self-destructive behavior into offseasontackletinkering. I ran the last words together so your PCF fisherman wouldn't understand, like spelling out words so the kids don't know you're talking about s-e-x.

To start the rehabilitation process, drop hints at the dinner table about how nice it would be to start the next fishing season with ALL the guides on a rod, and a reel that doesn't have to be turned with a pipe wrench. And wouldn't it be nice if company didn't have to trip over those rusty, smelly tackle boxes in the middle of the living room?

And think of all the money that could be saved by molding bucktails and making lures! Most striper anglers don't want to know that the cost of lead pots, sinker and bucktail molds, hooks, deer tails, thread, paint, etc., elevates the cost of a single bucktail lure to over $20 each. (Family members, please don't mention cost at this delicate stage of negotiations).

Garages and cellar workshops can be too cold in mid-winter for tackle tinkering activities. And remember—PCF anglers need constant supervision. It is wise to move him (or—God forbid I shouldn't offend the anglerettes—her) into the living room, dining room, or kitchen, under the watchful eye of the family.

My own rehabilitation began when my wife insisted that I restore and make tackle right in the midst of family activities. Right where she could clong me on the head with my (heavy) copy of C. Boyd Pfeiffer's book, *Tackle Craft* if I displayed any signs of PCF. Boyd tells the winter workshop striper angler the right way to do things. He failed to mention there is a lighter side. Let me pass on some helpful, but off-the-wall hints about the way it's done around our house:

ROD REBUILDING can be done right in the living room while watching TV or chatting with company. Now, before you accuse me of not having my line threaded through all the guides, let me explain. A rod-wrapping lathe and thread holder can be clamped at a convenient height so one's back doesn't get tired.

"CLAMP IT WHERE?" wifey said, turning up the volume so the neighbors could hear.

"Why, hail," I replied softly, "we got a coffee table."

"Wood blocks," I explained, "prevent the C-clamps from marring the polished tabletop." (Much).

Once the surface clutter of books and magazines was tossed neatly under the table, there was room for an assortment of new rod guides, scissors, the brown jug of "rod varnish" with the XXX's on it, and other necessities.

Now: Tell me that *any* family would rather have this delightful, witty PCF entertainer in the cold cellar rather than in the warm midst of the witty family discussions that only rod-winding on the coffee table can stimulate.

POURING SINKERS AND BUCKTAILS was best done right in the bosom of the family circle. PCF anglers need watching during this dangerous work. After all, a pocket full of molten lead is nothing to sneeze at.

And where is most of the family, most of the time? Why in the kitchen, of course.

To get started all I needed was our electric stove, an aluminum pan to melt lead in, heavy gloves and potholders, some bucktail and sinker molds, and an old spoon to skim undesirable floating things from the surface of the molten lead. Read Boyd's book for the details, but a few simple hints are in order:

1. Run the kitchen exhaust fan or better yet, open all the windows while melting lead, particularly when melting wheel weights that contain burning pieces of rubber. Health authorities recommend adequate ventilation when melting lead.

2. Use heavy gloves plus a thick pot holder to grasp the pot handle. (You only forget this once). Since the pot handle is very close in temperature to the molten lead in the pan, failure to use a pot holder assures a quick lesson in the excellent heat conducting properties of aluminum.

3. Second thought: use two pot holders and thick leather gloves.

4. Thick layers of newspapers on kitchen countertops prevent burns (and fistfights). Utensils used for melting lead should NEVER be returned to kitchen use.

Some may argue that lead spills on the kitchen floor give the place a homey look. To avoid spills, I add a note of caution: The family should avoid making loud noises during the pouring process.

TYING BUCKTAILS (or flies, if you lean that way). I found this procedure was best done at the convenient height of the dining room table. Lead jigs previously poured were firmly held in a small vise clamped to the edge of the table. Wood blocks prevented some marring of the shiny table top. Piles of jigs, deer tails, thread, ultrasharp razor blades, and a jug of XXXX rod varnish, were placed conveniently at hand, leaving plenty of room at the other end of the table for family dining. To accommodate company without unduly disturbing the person tying bucktails (don't make loud noises around fly tiers, either), we added a leaf to the table.

Pass the absorbed PCF angler some food occasionally. If the moon is full, or his therapist insists on it, take away the sharp razor blades and substitute dull scissors.

Lead-head lures were dipped in paint, not because fish insist on it, but because it seemed to satisfy my sense of esthetics. After dipping lures in the can of paint, hang them on the table edge to dry. Newspapers on the carpet catch paint drips. (Good hints like these won't be found in Boyd's book).

Permit me a small detour to warn the Family Treasurer about bucktail hair. Bucktail hair, the real stuff, is the very best for striper lures. Bucktail hair is found in two places: Fishing tackle catalogs, and at one end of a deer. Get the drift?

Deer hunting is a healthy outdoor sport that provides temporary relief from winter PCF. Before the Treasurer makes any rash decisions, she must weigh the fisherman's mental health against the start-up expenses for a new hobby: A deer gun. Shells. Licenses. Hunting property rental (or purchase). A camping trailer. Factoring in these necessities could run the cost of an individual bucktail lure up over $100, still a reasonable cost for any striperman.

One way to dissuade the angler from taking up this new avocation is to show him how cheap deer tails are in the tackle catalogs. Let him order to his heart's content (up the cost of a new deer rifle). Remind him how uncomfortable he will be perched on the limb of a tree in a blinding snowstorm with his hand frozen to the new deer gun. Quietly dispose of all catalogs that show deer hunting goodies.

LURES that survived the previous summer's abuse can often be rejuvenated. Chrome spoons can be restored, unless badly scratched, by washing with soap and polishing with Brasso. Badly chipped paint on bucktail jigs can be redipped in the paint of choice and hung by the hook on a wire to dry. Rusty hooks on striper plugs can be replaced, and new split rings should be installed at the same time. After all, what does it profit a man to have shiny new hooks if a rusty split ring lets the World Champion Striper swim away with them? Badly scratched or chewed paint on plugs can be touched up by those who consider themselves proficient with an airbrush.

Lisa Hughes with a Rebel Minnow sent back to the factory for rejuvenation. Imagine the tacklebox!

REEL CLEANING implements include a small container of kerosene (keep away from open flames), DO NOT USE GASOLINE!, a toothbrush borrowed from the bathroom, an empty egg carton to hold parts, the XXXX rod varnish, some reel grease, and screwdrivers and wrenches to suit. Spread newspaper on the kitchen table first. Careful, kerosene does funny things to wood surfaces. Not ha-ha funny. The kind of funny that has precipitated homicides.

As the reel is disassembled the parts are dipped in kerosene and scrubbed vigorously with the toothbrush to remove old grease and dirt before the parts are stored in their sequential niche in the egg carton. Upon reassembling the reel in the reverse sequence, use plenty of new grease so there will be lots of work for the toothbrush next year. Wives always have nice things to say about the homey smells of kerosene and reel grease in the kitchen.

Through all of this supervised winter time therapy, encourage the PCF angler to wear a long-sleeved T-shirt. At the peak of the full moon you may find your PCF angler standing outside in knee-deep snow casting one of his new bucktails into the still-frozen birdbath. The long sleeved T-shirt makes a handy emergency strait jacket when the nice guys come to take him away for a rest.

22

RECIPES BY CAROLE WALTERS

When you take home your catch and your better half asks you "what do I do with these? Show her this chapter. My wife, Carole, consented to include her favorite recipes she has used over the years to fix rockfish. Although the recipes are written for rockfish; perch, spotted sea trout, flounder, weakfish, or other white flaky fish can be substituted.

There are fish recipes (baked, fried, or poached) along with suggestions and recipes for food to serve with fish as well as delicious desserts. In other words, complete menus.

When I caught my 32-pound 8-ounce rockfish back in 1964, what a dilemma to present a wife. We had just a small freezer, so she had to cook that monster. She said "O.K., as long as I don't have to look at the head and eyes." She baked it (see the Baked Stuffed Rockfish recipe which she pared down to a 5 pound size for this book) and we invited all of our neighbors to share that culinary feast. Don't know if the neighbors still remember that dinner, but I sure do.

Enjoy these recipes as much as I have over the past 35 years.

Keith Walters

FREEZING YOUR CATCH

Unless I am planning a company dinner, and want a whole dressed fish to stuff and bake, Keith fillets and skins all the fish we catch—even perch. This saves scaling them first.

Whole fish do not keep as well as fillets. To freeze a whole fish you will need to scale it, cut off the head, then cut open and clean out the stomach cavity. Rinse well with cold water. Place fish in plastic bag then wrap in heavy freezer paper. Store in freezer one to two months.

There are many books available to show you how to fillet a fish. Buy a good stainless steel fillet knife, a plastic fish-cleaning board that clamps the tail of the fish down, and a book with diagrams on filleting fish.

Fillets are rinsed again in cold water and put in clean, empty milk cartons, plastic margarine tubs, or any kind of plastic or waxed container. Put in enough fillets for a meal and fill the container with cold water, making sure the fish is well covered. Leave about an inch of space at the top of the container for expansion when the water freezes. Tape or staple closed. Label and date the carton for the freezer.

Freezing in water avoids freezer burn which will ruin your fish. We've been using this method for 20 years or more. Fish will stay fresh up to a year—in fact we think they taste like fresh fish.

To thaw for cooking, remove the "block of frozen fish" from its container and place in a bowl of cold water, changing the water often. Never use warm or hot water. Drain thawed fillets on paper towels then cut out the dark strip of meat (if you didn't do this when you filleted them) and they are ready to use in Carole's Recipes.

FISH BASICS

Whole or round: Fish as it comes from the water. It must be scaled and eviscerated (internal organs removed) before cooking.

Dressed or pan-dressed (1): Eviscerated and scaled fish that usually has the head, tail, and fins removed. For small fish, the term pan-dressed is often used.

Fillet (2): A piece of fish, generally boneless, cut lengthwise from the sides and away from the backbone. If skin is removed you do not have to scale the fish.

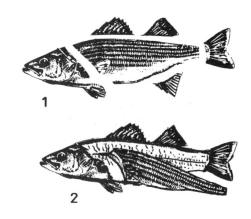

SUNDAY DINNER

Baked Rockfish

1 five-pound rockfish, cleaned and dressed
Salt and pepper
1 medium onion, sliced
1 tablespoon lemon juice
2 tablespoons corn oil margarine, melted
2 tablespoons corn oil
Parsley, 2 teaspoons

Wash thoroughly and pat dry with paper towels. Salt cavity. Stuff cavity of fish loosely with stuffing (see "Bread Stuffing" which follows). Foil-line a baking pan. Spread part of the margarine and corn oil in the pan, then sliced onions. Place fish on top of onions. Bake at 350 degrees, basting often, until fish flakes easily when tested with a fork—approximately 45 to 60 minutes.

Bread Stuffing

$1/2$ cup corn oil margarine, melted
3 tablespoons onion, finely chopped
$3/4$ cup celery, finely chopped
4 cups bread cubes
1 teaspoon salt
$1/8$ teaspoon black pepper
$1/2$ teaspoon sage
$1/3$ cup hot water (optional)
1 egg (optional)

Sauté onion and celery in margarine until soft and translucent (not brown). Add seasonings and stir thoroughly. Pour over bread cubes in large bowl and toss lightly. Slightly beat the egg and water together and add to bread mixture if you prefer a moist stuffing. Extra stuffing can be baked in a greased, covered casserole dish for about 35 minutes at 350 degrees.

Broccoli Salad

3 ounces cream cheese, softened
1 egg
2 tablespoons cider vinegar
2 tablespoons sugar
2 tablespoons corn oil
1 tablespoon prepared mustard
1/4 teaspoon salt
Pinch of garlic powder
Dash of black pepper
6 cups chopped fresh broccoli
1/2 cup raisins
2 tablespoons minced onion
1/2 pound bacon, cooked and crumbled
Chopped sweet red pepper for garnish

Combine first 9 ingredients in blender & mix until smooth. Combine broccoli, raisins, & onion in large bowl; add cream cheese mixture and toss gently. Cover and chill at least 3 hours. Garnish with bacon and red pepper. *Serves 6.* HINTS: Place bacon on a rack and pan and Bake in 375 degree oven for 15–20 minutes then cool and crumble. To make salad a day ahead, follow directions except do not pour dressing over salad until the next morning. Put the cooked & crumbled bacon under the broiler for a few seconds, then drain and sprinkle over salad and add red pepper just before serving.

Judging Doneness of Fish

During cooking, the flesh of fish gradually turns from translucent, pinkish-white to opaque white. To test for doneness, place fork tines into the fish at a 45-degree angle. Twist the fork. If the fish resists flaking and still has some translucency, it's not done. Fish that flakes apart easily and is milky white has reached the just-right stage. Overcooking results in mealy, tough, dry fish.

Rule of Thumb: Cook 10 minutes per inch of thickness.

Baked Pineapple

1 16-ounce can crushed unsweetened pineapple,
    drained (reserve juice)
1/2 cup sugar
2 tablespoons corn starch
2 eggs, beaten
1/4 cup pineapple juice
1 teaspoon vanilla extract

Mix and cook in saucepan to boiling. Pour into buttered casserole, sprinkle with cinnamon and bake uncovered at 350 degrees until there is a slight crust on the top—about 15 to 20 minutes.

Sweet Potato Pie

1/4 cup brown sugar
1/4 cup granulated sugar
1 teaspoon cinnamon
1 teaspoon nutmeg
pinch of ginger
1/4 teaspoon lemon juice
2 tablespoons butter or margarine
2 cups steamed sweet potatoes, strained
1/2 cup evaporated milk
1/2 cup water
2 eggs, slightly beaten
9" Unbaked pie shell

Combine dry ingredients and mix with whipped potatoes. Mix milk and eggs and combine with sweet potato mixture. Line pie pan with pastry and pour in filling. Bake in very hot oven (450 degrees for 10 minutes), then reduce temperature to 350 degrees and bake 35 minutes longer or until knife inserted in center comes out clean. *Serves 6.*

DOWN HOME FARE

Beer Batter Rockfish Fillets

2 lbs. Rockfish Fillets, skinned, & cut in large pieces
    (drain on paper towels)
1 cup regular flour
1 teaspoon lemon juice
1¼ teaspoons salt
2 teaspoons paprika
1 cup regular beer (not lite beer)

Mix flour, lemon juice, & seasonings. Slowly add beer and beat in with a small whisk or fork. Dip fish in batter and fry in Crisco at 375 degrees until golden brown and fish flakes easily. Drain on paper towels. *Serves 6.*

Note: If shortening is not hot enough or you crowd the pan, the batter will not be light and crispy.

Florence's Fritters

1¾ cup flour
3 teaspoons baking powder
½ teaspoon salt
1½ tablespoons sugar (for fruit fritters only)
1 egg, slightly beaten
1 cup milk
1 tablespoon corn oil

Mix dry ingredients. Combine beaten egg, milk, and corn oil; pour into flour mixture and stir just until smooth. *Serves 6.*

Fruit Fritters: Stir in 2 cups chopped apple. Drop by tablespoonfuls into hot Crisco (375 degrees) and fry just until golden brown on all sides. Drain on paper towels.

Corn Fritters: Stir in 2 cups canned corn (drained) and cook as above. Omit sugar in the recipe. Fritters can be frozen after frying. To serve, thaw, spread fritters in a jelly roll pan, cover with foil and reheat in a 350 degree oven for 15 to 20 minutes. They're delicious for breakfast!

Carole's Cole Slaw

1 small head green cabbage (discard a few outer
    leaves)
1 large carrot
1/4 cup onion, chopped fine
1 teaspoon celery seed (optional)
6 small sweet pickles, chopped, approx.
1/2 cup sweet pickle juice
2 tablespoons sugar
1/2 cup–3/4 cup Miracle Whip or your favorite
    mayonnaise

Cut cabbage in eighths. Trim core leaving just enough to hold cabbage to the core. Place about 3 sections (points down) in blender. Cover with water and liquefy for 1 or 2 seconds. Pour into a colander to drain. Repeat until you grate all the cabbage. Slice carrot and grate in blender with a little water added. Chop onion and pickles (not in the blender). Toss ingredients together in the colander. Sprinkle sugar on top. Pour about 1/2 cup sweet pickle juice over sugar. Toss again. Drain. Fold in about 1/2 to 3/4-cup mayonnaise (depends on the amount of cabbage). Keep refrigerated. *Serves 6.*

Jean's Blueberry Pie

1 cup sour cream
2 tablespoons flour
3/4 cup sugar
1 teaspoon vanilla
1 egg
1/4 teaspoon salt
1 1/2 cup blueberries
1 unbaked pie shell

Combine all ingredients except berries in blender and mix for about 5 minutes. Pour into large bowl. Fold in berries with rubber spatula. Pour into pie shell and bake in a 400 degree oven about 25 minutes. *Serves 6.*

LAZY DAY PORCH SUPPER

"Mock Crab" Salad

2 cups poached rockfish, flaked (See directions below)
1 cup celery, diced fine
1/4 cup minced onion
1/3 to 1/2 cup mayonnaise
1 teaspoon lemon juice
Salt to taste
1/4 teaspoon Old Bay Seasoning

Mix celery, onion, mayonnaise, lemon juice and seasoning together; fold into rockfish gently. Refrigerate. Serve on greens. *Serves 4.*

To poach rockfish: Place skinned fillets in pan with enough boiling water to just barely cover. Season water with parsley, stalk of celery with leaves, onion, & a few whole black peppercorns. Simmer, covered, until fish flakes easily with a fork about 10 minutes or less.

Rule of Thumb: Cook fish about 10 minutes per inch of thickness.

Tomato Aspic

3 cups tomato juice
1 stalk celery, chopped
1 small onion, chopped
2 lemon slices
1/2 teaspoon salt
1/8 teaspoon pepper
2 envelopes unflavored gelatin
1 cup cold tomato juice
2 tablespoons vinegar

Combine 3 cups tomato juice, celery, onion, lemon, salt & pepper. Simmer uncovered 10 minutes; strain. Meanwhile sprinkle gelatin over cold tomato juice and vinegar to soften. Stir into hot mixture until dissolved. Pour into 1 1/4 quart ring mold. Refrigerate at least 4 hours. Serve with creamy blue cheese dressing. *Serves 6.*

Blue Cheese Dressing

$^1/_4$ cup blue cheese, crumbled
$^1/_2$ cup sour cream
2 tablespoons mayonnaise
2 teaspoons minced onion (optional)
1 teaspoon lemon juice

Fold all ingredients together. Salt to taste. Let stand at least 1 hour in refrigerator for flavors to blend.

Trio Pasta Salad

$1^1/_4$ cups corkscrew tri-colored noodles, cooked & drained
2 cups broccoli flowerets, cooked & drained
2 medium tomatoes, cut into thin wedges
8 ounces mild cheddar cheese, small cubes
1 teaspoon dried basil leaves
1 garlic clove, minced (or garlic powder)
$^1/_4$ cup chopped parsley (or 1 teaspoon dried parsley)
$^1/_2$ cup mayonnaise

Cook noodles according to package directions. Rinse in cold water & drain. Combine mayonnaise and seasonings and mix well. Mix cheese, broccoli, tomatoes and noodles. Fold in mayonnaise mixture. Refrigerate. *Serves 6.*

Cookies 'N Cream Cupcakes

2 cups of broken cookies—your favorite kind; e.g., Pecan Sandies, chocolate chips, vanilla wafers, etc. This is a good way to use up those little pieces of cookies in the bottom of the bag. Handy to have in the freezer for unexpected guests.
$^1/_4$ cup margarine, melted
$^1/_2$ gallon of your favorite Ice Cream or Frozen Yogurt

Place cookie pieces in plastic bag and crumble with a rolling pin. Stir cookies and margarine together. Pat into pleated paper muffin liners inserted in cupcake pan. Fill with ice cream or frozen yogurt. Cover with plastic wrap & freeze right in the pan. After the dessert is frozen, remove from pan and place in freezer container. Before serving "cupcake," remove paper liners. *Makes 12 cupcakes.*

EASY OVEN DINNER

Barbecue Baked Fish

2 pounds rockfish fillets, skinned
¼ cup corn oil margarine
⅓ cup brown sugar, packed
1 cup catsup
1 teaspoon dried mustard
2 tablespoons cider vinegar

Wash fillets and pat dry with paper towel. In small pan, melt margarine and add sugar, catsup, mustard and vinegar. Pour ½ of sauce in shallow foil-lined pan. Place fillets in single layer in the sauce. Pour remaining sauce over fish. Bake 25–35 minutes at 350 degrees until fish flakes easily when tested with a fork. *Serves 6.*

Corn Pudding

2 cups corn (fresh, canned, or frozen)
1 tablespoon flour
2 tablespoons sugar
2 eggs
½ teaspoon salt
Pinch of white pepper
½ cup milk
¼ cup corn oil margarine

Put all ingredients in blender & mix 5 seconds at high speed. Pour into well greased baking dish and dot with butter. Bake 40–45 minutes at 375 degrees. *Serves 6.*

Short Cut Biscuits

¼ cup Crisco
2 cups self-rising flour
¾ cup milk
Corn oil margarine, melted

Cut shortening into flour. Stir in just enough milk until dough forms a ball Turn dough on to ungreased cookie sheet and pat into a 6-inch square. Cut into squares through dough. Do not separate. Brush with margarine. Bake in 450 degree oven about 15 to 20 minutes. Remove from cookie sheet; cool 5 minutes before pulling biscuits apart. *Makes 9.*

Suggested Addition to Menu: Tossed salad with blue cheese dressing.

Old Virginia Applesauce Cake

1½ cups applesauce
½ cup margarine
2 cups sugar
1 egg
2½ cups flour
¼ teaspoon salt
½ teaspoon cinnamon
½ teaspoon cloves
½ teaspoon allspice
2 teaspoons baking soda
½ cup boiling water

Cream margarine & sugar. Add egg and applesauce. Dissolve soda in boiling water. Add alternately with flour and spices. Bake in greased and floured tube pan at 350 degrees for 50–60 minutes or until cake tester comes out clean. Cool in pan for 10 minutes, then remove from pan. (Two 8" layer pans—bake 40–45 minutes).

ELEGANT ENTREÉ

Rockfish Thermidor

1 pound rockfish fillets, skinned
1 small onion, quartered
Lemon slice
1 can condensed cream of shrimp soup
3 tablespoons flour
$\frac{1}{4}$ cup milk
$\frac{1}{4}$ cup dry white wine
$\frac{1}{4}$ cup (1 ounce) shredded mozzarella cheese
2 tablespoons snipped parsley
$\frac{1}{2}$ cup soft bread crumbs
2 tablespoons grated parmesan cheese
2 teaspoons margarine
$\frac{1}{2}$ teaspoon paprika

Cut fish into $\frac{1}{2}$-inch cubes. Place fish, onion, and lemon in greased skillet. Add water to cover. Simmer, covered 5 minutes. In a saucepan, blend soup and flour; gradually stir in milk and wine. Cook and stir until thickened and bubbly. Stir in mozzarella cheese & parsley. Heat through. Drain fish well. Fold into sauce. Spoon into 4 greased baking shells. Combine bread crumbs, parmesan, margarine, and paprika. Sprinkle over fish mixture. Broil 3–4 minutes. *Serves 4.*

Tomatoes 'N Stuffing

$\frac{1}{3}$ cup margarine
$\frac{1}{2}$ teaspoon salt
1 teaspoon basil leaves
$\frac{1}{8}$ teaspoon ground pepper
$\frac{1}{2}$ cup chopped celery
$\frac{1}{2}$ cup green pepper strips
$\frac{1}{4}$ cup chopped onion
$\frac{1}{2}$ teaspoon ground sage
2 cups bread cubes
2 medium tomatoes, cut in wedges
2 teaspoons sugar (optional)

In large heavy skillet melt margarine, add seasonings. Sauté celery, green pepper, and onion over medium heat until crisp tender. Add bread cubes; then tomatoes and sugar; toss gently. Cover, cook another 10 minutes until tomatoes are hot yet firm. *Serves 4.*

Mixed Vegetable Casserole

24 ounces frozen mixed vegetables
1 10-ounce can condensed cream of chicken soup
1 cup shredded sharp cheese
1½ cups corn flakes, crushed
2 tablespoons melted margarine

Cook vegetables according to package directions. Combine with soup & cheese. Mix crushed corn flakes & margarine; sprinkle over vegetables. Bake at 350 degrees for 25 minutes. *Serves 6.*

Curried Peach Bake

1 16-ounce can of peach halves, drained
1 cup dark raisins
3 tablespoons butter
½ cup brown sugar
½ teaspoon curry powder

Melt butter in 9" baking pan. Stir in brown sugar, curry, and raisins. Drain peaches on paper towels, then place in sugar-curry mixture. Spoon over peaches. Bake in 350 degree oven for 35 minutes. *Serves 6.*

Hot Milk Cake

4 eggs
2 cups sugar
1 stick of butter or margarine
1 cup of milk
2 cups of flour
¼ teaspoon salt
2 teaspoons baking powder
1 teaspoon vanilla

Bring milk to boiling point and melt butter. Beat eggs until fluffy, add sugar and beat. Add flour & salt sifted together, then add hot milk & butter. *Lastly*, add the baking powder & vanilla. Bake at 350 degrees in a greased and floured tube pan 45–50 minutes. Toothpick inserted into center of cake should come out clean. Do not press down on cake to test. Let cake cool in pan 10 to 15 minutes before removing.

AUTUMN DAY SUPPER

Rockfish Stew

1 pound rockfish fillets, skinned & cut up
1 small beef marrow bone
1 medium onion, chopped
$^1/_2$ cup celery, chopped
2 or 3 sprigs of celery leaves, chopped
1 10-ounce package frozen mixed vegetables
2 large potatoes, peeled and diced (2 cups)
4 cups water
1 28-ounce can tomatoes, undrained
$1^1/_2$ teaspoons salt
1 teaspoon basil
$^1/_2$ teaspoon dried parsley
$^1/_4$ teaspoon pepper
$^1/_4$ teaspoon sugar

In 4-quart stock pot, over medium heat, cook onion, celery, celery leaves, potatoes, and frozen vegetables in 4 cups of water until potatoes and vegetables are tender (20 to 30 minutes). Stir in tomatoes, salt, basil, parsley, pepper, & sugar. Heat to boiling over medium heat. Reduce heat to low and simmer 10 minutes, stirring occasionally. Meanwhile, cut fish fillets into bite-size pieces; add fish and simmer 5 to 10 minutes or until fish flakes easily. Serve in soup bowls. *Serves 6.*

Peach Melba

3-ounce package raspberry Jello
1 cup boiling water
4 ice cubes ($^1/_4$ cup cold water)
1 16-ounce can sliced peaches in syrup
3-ounce package peach Jello
$^2/_3$ cup undiluted evaporated milk

Dissolve raspberry jello in boiling water; stir in ice cubes until dissolved. Chill (about 75 minutes) until slightly thickened. Drain peaches, reserving syrup. Arrange 8 peach slices in bottom of $4^1/_2$-cup mold. Spoon partially set raspberry Jello over peaches. Puree remaining peach slices in blender. Combine puree & syrup to make 1 cup; add peach Jello and heat to dissolve gelatin. Stir milk into peach mixture. Pour over raspberry Jello already in mold. Refrigerate at least 4 hours. *Serves 6.*

Uncle Bruce's "Pan Bread"

1 tablespoons corn oil
1 cup buttermilk
2 eggs, slightly beaten
1 cup self-rising corn meal
1/2 cup boiling water

In the oven, heat corn oil in an 8-inch square baking pan. Mix buttermilk and eggs; add to corn meal. Mix until smooth. Stir in boiling water. Pour into hot pan with oil. Bake in 450 degree oven for 20–25 minutes. Makes a moist corn bread. *Serves 6.*

Easy As Apple Pie

6 cups sliced Granny Smith apples (or your favorite
    tart apples)
1 1/4 teaspoons cinnamon
1/4 teaspoon nutmeg
1 cup sugar
3/4 cup milk
1/2 cup baking mix
2 eggs
2 tablespoons corn oil margarine
Streusel

Heat oven to 325 degrees. Grease 10 x 1 1/2 " pie plate. Mix apples, sugar and spices; turn into plate. Blend milk, eggs, & margarine in blender on high for 15 seconds. Pour over apples. Sprinkle with streusel. *Serves 6.*

Streusel: Mix 1 cup flour, 1/3 cup margarine (softened), 1/3 cup brown sugar, and 1/2 teaspoon cinnamon. Blend with pastry blender or fork. Bake for 50–60 minutes until knife in center comes out clean. Use cookie sheet or foil on oven rack below pie in case filling bubbles over.

EASTERN SHORE FARE

Just Plain Ol' Fried Fish

2 pounds rockfish fillets, skinned
lemon juice
salt (to your taste)
paprika (to your taste)
George Washington Self-rising Corn Meal

Sprinkle lemon juice, salt, and paprika over fillets then dip into corn meal. Fry in Crisco in heavy skillet (375 degrees) until brown on each side. Drain on paper towels. Fish should flake with a fork when tested for doneness. *Serves 6.*

Curried Beans

6 slices of bacon, cooked and crumbled
1 medium onion, chopped
1 green pepper, chopped
3 cans (16 oz.) of red kidney beans, drained
    (reserve liquid)
1 can (16 oz.) tomatoes, drained
    (reserve juice)
4 tablespoons of tomato juice
3 tablespoons of maple syrup
1 tablespoon catsup
1 teaspoon curry powder
1 teaspoon dry mustard
1 small can of Deviled Ham (optional)

First, cut up and brown the bacon, onion and green pepper. Drain on paper towels. Add these to remaining ingredients. Bake in uncovered casserode in 350 degree oven for 1 hour. Add remaining tomato juice and some of the bean liquid if casserole is getting too thick. *Serves 6.*

Suggestions: Serve with sliced tomatoes, corn on the cob, and cucumbers.

Summer Peach Cheesecake

8 ounces cream cheese, softened
$^1/_3$ cup sugar
1 cup sour cream
2 teaspoons vanilla
8 ounce container of Cool Whip
1 butter crumb Ready Crust
Sliced fresh peaches

Beat cheese until smooth; gradually beat in sugar. Blend in sour cream and vanilla. Fold in Cool Whip, blending well. Spoon into crust. Chill at least 4 hours before serving. Garnish with fresh peaches just before serving. *Serves 6.*

COMPANY'S COMING

Fish Fillets with Stuffing

2 pounds fillets, skinned
$1/4$ cup chopped celery
2 tablespoons chopped onion
1 tablespoon chopped green pepper
1 tablespoon chopped red pepper
1 pinch of garlic powder
$1/4$ cup tub margarine
2 cups soft bread cubes
$1/2$ teaspoon salt
$1/4$ teaspoon dried thyme
$1/4$ teaspoon ground sage
$1/8$ teaspoon black pepper
2 tablespoons lemon juice

Sauté celery, onion, green pepper in margarine. Add seasonings. Pour vegetables over bread cubes and toss lightly. Sprinkle lemon juice over fillets. Place half of the fillets in the bottom of a lightly oiled baking dish; top with bread mixture, then rest of fillets. Garnish with red and green pepper. Bake in 350 degree oven for 30 minutes or until fish flakes easily with a fork. *Serves 4.*

Quickie Version: Omit all ingredients above except fish and lemon juice. Use 1 package Pepperidge Farm Distinctive Stuffing (I use either Spinach Florentine or Country Garden Herb). Follow Steps 1, 2, and 3 on the package directions, only and skip steps 4 and 5. Layer the fish & stuffing as directed above and bake for 30 minutes at 350 degrees.

Carrots with Orange Glaze

$1/4$ cup melted butter or margarine
1 teaspoon sugar
1 cup orange juice
1 lb. carrots, peeled and sliced

Combine all ingredients in a saucepan. Cover and simmer 15–20 minutes or until carrots are tender. Uncover and cook until liquid is absorbed. *Serves 4-6.*

Hash Brown Potato Casserole

2 cups shredded cheddar cheese (8 oz.)
1 10-ounce can condensed cream of chicken soup
1 cup sour cream
½ cup onion, finely chopped
¼ cup margarine, melted
¼ teaspoon salt
¼ teaspoon black pepper
32-ounce package of frozen hash brown potatoes, *thawed*
2 cups crushed corn flakes
2 tablespoons butter, melted

Combine first 8 ingredients and mix well. Fold into potatoes. Put into greased 8" x 11½ " baking dish. Toss corn flakes and margarine together. Sprinkle over potato mixture. Bake at 350 degrees for 1 hour or until golden brown. *Serves 6.*

Pear Crumb Pie

1 unbaked 9" pie shell
1 cup flour
⅓ cup light brown sugar, firmly packed
⅓ cup butter or margarine
2½ lbs. firm-ripe Anjou or Bosc pears
1 tablespoon lemon juice
⅔ cup granulated sugar
1 teaspoon cinnamon
¼ teaspoon ground nutmeg
1 tablespoon flour
Prepare pie crust for a 9-inch pie shell with fluted edge.

Combine 1 cup flour & brown sugar. Cut in butter with a pastry blender until you have coarse crumbs. Set aside. Peel & slice pears into a large bowl; sprinkle with lemon juice. Combine the granulated sugar, spices, and 1 tablespoon flour then sprinkle over pears. Toss gently to mix then spoon into pastry shell. Sprinkle with brown sugar topping. Bake at 400 degrees for 40 minutes, or until pears are tender. Test by inserting knife into pears in the center of pie. If pie is browning too quickly after 20 minutes, cover top loosely with foil and remove about 5 minutes before end of baking time. Cool on wire rack. Serve warm. *Serves 6.*

Epilogue

IN SEARCH OF A STRIPER

The angler picked his way carefully along the slippery rocks on a point at South Harpswell, Maine. His wife followed close behind, carrying a camera. Marylanders touring Maine, they were dressed more for sightseeing than fishing. His short-sleeved dress shirt and blue cord slacks somehow didn't go with the 8-foot fishing rod he carried. His dress trouser pockets were stuffed with $1\frac{1}{2}$ ounce popping plugs armed with single hooks. A small release gaff hung from his dress belt.

The angler's lady wouldn't have chosen a sweater and skirt, had she known they would be chasing his dream of striped bass across a rocky Maine coastline.

"Well, why not?" she thought. "He's chased the striped bass (called "rockfish" back in Maryland) ever since we were married."

It was a picturesque point, and fishy looking, too, the angler thought. Perfect. Smells of seaweed and the Atlantic ocean combined to fill his nostrils. The air was crisp and dry, as it should be when striper fishing is at its best. It seemed that each cloud in the darkening sky arranged itself to show off the setting sun. His wife settled down on a rock to enjoy the sunset, pulling her sweater around her shoulders.

Early mornings and late evenings in the 1960s and 1970s would find him casting popping plugs along shallow Chesapeake shorelines. In those days big stripers, the gamest of fish, smashed the angler's surface lures, knocked them into the air in the midst a great swirl, then grabbed them when they fell back to the water. And, late on the darkest nights, hard fighting 20- and 30-pound stripers provided him special thrills when they struck live eels fished near Chesapeake Bay Bridge pilings. Those were the Good Old Days, the halcyon days of striped bass fishing. The angler thought they would never end.

Then, in the late 1970s and early 1980s, something went wrong. The Chesapeake Bay striped bass that once supplied 90 percent of Atlantic coast stocks were not reproducing. Scientists studied the problem, tagged fish, tried to re-build the spawning stocks with hatcheries. Some thought it may be too late, that the striper had been overfished almost to extinction.

Here on the Maine coast, South Harpswell locals had told the angler the rocky point was a likely place to hook a striped bass. Back home in Maryland, there was a moratorium on stripers, so he couldn't fish for them there.

The angler wanted badly to catch a Maryland-tagged striper in Maine. Yearling fish had been tagged in January, 1985, not far from the angler's home on Maryland's Choptank River. Later that summer a few of those tags were returned from stripers caught in Maine's Kennebec and Penobscot Rivers. Wouldn't it be something, the angler thought to himself as he walked out on the rocks, if I caught a bass with a Maryland tag? Not to keep the fish, understand, but to clip the tag and return the fish to the water, or at least record the tag number. A single-hook plug would ease the release, and his lip gaff wouldn't hurt the fish. He felt striped bass populations were in too much trouble to keep even one of them.

Fishingwise, the point presented some tactical problems. Only a few spots could be reached with a long cast; most of the area was shallow and weedy at low tide, except where the rocks dropped off into deeper water. Hip boots (hanging in a garage in Maryland) would have solved that problem. The water here was too cold to wade barefoot. And, once a fish was on, a nearby rocky crest, shaped like a dinosaur's back, would surely cut the line. A likely-looking striper lie was within casting distance, though. It was a place that a structure-oriented bass would like, out of the current, where the tide carries bait past. It was worth a try.

The striped bass was in her seventh summer, a healthy 1982 year class fish. Measuring 32 inches long, and weighing over 20 pounds, she was sexually mature. She would return to Maryland's Choptank River in the spring to spawn, not knowing that her 1982 year class was the best Chesapeake Bay hatch in the last decade, and that the future of coastal striped bass could depend on her.

The tag placed in her back in January, 1985 was only mildly irritating now. Looking like a piece of yellow spaghetti when it was new, the tag was now covered with marine growth, and the numbers on it were hard to read.

Her summer along the rocky Maine coast had been idyllic. She fed in a school with others of her size for much of the summer, chasing vast shoals of menhaden and other small fish.

Now she needed bigger meals, perhaps eels, softshell crabs, or a shedding lobster. She needed to conserve energy and gain weight. It was time to feed alone. Knowing nothing of her importance to the future of striped bass, she was motivated only by the urge to feed.

She selected her lie carefully. To conserve energy, she looked for an indentation in the rocks, just out of the current, so she could dart out and grab meals as the tide carried them past. If she swam constantly and caught little food, there would be a negative calorie balance. If it cost more energy to catch the food than the nourishment it supplied, she would not be healthy enough to winter off the North Carolina Capes, and return in springtime to spawn in the Chesapeake, when the ripening eggs in her belly told her it was time.

Her lie was a pocket in the rocks about the size of a bathtub, at the end of the point at South Harpswell. It was unoccupied, although countless other bass had used it for eons. She swam into the lie and positioned herself facing the current. The rumbling diesel engine of a lobster boat passing near the end of the rocks nearly panicked her into diving into the deep water off the point.

The angler cast his lure way beyond the bass' resting place, out into the channel, almost touching a passing lobsterboat. Slowly, he swam the lure back, occasionally popping it on the calm surface like a baitfish in trouble.

Successive wakes from the lobster boat rolled past the lure and broke on the rocky razorback. The angler popped the plug more vigorously as it passed over the spot where he thought a striper might lie in wait.

Odds were incalculable against catching a fish that had travelled so far from its home river in Maryland, perhaps a thousand miles along sandy and rocky coastlines. Why should there be a bass in this one hole out of a million others exactly like it? And if it did strike, could he manage to work it around the razorback and land it to check for a tag?

Was that a bathtub-sized swirl behind the lure, or wave action? The angler wanted to believe it was a fish striking short, perhaps more out of irritation than a feeding urge. Other swirls exactly like that one had kept the angler casting for many long hours along shallow Chesapeake Bay beaches. The thrill of seeing a big striped bass take a surface plug has hooked all too many anglers. It has resulted in broken homes, lost jobs, robbed sleep, and drained savings accounts. Even those who are addicted cannot explain why.

The striper's senses were perfectly attuned to her surrounding lie, watching, waiting in the calm water for an easy meal to pass by in the moving current. Her lateral line sensed movement on the surface above, a splashing disturbance, like a baitfish in trouble. Slowly she drifted upward, watching for a clue.

Her eyes detected movement on the surface, but there was something different about this meal. It didn't behave exactly right. She followed behind and slightly below it for a few feet. She sensed the odor of human in the wake of the lure—and still another, more puzzling aroma. The first odor was only a few parts per million of oil from the angler's skin. She sensed that something was wrong.

With a swish of her tail, she powered back down to her lie, trying to analyze the faint second odor she had sensed. The lure had been fished in the river of her birth, Maryland's Choptank. Could she detect that nearly imperceptible aroma? Was that what stopped her from smashing the plug?

An eel swam past in the current, hugging the edge of the rock face for protection. Darting in and out of each irregularity in the rocks, the eel didn't see the striper's rush until too late. The bass made a rapid cartwheel and swatted the eel with her tail, stunning it. As the eel groggily tried to escape, the bass quickly turned and took it headfirst.

This is a good lie, she thought. She would stay here a while.

A dozen more casts produced no action for the angler. Slow and fast retrieves, different plugs—nothing worked. It was getting dark now, time to go. The angler and his lady left the way they came, slowly—hesitant to leave such a beautiful spot.

The angler looked back. Was that a swirl near the lie? In the dimming light, did a Chesapeake striper make that characteristic slurping noise as it broke the surface to catch its dinner?

The angler and the lady were hungry now. They picked their way over rocks and along the beach toward a cheerful, warm beacon of light shining from the windows of the nearby Estes Lobster House.

Inside, exposed beams and trestle tables gave the place a picnic atmosphere. Windows on every side framed the surrounding rocky shoreline outside and a harbor bathed in the warm glow of dusk.

It took the angler and his lady back 34 years, to other places, other times. They were kids again. They spoke of the days of saddle shoes, penny loafers, bobby socks, and the pony tail hair style she wore then. About their many fishing vacations. How many fish caught, how many fish lost?

Tonight he asked his lady—did she think a striper made a pass at his plug, and if so, did it detect the taste of Maryland's Choptank River on the lure? Could he have seen that same fish before? Caught it? Tagged it? Released it?

A bubbly, cheerful girl served them their lobsters. The waitress wore the same pony-tail-and-bangs hair style that the angler's lady wore in the 1950s. He mentioned it to his lady.

My cup runneth over, the angler thought. Who could ask for anything more? A wonderful woman who had followed him all these years, across countless rocky and sandy coastlines, and put up with his sometimes irrational zeal for striper fishing. This evening was perfect: The weather, the place, and the lobster. A chance to fish for striped bass was icing on the cake.

He noticed the waitress' name tag. Her name conveyed something we all seek, he thought, but, more importantly, something the striped bass must have many more of before the rebirth of its kind. . . .

The waitress' name was Spring.

We all need another spring, he thought.

Another spring.

References

Fishing and Conservation Organizations

Assateague Mobile Sportsfishermen's Association (AMSA)
P. O. Box 848, Berlin, MD 21811

Atlantic Coastal Conservation Association (ACCA)
4801 Woodway, Suite 220W, Houston, TX 77056
(713) 626-4222

Atlantic Sportfishing Association
P. O. Box 245, Natick, MA 01760
(508) 655-3995

Chesapeake Bay Acid Rain Foundation, Inc.
P. O. Box 1538, Easton, MD 21601
(301) 822-5398 or (301) 822-9150

Conservation Federation of Maryland
P.O. Box 15336, Chevy Chase, MD 20815
(National Wildlife Federation Affiliate)

International Game Fish Association (IGFA)
3000 E. Las Olas Boulevard, Ft. Lauderdale, FL 33316-1613
(305) 467-0161

Jersey Coast Anglers Association
P. O. Box 111, Spring Lake, NJ 07762
(201) 270-9102

Maryland B.A.S.S. Federation
P. O. Box 954, Beltsville, MD 20705

Maryland Fly Anglers
c/o Wayne Grauer, 2207 Ellen Avenue, Baltimore, MD 21234
(301) 665-6034

Maryland Saltwater Sportsfishermen's Association, Inc. (MSSA)
7626 Baltimore-Annapolis Boulevard, Glen Burnie, MD 21061
(301) 768-8666

Pennsylvania Federation of Sportsmen's Clubs, Inc.
2426 N. Second Street, Harrisburg, PA 17110
(717) 232-3480   (National Wildlife Federation Affiliate)

Sport Fishing Institute
1010 Massachusetts Avenue, NW, Washington, D. C. 20077-8104
(202) 898-0770

Striped Bass Emergency Council
6 Fort Avenue Terrace, Boston, MA 02119
(617) 445-4567

Stripers Unlimited
P. O. Box 3045, South Attleboro, MA 02703
(508) 761-7983

Fishing Magazines

Maryland-Delaware-Virginia-West Virginia
Fishfinder Magazine
Fishfinder, Inc. P. O. BOX 197, Winfield, PA 17889
(717) 524-4206
(Monthly)

The *Fisherman* Magazine
14 Ramsey Road, Shirley, NY 11967
1 (800) 343-7490
(Weekly – 4 regional editions covering Maine to North Carolina)

The *Salt Water Sportsman*
280 Summer Street
Boston, MA 02210
(617) 439-9977
(Monthly)

Trophy Striper
P. O. Box 386
Boone, NC 28607
(704) 265-3474
(6 issues per year)

Information Sources

Maryland Sport Fishing Tournament
Maryland DNR
Tawes State Office Building
Annapolis, MD 21401
(301) 974-3765

Virginia Saltwater Fishing Tournament
Suite 102, 968 Oriole Drive, South
Virginia Beach, VA 23451
(804) 491-5160

Striper (Tournament Trail)
P. O. Box 210768
Nashville, TN 37221
(615) 868-0012

Free Guides, Maps, & Fishing Ruler

Maryland Office of Tourism Development
217 E. Redwood Street, Room 904
Baltimore, MD 21202
1 (800) 543-1046

> Maryland Travel & Outdoor Guide
> Maryland Calendar of Events

Maryland Department of Natural Resources
Fisheries Division, C-2, Tidewater Administration
Tawes State Office Building
Annapolis, MD 21401
(301) 974-3765

> A Fisherman's Guide to Maryland Piers & Boat Ramps Map
> Maryland Highway & Natural Resources Map
> Tide Tables & Fishing Tips
> Maryland Tidewater Sportfishing Guide
> Happy Crabber
> Folding 24" Crab & Fish Ruler
> My Maryland Natural Resources Coloring Book
>   (To keep your kids busy)

DID YOU BORROW THIS COPY?

Now is the time to order your own copy.

Autographed? Yes _____   No _____

BOOK ORDER FORM

I would like to order _____ copies of *Chesapeake Stripers* by Keith Walters.

Number of copies _____ x $19.95 each   = $ _____

Maryland Residents:
  Add $1.00 Sales Tax per book   =   +

Shipping: Add $1.55 per book   =   + _____

Total enclosed: $ _____

Make checks payable to: AERIE HOUSE,
P.O. Box 279, Bozman, Maryland 21612

Ordered by: _____

Ship to: _____
                                    Name

_____
                              Street Address

_____
            City   State   Zip Code

Phone: _____

This page may be Photocopied

Bulk purchase inquiries invited.
AERIE HOUSE: (301) 745-2236